Georgetown ME

Happy Sailing

Judy Silva

THE VOYAGE OF
YANKEE
LADY

CIRCUMNAVIGATING
NEW ENGLAND ON A SAILBOAT

JUDITH SILVA

THE VOYAGE OF
YANKEE
LADY

CIRCUMNAVIGATING
NEW ENGLAND ON A SAILBOAT

TATE PUBLISHING
AND ENTERPRISES, LLC

This book is designed to provide accurate and authoritative information with regard to the subject matter covered. This information is given with the understanding that neither the author nor Tate Publishing, LLC is engaged in rendering legal, professional advice. Since the details of your situation are fact dependent, you should additionally seek the services of a competent professional.

The opinions expressed by the author are not necessarily those of Tate Publishing, LLC.

Published by Tate Publishing & Enterprises, LLC
127 E. Trade Center Terrace | Mustang, Oklahoma 73064 USA
1.888.361.9473 | www.tatepublishing.com

Tate Publishing is committed to excellence in the publishing industry. The company reflects the philosophy established by the founders, based on Psalm 68:11,
"The Lord gave the word and great was the company of those who published it."

Book design copyright © 2013 by Tate Publishing, LLC. All rights reserved.
Cover design by Rtor Maghuyop
Interior design by Caypeeline Casas

Published in the United States of America

ISBN: 978-1-62510-673-5
1. Travel / General
2. Sports & Recreation / Boating
13.03.05

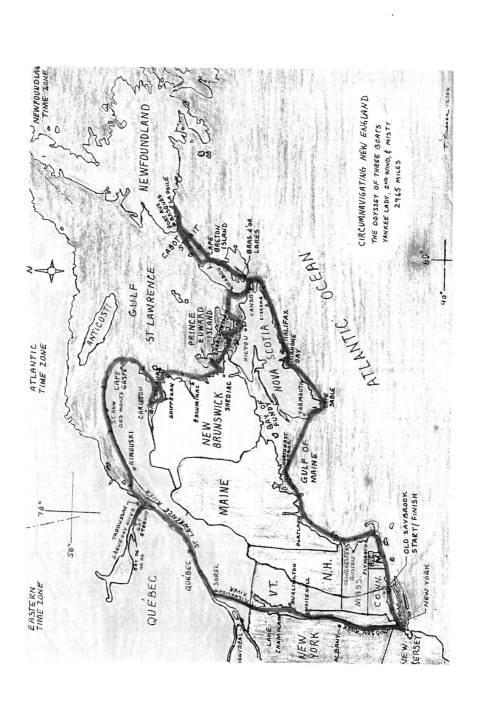

CIRCUMNAVIGATING NEW ENGLAND

THE ODYSSEY OF THREE BOATS
YANKEE LADY, 2ND WIND, & MISTY
2965 MILES

DEDICATION

To Jim,
this voyage belongs to both of us.

ACKNOWLEDGMENTS

This book could not have been written without the support and encouragement of so many people. My thanks go to all of them, named and unnamed.

Without Jim, this book never would have happened. It was his idea to circumnavigate New England aboard *Yankee Lady*. He was the instigator and he held the trip together through good weather and bad. His mechanical ability saved the rest of us a lot of frustration and kept us moving. His patience, encouragement and insightful suggestions helped me complete this project. Thank you.

Thanks to my step-sister and fellow author, Jenny Van Horne, who convinced me that I could write this story and helped me find my own voice.

I learned to write creatively and with feeling from Patricia Klindienst, one of the best teachers I have ever encountered. The compositions I wrote during the classes she taught became the nucleus of the first chapters of this book.

Barbara Frasca has spent hours carefully reading and editing this manuscript. As a sailor and participant on this voyage, her perspective has been invaluable. Her illustrations add a visual accent that words cannot express.

My son, Larry La Forge, has been my technical, computer advisor, answering all my computer "help" questions with patience and clarity.

My granddaughter, Ally La Forge, has read and commented on every chapter as I produced them. She has been my loyal supporter and fan and is a talented writer and budding journalist in her own right.

Thanks to Tom and Barbara Frasca and Tom and Rosie Isele for accompanying us on this trip and making it the fantastic voyage that it was.

Thanks to Tate Publishing for having faith in this first time author.

CONTENTS

INTRODUCTION

What do an educator, a mechanic, a salesman, a housewife, an engineer, and an artist have in common? This is the story of six very different sailors, all retired, who cruised three modest sailboats, on modest budgets, for just under three thousand miles along the Canadian and American waterways that surround New England. We found our way into almost ninety harbors and anchorages, most of them for the first time. Not everyone dreams of sailing across an ocean, but anyone who dreams of retiring and sailing into adventures will enjoy our lively, exciting, and sometimes funny experiences. A long voyage is taken one day at a time, and this book may convince you that such a six-month journey is possible. Our encounters with whales, stops at rural fishing ports, and experiences with friendly Americans and Canadians (both French and English speakers) will make you wish you were there. We coped with storms, solved mechanical problems, and viewed magnificent scenery. This book also offers a glimpse of our everyday cruising life—potluck suppers, anchoring and docking, and senior moments. Six people went on this voyage, each has a story to tell. This is my story.

THE VOYAGE BEGINS— CONNECTICUT RIVER TO THE ST. LAWRENCE RIVER

Every day is an adventure. This has been our guiding philosophy ever since Jim and I were married in 1996. Since then, we have spent winters cruising the Florida Keys aboard Jim's boat, *Albatross*, and summers cruising New England and the Bay of Fundy aboard *Yankee Lady*. During the winter of 2000, Jim suggested we go on a three-thousand-mile cruise around New England, and I enthusiastically agreed. We invited two other couples, close friends, and cruising companions to join us. Tom and Barbara Frasca would be aboard their boat *Misty*, a thirty-foot Pearson Wanderer, and Tom and Rosalie Isele would be aboard their boat *2nd Wind*, a thirty-foot Catalina. They had sailed with us on previous trips to the Maine coast, the Bay of Fundy, and the Hudson River. We planned to take two summers to complete this trip. Our plan for the first year was to cruise up the Hudson River through Lake Champlain, to the St. Lawrence River around the Gaspé Peninsula, to Northumberland Strait, and to the town of Shediac, New Brunswick. We would leave the boats there for the winter and return the next summer when we planned to cruise to Prince Edward Island, Cape Breton, Bras d'Or Lake, and Newfoundland returning along the Nova Scotia Coast, around Cape Sable to Yarmouth, across the Bay of Fundy to Northeast Harbor, Maine, and home to Connecticut.

June 14, the day of departure, finally arrived. For the last few weeks, we had sanded, rubbed, polished, and fixed various parts of *Yankee Lady*. Each boat had nine hundred dollars' worth of US and Canadian charts and as many cruising guides as we could find. We all had radar, GPS receivers, VHF radios, and compasses. We did not have the luxury of chart plotters or computer programs. *Yankee Lady* was ready, we were ready, and so were the others. We dropped our moorings at nine in the morning and proceeded single file through the narrow North Cove entrance channel. *Wow*, I thought, *we're really leaving, and I'm so excited I can hardly stand it*. I always dreamed about taking a long voyage like this, and now I was actually doing it. I had confidence in myself, Jim, and *Yankee Lady*; we were off on a grand adventure. We motored past the familiar Old Saybrook outer lighthouse. We would not see it again for two years.

Long Island Sound is located between the northern coast of Long Island and the southern coast of Connecticut and New York; it flows in an east-west direction. Starting at the Race at the easterly end, it continues for about one hundred miles almost to Hell Gate at the beginning of the East River. It is narrow at either end, which causes the water flowing in and out from the Atlantic Ocean to rip and boil. Both the Race and Hell Gate are famous for their swift currents, standing waves, and overall turbulence during times of maximum flood and ebb tides. We were used to the Race; it was part of our regular cruising territory. *Yankee Lady* is strong enough to power through most of its turbulence and adverse current, but it is uncomfortable to bounce around and barely make headway. We tried to avoid maximum flood and ebb tides. This would be true for Hell Gate as well.

We left the Connecticut River in a brisk southwest wind bound for the Thimble Islands, just off Stony Creek. *Misty* and *2nd Wind* set sail and heeled over smartly on this upwind day. The purist sailor in me and my competitive spirit wanted to do the same, but *Yankee Lady* was the smallest and lightest of the three boats. She was tender when sailing into the wind and would heel over farther than the other two boats. This could be fun when racing or out for a day sail but cruising gave me a different mindset. I didn't want to fix lunch and move around the boat at a thirty-five-degree angle. My comfort won out. We motor-sailed with a raised mainsail and no jib. Jim consented although he wouldn't have minded heeling over and balancing for four hours.

After negotiating our way through rocks, ledges, and confusing buoys, we motored smoothly into the slot between Pot and High, two of the Thimble Islands. Small and large summer cottages rose from the pink granite rocks that form these islands. One house, in particular, was perched precariously on a set of rocks that was little more than a ledge. It was a "hold your breath" setting. These rock-bound islands reminded me of my beloved Maine. But as I tried to imagine I was in the wilderness somewhere off the Maine coast, I realized there was too much civilization around me for that to be true.

Each island is privately owned and jealously guarded by its owners. I had anchored here one summer weekend; it was not a friendly place. Cruisers were not welcome to anchor or go ashore. But it was quiet this early in the season, and no one bothered us. We found three empty moorings belonging to assorted yacht clubs and picked them up. We rolled slightly in the wakes of a few passing powerboats, including the small passenger boat, which announced itself by a sign that said Ferry. Island residents, guests, and summer tourists used it to come out from the village of Stony Creek, Connecticut.

Our next stop was Stamford, Connecticut. This was a light-wind day, pleasant but no sailing. We motored between the two breakwaters and entered Stamford Harbor. We glided by the large, round barge mooring and anchored well clear of it. As the tide dropped, Jim and I watched rocks appear nearby. However, we had checked the chart and knew we were safe just off the main channel. Rocks in the water always seem threatening to me.

When I first sailed in Maine, I used to think (irrationally) that they would jump out and get me. This day, Jim and I motored our inflatable dinghy over some small submerged ones. The movement of the water over the rocks distorted and softened their sharp outlines; the refracted sunlight illuminated their black and brown colors. They were ominously beautiful, lurking only inches under the surface of the water.

Jim and I have been grounded on rocks just once. That was enough. We were on a previous cruise with *Misty* and *2nd Wind* near Norwalk, Connecticut. We arrived at the unfamiliar Norwalk Islands just as a squall was approaching. This added drama to a situation that didn't need any more drama. *Yankee Lady* was leading; I was at the helm. We found our way around the lighthouse and headed for Chimon Island, one of many shown on the chart. There was shallow water to avoid; we were supposed to anchor just before Chimon Island. I said, "I think we should go a little further." *Clunk, clunk, screech, clunk*; we had found the rocks, just below the surface. What a horrible noise! We waved the other two boats off, and they anchored. The sky had darkened; the wind was shrieking, and we were in the middle of the squall. We had to act immediately before the tide dropped any further. There was no time to talk it over or wonder what we should do. This was where our experience counted. I put the engine in neutral and turned to port away from the ledge. Jim pulled the jib all the way out on the port side, sheeted it tight, and let if fill with wind. "Come on *Yankee Lady*," I pleaded to myself, "*Get off!*" I don't know if it was our determination, skill, luck, or a combination of these, but *Yankee Lady* lay over on her side, which caused the keel to lift off the rocks. The bow swung to port, the keel scraped across the rocks and we were *off*. We motored toward *2nd Wind* and anchored. When the wind finally calmed, Jim dove in and swam under the boat to check the keel. There were three dents on the starboard side and a missing piece of fiberglass on the port side, but the keel did not feel loose. The dents could be fixed and the fiberglass repaired. I checked the keel bolts in the bilge; they were not loose, and no water was coming in. We could finally relax. As the tide went down, we saw a nasty group of rocks baring themselves. Our blue bottom paint was on two of them.

As I drifted in the dinghy that sunny day in Stamford, I asked myself, "Why do these submerged rocks seem so ominous?" Perhaps it was because they were hidden until we were over them. I remember thinking, *As with any difficulty in life, it's the hidden dangers that are the most terrifying.* I hoped that I would always have the necessary resources to face them.

Long Island Sound is a major waterway between New York City and the New England coast. It is prime cruising territory for all types of recreational boats, and it is a major route for commercial traffic such as tugs pulling barges. From our anchorage, I could see an occasional freighter or tug and barge. When I was a novice cruiser on these waters, I used to panic when I would see a barge and tug in the distance. Sailboats move slowly; tugs pulling barges cannot stop suddenly or turn quickly. I wanted to be able to plan ahead to stay out of their way. As I gained experience, I learned how to do it.

We passed Larchmont, where I first started sailing as a teenager; first in my 12 foot Penguin sailing dinghy, and then in my 16 foot Comet sloop. I felt a little like that young Judy sailing her Penguin. There was buoy number 42 (known as 42nd Street) near where the rudder kept floating off the boat. I thought, *Am I really here on this twenty-eight-foot boat with all its comfort and sophisticated equipment, a boat I could barely have dreamed about back then? I could never have imagined I would be going around New England with someone who could do this with me, someone I cared about.*

Sailboats, with white sails set, were gliding across the water. Small fishing boats were anchored near the shore while the fishermen, bobbing ever so slightly in the ripples, were patiently attached to their fishing poles whose lines disappeared into the water. This was Sunday afternoon on lower Long Island Sound, a peaceful scene right out of a sailing magazine.

The Sound narrowed as we approached the Throgs Neck Bridge. Throgs Neck marks the place where the Sound ends and the East River begins. There was an anchorage in the small harbor near the northeast shore of the peninsula. To get there, we needed to pass under the north span of the Throgs Neck Bridge. I worried about fitting under the span of the bridge to anchor close to the shore. The cruising guide said there was a fifty-foot to fifty-five-foot clearance under the sixth span from shore. But which shore? We chose the shore to port. *Yankee Lady* needed thirty-seven feet, *2nd Wind* needed forty-two feet, *Misty* was in between. Have you tried looking up at a bridge as you pass under it in a sailboat? Even if the bridge is very high, you will think that the mast is going to touch. Gingerly, Jim inched *Yankee Lady* through. I looked up anyway, but the cruising guide was right. We all passed under it with plenty of room to spare. We were in the greater New York City area. The land surrounding our anchorage was a cityscape of waterfront houses crowded together in company with the buildings of the NY Maritime Academy and the State University of New York.

The anchorage was not so peaceful at first. Sunday afternoon motorboat traffic kept us rocking and rolling. But as it became dark, the powerboats went back to their marinas, and the water calmed; we floated gently at anchor. Guarding the entrance to our harbor, the bridge, illuminated by hundreds of lights, was a study in grace. We gazed at the sweeping curves of the suspension cables and the angular outlines of the two towers outlined against the dark sky. The muted hum of traffic lulled us to sleep.

We left at 8:00 a.m. in order to carry a favorable current through Hell Gate. As we passed the end of the LaGuardia airport runway, a departing plane roared a few hundred feet overhead. The deafening sound of its engines vibrated through my whole body. Words disappeared in the fog of noise. I thought, *Not many people have heard or seen this "boats eye view" of a huge DC10 lumbering into the sky.* I said a little prayer for the safety of the passengers and crew.

We rounded the next curve and were met with a scene of blazing glory. Hundreds of east-facing windows in the forest of Manhattan skyscrapers reflected the gold of the rising sun. I once saw Van Gogh's original painting *Sunflowers* on exhibit at the Museum of Modern Art in New York City. The intensity of its vibrant colors reached inside my very being. This was a Van Gogh moment.

Hell Gate is where the Harlem River joins the East River, and it is known for its swift currents and chaotic waters. This would be our third time through it. We had consulted the current tables in our cruising guide, and our timing was perfect; we slid through on the ebb current with no hassle.

As we cruised down the East River, I watched morning joggers and walkers. I waved at some, determined to get a response from city people who seldom make eye contact with strangers. A few waved back. As we passed mid-Manhattan, I looked up the canyons of the cross streets to see the silvery Chrysler building and the tall Empire State building. We passed the UN buildings and motored under the Queensboro Bridge at Roosevelt Island, the Williamsburg Bridge, and the Brooklyn Bridge. We passed by the carefully preserved old ships of South Street Sea Port.

The river turned slightly to port, and there, ahead of us, was the Statue of Liberty, her torch glowing in the sunlight. She is an inspiration to me whenever I see her. In 1986, Jim and his beloved first wife, Carol, aboard *Albatross*, and I, aboard *Yankee Lady*, spent four days anchored in New York Harbor joining hundreds of other boats to watch the celebration of her one hundredth anniversary. After dusk on July 3, we watched as red, white, and blue laser lights illuminated her from her torch to her feet. Then as fireworks exploded around her and smoke partially concealed her, she stood there with her torch held high, a solid emblem of freedom. It was the essence of "The Star Spangled Banner" with the "rockets' red glare" revealing an unconquered symbol of liberty.

Entering the Hudson River was the beginning of the next stage of our journey. From here, we would cruise up the Hudson to Troy, New York, through the Champlain Canal and into Lake Champlain. We were entering a waterway system that once was a major transportation link between Canada and New York. Henry Hudson explored it, Americans and British fought on it, settlers set out for the west on it, and traders carried furs and other goods on it. I wondered, *What would happen to us on it?*

We stayed so close to shore as we rounded the Battery that I could read the hot dog signs in the park. The towers of the World Trade Center loomed overhead. As my gaze traveled to the tops of those twin towers, I felt like a tiny speck gliding through the water. I asked myself, "Who were we to be undertaking this audacious voyage in three small boats through rivers, canals, and potentially dangerous ocean all the way to Newfoundland?" But I reaffirmed that our philosophy has always been, "One day at a time," and that was how I approached this trip. Sadly, as I write this memoir, all that remains of those twin towers is a 9/11 tragic memory.

The sights of the West Side unfolded. New York Waterway commuter ferries crossed back and forth from New Jersey to Manhattan like darting dragon flies carrying commuters to their city appointments. We bounced in their wakes and continued on our way.

Midtown, we passed several decaying docks, which were all that remained of the glory days of the trans-Atlantic liners like the Queen Mary. We passed the World War II aircraft carrier *Intrepid*, which was permanently tied to a dock, a museum open to the public. We motored by the docks of three gigantic cruise ships, the new glory boats. Bright and shiny, they awaited a new class of pleasure seekers.

Cars hummed along the West Side Highway near Riverside Park and the 79th Street Marina. It was hard for me to imagine living on a boat in New York City, but there were several liveaboard vessels here. One must have belonged to a frustrated gardener. It was practically a floating flower garden.

What a different perspective it was to experience Manhattan from the water. From the water, there were no faceless crowds, dirty streets, honking taxi cabs. Navigation was easy without the mazes of busy streets. We traveled at a slower pace. Reading a chart was a lot easier than reading a Manhattan road map.

I didn't think the view had changed much since last year when we were on our first trip up the Hudson also with *Misty* and *2nd Wind*. Then we had picked up a mooring near the 96th Street exit of the West Side Highway. Jim and I had watched a promenade of people on the walk by the river. We saw a grandfather lying on a park bench while his two grandchildren sat in a stroller next to him. A fashionably dressed lady in black and white strode up to him, obviously the mother. Judging by her body language, I told Jim, "I think she's scolding him for falling asleep while he was supposed to be watching the children."

Jim replied, "I bet he said, 'I was just resting my eyes.'"

Bicycles, dog walkers, and pedestrians spread out across the grass and on the walk. I saw one lady pushing a wire cart with a pillow in it. She was accompanied by a small, fluffy white dog. The pillow appeared to be the bed for "fluffy" when she (wearing a pink ribbon) became tired. A brown mongrel dog was racing around the grass, daring his owner to catch him. He spied "fluffy" and ran over eagerly. The woman tried to pull her dog closer, but there was no need to. Life in the dog world is not based on social appearances. The two dogs exchanged sniffs and other pleasantries, and then the mongrel and his owner went on their way. It was "Lady and the Tramp" in Riverside Park.

As we approached the George Washington Bridge, we could see the famous Riverside Cathedral and Grant's Tomb on our right. Motoring under the bridge, we passed a small lighthouse on our starboard side nestled against a pillar of the bridge. The lighthouse is obsolete now, dwarfed by the tall spire behind it. But it stands there, the symbol of a past way of life when mariners relied on it to protect them from danger. Time moved on; the mighty bridge whose spires point to the sky supports a different kind of transportation and a different mindset. Busy travelers drive over it, sometimes bumper to bumper; they don't have time to marvel at the beauty of it. But passing under it at sailboat speed, I was awed by the beauty of both structures and the juxtaposition of the old and the new.

The Palisades on our port side towered above us. They were impressive—some looked like giant totem poles and some like church organ pipes. Their basalt cliffs dropped steeply to the shore. Trees capped the top and skirted the base of the cliffs all the way to the river. Piles of fallen rock lay on the slopes. The vertical cliffs of this natural wonder faced the civilized wonder of the tall buildings and street canyons of Manhattan.

We passed under the Tappan Zee Bridge, stopped at Tarrytown Marina for fuel, water, and ice, and then motored across the river to Hook Mountain Yacht Club, one of the friendliest places we have encountered anywhere. We picked up three moorings courtesy of the Yacht Club.

The next morning, we were ready to leave at 11:00 a.m. *Yankee Lady's* and *Misty's* engines were humming. Tom Frasca was on *Misty's* bow ready to drop his mooring line. Then, Tom Isele called over to Jim, "My engine won't start," and so continued the story of the cranky engine.

We have been on several cruises with Tom and Rosie, and they are our good friends. Tom has spent time and money trying to keep *2nd Wind* in good repair. But sometimes, all his efforts seemed like a comic opera. No matter what he did, something was always breaking, and Jim was usually fixing it. Rosie would get frustrated with Tom whenever this happened, but after forty plus years of marriage and six children, I think Tom has adjusted to it. So now when Rosie said emphatically, "It's not up to Jim to fix this engine," Tom resignedly called the local boatyard to find a mechanic. The manager said, "My mechanic can look at it this weekend, but he won't be able to work on it for two weeks." Discouraged, Tom and Rosie considered their options. Should they leave the boat here and go home? Should they have *2nd Wind* towed home? Should they see if their Connecticut mechanic could come to Nyack? It looked like they wouldn't be able to finish the trip.

Then Jim said, "Let's take it apart to see if we can find the problem." I was so confident in Jim's mechanical talent that I never doubted he would find and fix whatever was wrong.

Because the engine, an Atomic 4 gasoline engine, was full of water, Jim assumed that there was a leaking head gasket. Over the course of the next two days, the three men took the engine apart, diagnosed, and rediagnosed. Hope soared; hope plummeted. Was it a cracked block? Was it a cracked manifold? Was it the head gasket? Jim saw no signs of a cracked block or manifold, which was a relief because *2nd Wind* would have needed a new engine. It had to be the head gasket. Tom bought a new one. He had the head resurfaced at a machine shop. Jim spent three hours install-ing the resurfaced head and the new gasket.

Working on a sailboat engine is not a comfortable task. The engine compartment of *2nd Wind* was under the seat in the main cabin. Jim had to remove the seat and then kneel and bend over the engine to reach the necessary parts. Almost finished, Jim tightened all the bolts in sequence. The last one broke! With remarkable patience, he drilled and removed the broken stud. He had to start the process all over again. Tom bought a new bolt. After another three hours of work, Jim was ready to tighten the bolts again. This time, someone from the yacht club had loaned him a torque wrench, which controlled the amount of pressure on the bolts. Jim handed the wrench to one of the Tom's, saying, "You do it. I don't want to break another one."

At last, victory! 2nd Wind's engine was purring smoothly. Tom ran it all morning while the rest of us went to town for more shopping and lunch. In appreciation for the hospitality of the yacht club, Barbara painted a scenic watercolor of Hook Mountain, which she gave to the commodore for the club's meeting room, and Tom Isele donated money to their Christmas fund.

We left at 2:15 p.m. Tom blew his horn in celebration as our little fleet glided out of the harbor. The Palisades ended as we approached Haverstraw Bay, the widest part of the river.

The Catskills, blue on the horizon, framed this summer day. Around the next point, the river narrowed. Steep-sided mountains, covered with layers of green forests, dropped to the shores on either side of us. This was the beginning of the section of river that has been justly called spectacular. We passed under the graceful spans of the Bear Mountain Bridge, watching a silver passenger train enter and leave the tunnel dug through the mountain on the east shore.

We wanted to pick up moorings at the Garrison Yacht Club, opposite West Point, but needed to ask permission. As frequently happened, Jim and I did the investigating. We tied up at the dock; *Misty* and *2nd Wind* circled in the river. Although he has been here all his adult life, the proprietor, Jim Guinan, was as Irish as a shamrock and sounded as if he had just returned from the Blarney Stone. He told us to pick up three empty moorings. I asked, "Is there any charge?"

With a twinkle in his eye, he replied, "What the eye doesn't see, the heart won't grieve. Enjoy yourselves."

The evening was calm and still, beautiful in the soft colors of twilight. West Point loomed across the river, massive and gothic. Tugs and barges passed by; the throbbing of the tugs' engines said work, work, work. Passenger trains sped by on the east side of the river, lumbering freight trains rolled on the west side. The freight trains approached with a dull roar, followed by the sounds of the cars rumbling over the tracks and then the haunting sound of the whistle as a train approached a crossing. Every now and then, one of these lengthy monsters stopped at West Point. The passenger trains slid more quietly into the station on the east side, gave two toots with their whistles, slowed to a stop, and hummed a little while the passengers stepped off.

We left the city of Newburgh to port, noting its red brick buildings that seemed to hug the hill right down to the shore. We motored under the latticed girders of the Newburgh Bridge. Across the river, the green skyline of nearby mountains sketched a gentle outline in the sky—nature and civilization, bridge and mountains. When this bridge was opened twenty-nine years ago, it replaced the last remaining ferry on the Hudson River. This is only the fourth bridge to span the Hudson since New York City, and it has made Newburgh an important transportation link along the river.

We arrived at Kingston and Rondout Creek, which is thought to be the best natural harbor between New York and Albany. Our destination was the anchorage just before the fixed bridge at the end of the Creek. This was where the Delaware and Hudson Canal began.

As we motored up the Creek, we passed marinas, a large dry dock for barges, and a crushed stone distribution plant. The cranes and towers that moved the stone looked like a giant erector set. If I had been here when my sons were young, they would have watched the activity all day; it was the stuff of a little boy's construction set dreams. Gravel poured out of conveyer belts leaving pyramids on the ground. Dump trucks moved the gravel from here to there. Docks waited for barges to come and load up. To me, it appeared to be one of the last vestiges of the commercial prosperity started by the building of the canal. It seemed out of place with the peaceful nature of the rest of the creek.

The end of the creek was rural and still. We elected not to pick up unknown moorings; instead, we anchored in front of a cleared, grassy field and a small beach. This was a perfect, quiet anchorage across from a small marina. The six of us motored our dinghies the short distance to the low bridge and dam. We "docked" against the rocks and climbed to the other side of the dam. We could see where the canal had been, but it looked more like a small creek. It was hard to imagine a prosperous commercial waterway; it was overgrown and narrow.

We needed to find a place to take our masts down in preparation for the low bridges of the Champlain Canal. I found a phone at the marina in Kingston and called Shady Harbor Marina in New Baltimore. They were too busy. Castleton Boat Club was a do-it-yourself place at a cost of thirty dollars. The price was right, but we didn't feel confident enough yet for "do-it-yourself." Troy required an appointment, and the price was one hundred fifty dollars. I was beginning to feel like Goldilocks trying to find the best bowl of porridge or the just right bed. Then the gentleman at Riverview Boat Yard in Catskill said, "We can do it tomorrow for sixty-five dollars per boat." Riverview also gave us a special dock price of seventy-five cents a foot. Although Catskill was farthest away from the low bridges, the price and timing were just right.

We arrived midafternoon in the middle of a rain shower. I was at the helm and motored *Yankee Lady* into her assigned dock against a brisk crosswind; Jim jumped off and tied the bow and stern lines around the cleats on the dock. These were not easy maneuvers since the wind was blowing *Yankee Lady* away from the dock.

The skills required to dock a boat, especially in crosswind conditions, cannot be overestimated. Timing is everything. I had to control the boat with the engine, and Jim had to jump quickly onto the dock before the wind blew the boat too far away for him to jump off. I recalled an incident at the Edgartown, Massachusetts, water barge when I was sailing by myself. There was a crosswind, and I had to plan ahead carefully. Before approaching the barge, I put the engine in neutral and attached the fenders to the port side of the boat. I placed the bow and stern lines over the lifeline amidships so that I could grab both of them at the same time. I returned to the helm, engaged the engine, and approached the barge. I had to use more power than usual so as not to be blown away from the barge. As *Yankee Lady* hit the barge too hard (she has a scar on her hull to prove it), I put the engine in neutral, hurried to the side, grabbed the lines, and leaped off. The boat had already started to drift away, and I had to hold the lines with all my might before I could secure them to the cleats on the dock. It was scary to think about what would have happened if I couldn't have held on to those lines or if the boat had drifted too far away in the middle of my jump.

I really didn't want to repeat that experience, and I should have appreciated the teamwork among us. We prided ourselves on being able to dock *Yankee Lady* by ourselves. We have observed many skippers who just aim at the dock and then throw their lines (sometimes wildly) at any person standing there. (However, there would be a time in Halifax when we would be glad to have Barbara helping on the dock.)

We acted as a team, but I felt that Jim resented my taking the helm to dock the boat. That was the glory part, and the captain should be doing it. He didn't doubt my ability, but he didn't want to take orders from me. I had the same problem: I didn't want to be ordered around either. I knew that we didn't think alike and had very different ways of solving problems (or approaching a dock). It was very difficult for me to let him do things his way if it conflicted with what I thought was right. It's probably a lesson every "back seat driver" has needed to learn, and I was trying, but it was hard; we would get into fights over it. Even though I worried about how my role as co-captain would affect us and I didn't like the tension, I knew that our teamwork was important.

The alarm clock rang at 7:00 a.m. Jim and I wanted to be up and ready for the boatyard crew by 8:00 a.m. We removed the sails. Jim loosened the turnbuckles and prepared to pull out the cotter pins. He put the wood supports for the mast in place. We had carefully stored them aboard since Jim made them in Connecticut. Jim and I never argued about anything mechanical. There was no competition; I never could do all those mechanical things. Without him, I never would have taken this trip, and I don't think *2nd Wind* or *Misty* would have either.

At 8:40 a.m., we nosed into the launch basin by the crane. By 9:30 a.m., *Yankee Lady* was done. She would be a pure motorboat for the next few days. *Misty* followed and then *2nd Wind*. By 12:30 p.m., the three boats were ready to leave the boatyard. We would remember its clean laundry and the showers that slammed you against the wall. Jim reminded everyone not to use their VHF radios. They would fry if used with no antenna because the outgoing signal would go back into the radio and put too much power in it. We switched to our handheld radios.

The river narrowed a bit. We passed marshes and islands, some with beaches and picnic tables, and continued through mostly rural countryside, passing several small marinas and boat clubs. Albany's commercial port was located just before the city proper. There were no freighters or barges tied up at the docks or oil storage facilities, and it did not look very prosperous. As we passed the city, I noticed the wind vane on top of the gothic New York University building, a model of Henry Hudson's vessel, *Half Moon*.

Henry Hudson explored this river in 1609. He was hired by the Dutch East India Company to find a water route through the northwest to Asia. Although he discovered no passage to Asia, his exploration provided enough information for the Dutch to establish New Amsterdam at the mouth of the river the following year. I like to think about the early adventurers; what was it really like to voyage into the unknown? It must have taken a lot of faith and courage to venture across the ocean and explore this river. I wondered what emotions Hudson must have felt when he realized he had not found the Northwest Passage? Even though we had engines, charts, and modern instruments, we would need to find strange harbors and face uncertain weather. I too felt like an explorer.

After motoring under two low bridges near Albany, we reached the Troy Federal Lock. I radioed the lockkeeper on Channel 13 and was instructed to prepare for a port side tie up. The green light flashed, and we entered the lock. I had no anxiety about this; Jim and I have transited many locks aboard *Albatross* on the Okeechobee Waterway in Florida. Jim motored *Yankee Lady* slowly to station 4, which was toward the front of the lock. I looked up at fourteen feet of rough, slimy concrete wall. We had placed fenders on *Yankee Lady's* port side, which would partially protect her hull from the rough concrete. But that would not be enough. There was a metal pole built into a recess in the lock wall. Jim looped a line around it and tied the line to a stanchion in the middle of the boat. As the water rose, the line would slide up the pole and steady the boat. Then Jim stood behind the wheel with one boat hook; I took another and went forward to the bow. The gate behind us closed. The one in front opened slightly; water gushed through. The narrow opening controlled the turbulence of the incoming water. As the chamber filled, the gate opened wider until at last the water levels were equal. Meanwhile, Jim and I used the boat hooks to fend off from the lock walls as the turbulence caused the boat to swing slightly.

It was cool and damp in the bottom of the lock chamber. Very little sunlight filtered down; it was a gray world. Sounds echoed; the lock gate behind us closed with a clang. We turned off our engines to keep from inhaling exhaust fumes. The incoming water hissed by *Yankee Lady's* hull. The water lifted us up; it seemed so effortless. The sunlight became brighter; roofs of buildings and the tops of trees appeared. At last, we saw the full view: lock buildings, the dam off to the side, and the surrounding countryside. The current stopped, the gate opened silently, and we were free to go.

Just before we untied, Jim called over to the small powerboat in front of us to ask if there was a grocery store with a dock nearby. They discussed this with two local Jet Skiers in front of them who said that just before the second bridge, there was a dock big enough for our boats. It was close to a Price Chopper supermarket.

We entered the New York canal system. I was not used to being in freshwater aboard *Yankee Lady*. If we went aground during this part of our voyage, there would be no high tide to lift us up. In fact, there would be no tide at all until we reached the St. Lawrence River. Ahead, I saw a waterway intersection with a sign on the shore: Erie Canal (arrow pointing left) and Champlain Canal (arrow pointing straight ahead). I mused, *How unusual to see navigational directions from a land sign. We were on boats, not in cars.* We were used to sailing in the open water; the character and mood of this canal seemed so different. The Erie Canal could take us all the way to the Great Lakes, and it was a beckoning path, the road not taken. I thought, *Maybe another time...*

After we passed the first low bridge, both Jet Skiers came over and pointed out the grocery store dock. We waved our thanks. We managed to dock all three boats at this somewhat flimsy dock. After our grocery store trip, we ate supper on the boats and then anchored for the night just off the dock.

Jim and I reviewed our cruising guides while the others went to church and breakfast. We were both excited. We looked at each other, and I asked, "Are we really on our way to Lake Champlain and the St. Lawrence River?" We would travel the next sixty miles through locks and canals to Whitehall, New York, which was considered the beginning of Lake Champlain.

Locks number 1 through number 8 lifted us up, anywhere from 10 to 19 feet. After Lock number 8, the canal was 140 feet above sea level. We descended locks number 9, number 11, and number 12 toward Lake Champlain. Even though there were only eleven locks to negotiate, the last lock was labeled number 12. When the locks were built, the engineers found they didn't need a lock number 10, but no one bothered to renumber them. We passed under several low railway and highway bridges; they were so close overhead that I felt like ducking. We motored through rural countryside, passing by a few summer camps, groups of small homes, and forests.

Just before lock number 3, we saw the new free dock at Mechanicville and decided to stop. We noticed ladders built into the wall at evenly spaced intervals. Each crew selected a ladder and tied up to the dock with the ladder amidships. I didn't realize it then, but before the end of this voyage, we seniors would become expert ladder climbers. I never expected to climb straight up or down fifteen feet or more of a ladder and think no more of it than walking across a parking lot, but that is what we did on the St. Lawrence River. Here all we needed to do was climb three feet to get onto the dock. We explored the town, shopped, ate out, stayed overnight at the dock, and left in the morning.

After lock number 4, we passed a sign, Saratoga National Historical Park, one of the many historic sites in this area. High on the hill to the west, a series of cannons faced the river. These were part of the Saratoga Battlefield, site of British General Burgoyne's defeat in October 1777 during the Revolutionary War. It was the first major victory for the Americans and a turning point in the war.

It rained on and off during the day; there was still no break in the humidity. We looked ahead as we rose through lock number 6 to see an ominous, threatening black sky. We quickly decided to tie to the wall after the lock to wait the weather out. Both Jim and I have been on the open water in many thunderstorms, and it was no fun. Pelting rain reduced visibility, strong winds made the boat difficult to control, and I always hoped that *Yankee Lady's* mast would not attract lightning. At least for this storm, *Yankee Lady's* mast was safely stowed on deck.

There were ropes attached to the wall, but they were too far apart for our twenty-eight- to thirty-foot boats. I knew I could depend on Jim to figure something out. He grabbed one rope from the wall and slid one of *Yankee Lady's* ropes through its eye, jumped on shore, passed our stern line through a cleat, and we were secure. It was an acrobatic maneuver that I could never have done. The others managed in various ways to get tied up also. Sharp streaks of lightning hit the ground near us, thunder crackled and boomed, the wind howled, and rain fell slantwise across our cockpits. We were glad we waited it out.

Just before lock number 7, we saw a marked side channel, which would take us to Fort Edward. We radioed the lockmaster to ask if the water was deep enough for our keels. He said he thought so although we might bump a little. We didn't bump, although it was close in a couple of places. *Misty*, with her three-foot draft, led in. If she touched bottom, *Yankee Lady* and *2nd Wind* with five feet under each of them, would go aground. We tied up at another long cement dock, also free, set against a very attractive park.

We asked a local couple walking on the dock about a restaurant. They told us they drive especially to Fort Edward to eat at Vickie's, across the street from the docks. Vickie's was, indeed, the popular local eating place. There was an extensive menu, which included homemade bread and pies. I've always felt that eating out provided a view of the local life in the town we were visiting. In this case, I hoped it provided some justification for buying 105 dollars worth of groceries at Price Chopper and then eating out for the next few days.

There were two more up locks, number 7 and number 8. After lock number 8, the canal was higher than the countryside. From *Yankee Lady's* cockpit, I looked *down* at fields and *over* housetops to see farmland.

Going down locks number 9, number 11, and number 12 was easier and quicker. There were no whirlpools created by incoming water, which caused the boats to shudder and shake, and it didn't take as long to drain the locks. As we motored between these locks, the canal became quite narrow in spots. I saw the former towpath, now a dirt road, and railroad tracks along the forested shores. *Yankee Lady* was in the lead followed by *2nd Wind* and *Misty*. It was just the three of us floating over a deserted watery highway. I could smell the fragrance of the north woods balsam trees. I love that piney smell; it reminds me of family times, hikes in the woods, and Christmas celebrations.

Lock number 12 at Whitehall marked the end of the Champlain Canal System and the beginning of Lake Champlain.

Lock number 12 marina was a small marina on the east side of the waterway. We docked there for the night in preparation for putting our masts up the next day. There were a restaurant and inn, a small ships store, clean bathrooms and showers, fuel and pump-out services, and the crane for putting up the masts. The crane was hand-operated by the owner. He reduced the price when he found that our now experienced crews were able to rig the boats after the masts were raised. We settled in for the evening and anticipated turning our boats back into sailboats in the morning.

Social life for many boaters involves late afternoon cocktails and appetizers. This life was not for me. I was very happy that none of us were big drinkers. Instead, we established the custom of getting together for dessert on one of our boats.

This night, Jim and I ate supper on *Yankee Lady* and then gathered on *2nd Wind* for dessert, a raspberry pie Rosie had bought at Vickie's. Big surprise, the six of us were fond of desserts. I loved to cook, Rosie loved to buy treats, and we all loved to eat.

All six of us spent the morning getting ready to leave. After the marina owner lifted *Yankee Lady's* mast with the crane, Jim had to connect the radio and electric wires that hung out of the bottom of the mast to the wires from the boat. I was nervous when he did this because the mast was suspended only inches above the deck of the boat. Jim had to put his hands under the mast, grab the hanging plugs, connect them to the wires extending out of the boat, and wrap them in electrical tape. Only then could he remove his hands and signal the crane operator to lower the mast. I always held my breath a little until this job was done.

We finished rigging *Yankee Lady* and stowed the wood braces for the next canal after Lake Champlain. We dumped the trash and bought ice and fuel. The others followed just about the same procedures. It was sunny; there was no shade on the dock. We were all hot, wilted, and ready for a lunch out before leaving.

Rosie treated us all at Finch and Chubb Restaurant and Inn. I had mixed feelings about this restaurant because last night, while making a phone call near the inn, Jim and I saw a beagle inside the door. One of the employees told us that she is left alone overnight as the "guard dog." Ever the dog lover, I was sure I heard her say in beagle, "Don't leave me, don't leave me," as the last employee left and closed the door. Nevertheless, the food was good. Even better than the food though was the unlimited ice water to drink in this hot, humid weather. Unlimited ice water is not a commodity on a small cruising sailboat.

We left at 3:00 p.m. The marina owner cautioned us to stay to the left near the Poultney River. *Yankee Lady* touched bottom once as we left the marina, but there were no other problems. This lower part of the lake seemed more like a narrow, winding river; we followed the buoys carefully as we passed green, grassy meadows on the shore and a forest of trees climbing the steep mountains behind them.

Twenty miles later, shortly after rounding a curve near Mount Defiance, we looked up and saw the imposing ramparts of Fort Ticonderoga. A symbol of strength from a past era, its walls bristled with cannon aimed in our direction. We anchored in the small bay to the south, just our three boats until joined by one other after dark. The first thing Jim and I did was to go swimming. He, of course, dove in; I followed more slowly down the ladder. What beautiful, cool, refreshing water.

Sometimes, I think that Jim is part fish. He loves to swim, and it seems as if he can stay underwater forever. He has used this skill many times to inspect the hull below the waterline. I remember one time when *Albatross* was anchored off Mid Cape Beach, part of the Florida Everglades. Jim had noticed a vibration in the shaft as we motored toward the anchorage. It was a calm, hot, sunny day. The sandy beach was one hundred yards in front of us, and the whole Gulf of Mexico spread out behind us. Jim dove in and swam under the boat. He diagnosed a loose zinc attached to the shaft. He returned to the surface, asked for a screw driver, put it between his teeth, and dove again under the boat. It seemed like forever before he resurfaced while I tried not to think about sharks and other creepy-crawlies. He fixed the zinc and climbed back aboard. Then we looked toward the beach with our binoculars. What had looked like logs lying on the beach were really crocodiles sunning themselves! There was no need to worry about such things in Lake Champlain even though the lake has a reputation for its own monster, Champy, probably a cousin of the Loch Ness monster in Scotland.

We relaxed in the cockpit, enjoying the cool breezes and the rosy colors of evening. How nice it was to share such an evening with a loving partner. We planned for a quick tour of the fort tomorrow.

In the morning, we took our dinghies ashore through the shallow water. Jim and I started out using the motor, but soon we had to switch to the oars because of the "algae soup" that fouled the propeller. Poling and paddling, we arrived at the shore and found the path leading through a grassy field to a steep set of stairs next to the Fort. There were signs saying, Caution, Live Artillery on the overgrown field to our right. Never mind, we won't go there. The last time I had been to Fort Ticonderoga, I was teaching sixth grade in Hinesburg, Vermont, and had brought the class here on a field trip. It was a two-hour trip in a basic yellow school bus. Although I'm sure the students gained some historical knowledge, I could have done without the two-hour rendition of "ninety-nine bottles of beer on the wall" that it took to get here.

This day as I stood in front of it, the fort was impressive. It had been built by the French in the shape of a star, the shape which gave the most opportunity for soldiers to shoot at the enemy. It had been the ultimate defensive weapon of the eighteenth century. How simple that seems now.

On May 10, 1775, three weeks after Lexington and Concord, Ethan Allen and Benedict Arnold converged on Ticonderoga with the same idea—to recapture the fort. Together, they marched on the fort, entered, climbed the stairs to the commander's headquarters, and knocked on the door. When the door opened, Ethan Allen ordered the British officer to "Surrender in the name of the Great Jehovah and the Continental Congress." The surprised commander surrendered without a shot being fired. This was the first American victory in the Revolutionary War.

We visited the museum with its memories of a distant time, looking at instruments of battle, daily living tools, and paintings of battles. Of interest to me was a rope bed on display. It had a twisting device, which was used to adjust and keep the ropes tight in order to support the sleeper. Now I knew where the saying "Sleep tight" originated.

The next segment of our voyage would take us to Malletts Bay in the Burlington, Vermont, area where we planned to spend two weeks. Jim's friend, Ken Stevens, had offered a free mooring to each boat. I needed to fly to Denver, Colorado, for a weekend meeting, and I knew I could conveniently fly out of the Burlington airport while we were moored in this harbor in Lake Champlain.

We planned to stop first at Vergennes, Vermont, a day's journey from Ticonderoga. We studied the chart carefully in order to see if we could take the boats up Otter Creek into Vergennes.

The chart showed the basin in Vergennes to be four feet, which was not enough depth. The cruising guide indicated six or seven feet. Further research solved the mystery. The chart was based on the low water lake level of ninety-three feet. I called the Coast Guard on the radio to determine the present level. They quoted the National Weather Service statement of almost ninety-five feet, which meant we could add two feet to the levels shown on the chart. There would be enough water.

We left around eleven the next morning, anxious to get to the safety of Vergennes before the predicted high winds and rain would arrive that night. We passed by Button Bay, found small green can 53 off a pile of rocks called Scotch Bonnet, and passed by Basin Harbor, all on the Vermont side. We needed to avoid the shallows of Fields Bay while finding can 51 to indicate the turn into Otter Creek. Otter Creek splits a small peninsula and is not easily visible from the lake. There were no buoys to mark it, but Jim saw a small motorboat enter and disappear behind the land. He concluded that this must be the entrance. The wind was blowing twenty knots as we made the turn, heeling us over slightly. It would not be a good time to run aground to leeward because the wind would force us further into shallow water. *Misty*, drawing only three and one-half feet, cautiously led us in. We really didn't know if it was the right entrance until we were there. This was what sailors call gunkholing—cruising into small and "out of the way" places. The cruising guide said that Vergennes had free dock space with electricity and water. We motored seven miles through meandering Otter Creek, not sure what to expect. How many people knew about this creek? Would there be space available? Would we have to anchor? We arrived to find one sailboat and three trawlers tied up at the dock. There was enough room for *Misty* and *Yankee Lady* to tie up also. *2nd Wind* rafted to *Yankee Lady*, and we were all secure.

The docks were in a small basin formed by a spectacular dam and waterfall. There was an old factory and an old mill at the top of the falls. We walked five minutes up the hill to the city, the third city to be incorporated in the United States. The term "city" seemed a misnomer because the main street with shops, restaurant, and a library was only three blocks long.

That night, it blew a gale and poured torrents of rain, but we felt safe and secure at our somewhat flimsy but adequate dock. Because we were in a narrow river, there were no waves to bounce us around, something to be very grateful for since we all have experienced many a wave-bumpy harbor in storms. It cleared by midmorning and turned hot and muggy. We climbed the hill to town and checked out the shops. Jim and I ate at the deli and stopped at Luigi's for ice cream. Back at the dock, Jim patched the dinghy, which had developed a leak.

In the morning, we retraced our path through Otter Creek, a little more confident on the way out. The creek was about two hundred feet wide. We stayed in the middle where we found depths from six to eighteen feet. The creek was lined with trees, a few summer camps, ramshackle docks, two small marinas for fishing boats, and some year-round homes. Fallen trees hung out over the water. The spaces between the trees revealed meadows dotted with blue chicory, yellow tiger lilies, and other colorful wild flowers. There were menacing deadheads on either side of the creek. These heavy water-logged branches or small trees have partially sunk to the bottom with only a small portion appearing above the water. They could do serious damage to a boat hull if hit the wrong way. This creek felt more appropriate for a canoe than a saltwater cruising sailboat. I recalled that boating in a canoe is an intimate and personal way to experience a river. Although I was in an ocean-going sailboat, this river evoked some of the same feelings.

As we headed north on Lake Champlain, familiar mountains appeared on the skyline. They reminded me again of my life in Vermont. There was Mount Abraham where I picked raspberries and stepped on a snake; Camel's Hump, everyone's landmark;

and Mount Mansfield, where my family and I have skied and hiked. The Burlington skyline appeared with the tall buildings and spires of the University of Vermont crowning the hillside. I remembered walking across that campus from the parking lot to classes, especially to an 8:00 a.m. geology lab, on below zero, windy, winter mornings.

Jim and I charted a GPS course for Colchester Shoal, rounded it with no problem, and entered a way point into the GPS for the railroad cut that leads into Malletts Bay. The water on the south side of the cut was grassy and shallow. *Misty* and *2nd Wind* headed to the north; staying away from the shallow section, we followed and entered Malletts Bay. We headed 120 degrees to the inner bay and aimed for the three radio towers as we had been directed by our host, Ken. We asked several boaters for the location of Hazelett's moorings. One pointed us in the right direction; we found them and each crew picked up a mooring. Jim took the dinghy ashore to contact Ken who worked for the Hazeletts. He appeared in a small runabout and led us to the three moorings that had been set aside for us. Ken also gave us the use of his truck.

The atmosphere was pure Fourth of July holiday weekend. Sailboats tried to sail in hardly any wind, powerboats churned up the water, and families on their moored boats jumped in the cool water and cooked on their barbecues. The bay was rimmed with hills and mountains. We jumped into the cool water. This would be our home for the next two weeks. Jim and I went to Ken's house to call my daughter, Cathy. She and her husband, Jon, would drive from New Hampshire to meet us at the boat the next day.

Cathy and Jon arrived at noon in the humid heat and very little wind. We motored around Malletts Head over to Porters Point until the water started to get a little shallow. We passed near the camp that belonged to my friend, George. I kept an eye out because this was a sentimental spot where I had started sailing again over twenty years ago.

George had let me keep my new Boston Whaler Harpoon sailboat on a mooring here for two summers. My children and I spent many happy days sailing in this bay before I moved permanently to Connecticut. One particularly memorable time was when my son, Larry, and I were sailing downwind on a breezy day. I pulled up the centerboard, and we went flying across the water, barely skimming the surface. We held on and enjoyed the ride.

Jim and I anchored *Yankee Lady*, and all four of us went swimming. Jim and Jon practiced diving and cannon balling while Cathy and I each floated serenely on square blue flotation cushions. After we climbed back on board, the breeze freshened; we raised the sails and, with a smiling Jon at the helm, sailed in the bay for two hours. Close hauled, *Yankee Lady* heeled over smartly and achieved seven knots. It was a perfect afternoon.

After we returned to the mooring, Jim took the dinghy ashore to pick up Ken and his wife, Ann, so they could join us for a potluck supper. Because we were ten people in all, we rafted with *2nd Wind* so everyone would have a place to sit in relative comfort. Cruising sailboats don't have group accommodations. After dark, we watched the fireworks. The booms and the exploding, cascading lights celebrated Independence Day.

The next day was a glorious rest and relaxation day for all of us. We didn't plan to go anywhere until late afternoon when we drove over to Ken and Ann's for a cookout at 4:30 p.m. What a pleasant evening, a perfect summer barbecue followed by pleasant conversation. Ann treated us to a display of clog dancing, her flying feet, and intricate steps tapping out the beat of the Gaelic music. We returned to the boats just before a different kind of fireworks display, thunder and lightning.

The next two weeks were filled with a variety of activities and adventures. We met a summer liveaboard couple who joined the six of us on *Yankee Lady* to show us their favorite charted anchorages. All eight of us were enjoying ourselves when someone looked outside to the west. We saw a long, dark wall of clouds, which looked like a cliff rising above the water. That wall was moving quickly toward us—an approaching squall. Six people scrambled into their dinghies. They reached their boats with five minutes to spare. Jim and I closed our open ports and hatches. The shrieking wind, forty-five knots at peak, arrived first, followed by torrents of rain. White caps churned the lake that had been flat calm; raindrops pelted the water, splashing and forming staccato patterns across the surface of the waves. *Yankee Lady* swung back and forth on her mooring, straining against the wind. Then, after forty-five minutes, the front passed, and all was calm again. We were grateful for our secure moorings!

One evening, after dinner, Jim and I watched a mother duck and her eight fluffy babies come over for a hand-out. All enjoyed bread crumbs until four ducklings were separated from Mom by the trailing dinghy. Immediately, all four set up a plaintive cry of "Peep, peep, peep," until Mom found them.

My son, Larry, and granddaughter, Allyson, age five, arrived from New Hampshire to stay overnight and go sailing the next day. After a good night's sleep and breakfast, we raised the mainsail and sailed off the mooring. The water was calm in our protected bay. I pulled out the jib, and we sailed toward Malletts Head. As we rounded the first point, *whoosh*, a major gust of wind hit us. Larry, veteran of sailing the Harpoon on this lake, said, "That's Lake Champlain for you, never a steady wind. It's always gusty between these two points." We reefed the jib and continued. We saw the next gust coming across the lake. It heeled us over until the rail was almost in the water. I was deciding that we should reef the main when I looked up. The sail had solved the problem for us—one of the batten pockets had ripped out. That was the end of sailing for the day. Jim released the main sheet to get the wind out of the mainsail. I let go of the wheel and reached over to start the engine. The wheel spun around, the bow swung through the eye of the wind, and the wind filled the back side of the jib so that we heeled sharply over on the other side. The sails were flapping wildly as the boat righted itself. Larry and Ally tried to stay out of the way, while Jim went forward to pull the mainsail down and secure it to the boom. I released the jib sheet. The jib whipped noisily back and forth, flapping wildly until I could grasp and pull the furling line with all my strength, which rolled the flapping jib tightly around the front stay. Quiet was restored. *Yankee Lady* was upright and under control. That was enough excitement. We looked at the building white caps and decided to return to the mooring.

The next day, Jim, Larry, Ally, and I went ashore to try to find a sailmaker. Someone at The Moorings recommended Shore Sails on Pine Street. We drove there, but they weren't open this Saturday afternoon. The weather deteriorated to cold and rain. We had left our warm clothes on the boat. When we returned, we warmed up with the help of the alcohol heater. Snug again, we ate the spaghetti dinner, salad, and chocolate cake that tasted especially good.

At the same time we were fighting the elements, the four others aboard *2nd Wind* were trying to sail and motor out of Malletts Bay across the lake to Plattsburgh. The waves were so steep and the wind so strong against them that they were making only two to three knots headway. They agreed that it would take forever to get there and that they were not having fun. So shortly after us, they returned to their mooring and took Ken's truck to Burlington for shopping and supper out. They were smart enough to wear warm coats.

Sunday was beautiful with a clear blue sky, puffy white clouds, and calm water. We motored *Yankee Lady* out of the bay, crossed a five-foot shallow section, circumnavigated Stave Island, which was owned by Ken's bosses, the Hazelett brothers, and picked up one of their moorings on the protected east side. The New

York Adirondacks and the Vermont Green Mountains framed a spectacular view.

On our return, we figured out a way to do some sailing even though we didn't have the mainsail. After all, the jib was still okay. So we motored toward the railroad cut that enters the bay, turned down wind, and unfurled the jib, which bellied out in front of us, full of wind. We sailed into the bay, enjoying the no-motor quiet. I was content—peaceful sailing, glorious views, and perfect companionship.

Almost back, I furled the jib and motored to the mooring; Jim picked up the mooring line with the boat hook. Since my early sailing days I have always tried for perfection when approaching a mooring. The concept is the same whether under sail or motoring, but there is more control with the motor. The idea is to get to the mooring line by heading into the wind. There should be little or no speed left so that the boat does not zoom past it. Of course, with the motor, you can always add extra speed at the last minute or put the engine in reverse if your speed is too fast. Depending only on the sails requires more skill and better timing.

It was time for Larry and Ally to leave. Larry packed up, and Jim took them ashore. I was also glad that, in spite of the big wind and the ripped mainsail, Larry was able to experience the quiet joy of sailing when we unfurled the jib.

After Jim returned to *Yankee Lady*, we watched our neighbors in their forty-foot racing boat return and pick up their mooring under sail. The boat had no engine. They timed it perfectly, and we were impressed. Then we saw *2nd Wind* approaching, also under sail. They appeared to be doing the same thing. Jib furled, main luffing, with Barbara at the helm, they rounded into the wind and glided to the mooring. Tom Frasca picked up the mooring line. "Yay," I called over, clapping my hands, "good job."

But Rosie was poised to go over the side, and Barbara shouted, "We're on fire." In an instant, Jim grabbed our fire extinguisher and was in the dinghy. Smoke was pouring into *2nd Wind's* cockpit and out the hatches. When he reached, *2nd Wind* Tom Isele told him that it appeared to be an electrical problem with lots of smoke, but fortunately, there were no flames. He turned off the batteries, and the smoke died down. More than a little shaken, Rosie and Barbara motored *2nd Wind's* dinghy over to join me on *Yankee Lady.* They needed to regroup and get some fresh air while the men diagnosed *2nd Wind's* problem.

What had happened? They had been sailing in the gusty wind when they decided that it was too uncomfortable to continue. Leaving the sails up, Tom started the engine to motor back to the mooring. Before starting this trip, Tom had the boat rewired, but evidently, the string of wires had not been secured properly. When the boat heeled over with the engine in gear, the wires fell toward the spinning shaft. A nut on the shaft caught the wires and pulled them out of the battery. There was a loud bang, the engine stopped, and smoke started pouring out of the engine compartment. Fortunately, this happened a short distance from the mooring although at one point, Barbara wondered if they should anchor and leave the boat. But there were no gas fumes from the engine, and there was no flame. Tom decided to continue toward the mooring. While he attended to the emergency, he handed Barbara the wheel and said, "Take her in," which she skillfully did.

Barbara was determined to go on this trip from the very beginning. Her sense of adventure is notable; she calls herself a gypsy at heart. Although she and Tom have owned *Misty* for thirty years, she has done most of the boat handling. Tom is more cautious and deliberate. Instant problem-solving is difficult for him, and emergency situations could be a major challenge. He was the most reluctant to undertake this voyage. In some ways, he and Jim are opposites. Jim is seat-of-the-pants Mr. Independent while Tom prefers to study a problem thoroughly before reaching a decision. Jim would sometimes become impatient with this approach.

Monday became the day for solutions. We called Bacon Sails in Annapolis. Yes, they had a brand-new sail that would fit *Yankee Lady* for $650.00. It would be mailed overnight. Ken put Tom Isele in touch with a mechanic who could rewire *2nd Wind* on Tuesday.

With calm restored on *2nd Wind*, Rosie invited us all for dinner. For an excuse, she said she wanted to use up some of the food she had bought on sale at the grocery store last Saturday. That's Rosie, always buying extra food and then inviting us over to share it. Rosie is everyone's hostess. She admitted that "she was just along for the ride" and claimed no skill at boat handling or navigation. But she has a keen sense of adventure and is always ready for any of our sailing trips. She could steer *2nd Wind* in the direction that Tom pointed out, but she made no decisions. More than once, when Jim and I were following *2nd Wind* in Maine, we watched Rosie motor straight over lurking lobster pot buoys. We marveled that she never snagged one in *2nd Wind*'s propeller. Tom was essentially single-handing the boat.

There were still more challenges. Tuesday, *Yankee Lady* had a suspicious smell. Jim dug everything out of the aft hatch to reach the holding tank. Yes, it looked like there was a small leak. Ugh. He cleaned out the compartment, disinfected it, changed and caulked one of the fittings. After moments of extreme discouragement—should we continue this trip—we hoped the problem was solved and/or we'd manage somehow until we got to open water. Dealing with marine sewage is something no one wants to talk about. Dumping of sewage in Lake Champlain is absolutely forbidden. In fact, we had to seal our overboard discharge systems before entering the lake. We used the pump-out facilities at nearby marinas and were glad to help keep the lake clean. This was not the place for a sewage problem. At the same time, Tom Frasca dinghied over to consult Jim about a fuel leak on *Misty*. Later, Jim went over to help. They found a leaking diaphragm in the fuel pump, certainly fixable although Tom would need parts from Wests Marine store.

Will *Yankee Lady* get her sail?
Will *Yankee Lady's* holding tank need repair?
Will *2nd Wind* get her wiring fixed?
Will *Misty* get the fuel leak fixed?
Will the half dozen adventurers get under way again?

Jim had a senior moment when we went to the ATM machine to get cash and change it into Canadian money. He couldn't find his debit card. We checked our records and found the last place he had used it was in Vergennes. That ATM had argued with him about how much money he could take out. When he finally got the cash, he forgot the card. The manager of the Merchants Bank in South Burlington kindly called the Chittenden Bank in Vergennes. Yes, it was there; what a relief. The six of us took an unexpected drive to Vergennes in Ken's vehicle.

I flew to Denver for my annual association meeting. While I was gone, the weekend was filled with a variety of activities and visitors, most of whom spent lots of time in the lake to keep cool. Mother duck entertained all by allowing them to feed bread to her eight babies. The babies would jump up and take the bread out of their hands, not environmentally correct, but irresistible. Mother stayed back and watched. The babies grew bigger every day. When I returned, we figured out the answers to the questions above.

We bought a used sail from Bacons in Annapolis, half the price of a new one. It fit perfectly.
Jim fixed the holding tank connections.
2nd Wind was rewired by a local electrician in two days, reasonably.
Tom Frasca fixed *Misty's* fuel leak.
The six adventurers would be leaving tomorrow.

We left in the morning for Stave Island. This was not a long trip, only seven miles, but we had left Mallets Bay! Psychologically and physically, we were on our way again toward our goal of circumnavigating New England. We entered the small cove, which marked the entrance to the island, and picked up three moorings courtesy of Hazeletts. Ken had told us the moorings were close to shore but that there was plenty of water at nine or ten feet. We were about thirty feet from the rocky shore. The land was capped by fragrant cedar trees and wild flowers. It was breezy and started to rain shortly after we arrived, but by evening, it was calm and beautiful. We were still feeling like intruders to this private space when the caretaker and his wife motored over and invited us to walk around the island. It seemed we three boats were well known to the Hazeletts even though we never met them. After thanking the caretaker, we decided to wait until morning.

At 4:00 a.m., we suddenly started bouncing. The sky was clear, but the wind was blowing around twenty-five knots, a passing cold front. We were slightly protected by the point, but I said to myself, "Ken, you better be right about this new mooring system." It was developed by Hazeletts specifically for Lake Champlain waters. Each mooring consisted of a two-thousand-pound block of concrete that was attached to a bungee cord, one and one-quarter inches in diameter. This was connected to a floating aluminum tube attached to a mooring pennant. That rocky shore was awfully close, but we stayed put, no problem.

By breakfast, the wind had died some. The waves were still choppy as we motored ashore in our inflatable dinghies. Inflatable dinghies are wonderfully stable and fun to zoom around in. Sitting on a rubber tube is relatively comfortable when it's calm, but in choppy conditions, whatever part of your body that is hanging over the edge will get wet. We all arrived slightly damp from the splashing waves. The small harbor was made secure by a concrete breakwater; it was calm inside. The harbor contained two sea planes tethered to moorings, a small floating dock, an imported sandy beach, and a docked sailboat. These were some of the Hazeletts' toys that Ken was employed to maintain. We landed at the floating dock. The main house was up the hill, slightly to the right, nicely landscaped with flowers, lawn, and trees. It faced New York State and the sweeping Adirondack Mountain range. We understood that the house now has indoor plumbing, but when Ken first came to work here, it did not. Instead, he told us, there was a double-holer outhouse with French doors. The top half of the doors opened to the great outdoors. One could enjoy a panoramic view of the Adirondacks while doing the necessaries.

We walked up the small hill and turned left onto a gravel path. Shortly, we arrived at a steep path with stone steps. We stayed on the gravel path and continued walking around the island. Sumacs, red and orange chokecherries, tall grass, and bushes lined the path. We reached the farmhouse on the Vermont side of the island with its wide-screen view of the Green Mountains. We crossed the yard and headed toward the lake where we found a narrow path through the woods. Brushing aside the spider webs, we walked up and down through cedar and pine. Breaks in the trees yielded a variety of views of the water. What a privilege to be on this private path, just the six of us. We took pictures of the boats from the rocks next to the trees, kept walking, and arrived back at the harbor.

Seeking the view from the fire tower, we retraced our way to the steep stone steps. We climbed them, and then holding onto the hand rails, we climbed the tower. What a 360-degree clear day view of the Green Mountains, the Adirondacks, and Lake Champlain. Sailboats and powerboats, appearing small in the distance, dotted the sparkling lake. We would be part of that scene tomorrow.

It was time to leave. We dropped the moorings, rounded Providence Island, and headed north on the broad lake toward the marina at Rouses Point where we could take our masts down in preparation for the Richelieu River and Locks. We avoided the ferries crossing the lake between Cumberland Head, New York, and Grand Isle, Vermont.

We were now leaving the mountains astern. They appeared smaller and smaller on the horizon as we approached Rouses Point. We motored by Isle La Motte and called the Lighthouse Marina at Rouses Point to ask for directions and to arrange for overnight slips. The gentleman on the radio repeated the directions several times in English with a French accent. We were getting closer to French-speaking Quebec. He told us to go through the railroad trestle, find the buoys leading to the south of the island, which was little more than a large patch of grass, and then head for the blue roof.

Many of the shallow spots on the lake were filled with long weeds reaching toward the sun. The depth sounder would read two or three feet in seven or eight feet of water because the weeds confused it. We passed through patches of these weeds in the channel and at the Lighthouse Marina. We planned to unstep the masts here until we learned the cost, about ninety dollars *plus* labor. Tom Isele called Marina Gagnon in St. Paul de L'Ile-aux-Noix. The dock master said there was a do-it-yourself crane that we could use for no charge. We could use the dock for seventy-five cents a foot for each boat to stay the night. We were committed to Rouses Point for this night, but we would wait until tomorrow to do the masts.

After spending three weeks in the Lake Champlain area, we would be leaving Vermont. I lived in Vermont for fifteen years while my three children were growing up. I think part of me will always belong there; I have so many memories. This would be the last familiar territory to me until almost the end of the voyage when we reached Maine. In between, we would be exploring maritime Canada, unfamiliar to us and ripe for adventure.

We headed north, entered the Richelieu River, and said goodbye to Lake Champlain. I was excited as we entered Canadian waters. I thought to myself, *This is another milestone in our voy-*

age around New England. I was looking forward to cruising in Canada. I have always considered it to be my second country. My grandmother was a Canadian citizen until she married my grandfather in Buffalo, New York. I studied Canadian history and geography at the University of Vermont. I was excited by thoughts of sailing down the St. Lawrence River to Nova Scotia, Bras d'Or Lake, and ultimately to Newfoundland.

The six of us had sailed to Canada before. Rosie grew up in St. John, New Brunswick, and is still a Canadian citizen. Together, we had cruised to the Reversing Falls and the St. John River to visit Rosie's family. On that trip, we had cleared customs at Grand Manan Island in the Bay of Fundy. It was a simple process, done by telephone. Now, we didn't know what would happen; we would be meeting the customs officer in person. The customs dock was small with room for only one boat at a time. We took turns circling in the river until we were all cleared.

The customs officer was friendly. I showed him our paperwork and told him about our plans to leave the boats in Canada over the winter for "maintenance." We had received confusing information about leaving our boats in Canada. We understood that American boats were not allowed to winter over without paying duty or tax unless a bona fide boatyard provided maintenance work. What constituted maintenance needed to be clarified. The customs officer called someone who advised him to give us a pass for four months. We would have to solve the maintenance issue later.

After we left the customs building, we followed the buoys to the narrow channel that leads to St. Paul and L'Ile aux-Noits where we would take down our masts. We turned to port and found Marina Gagnon, our first French-Canadian port, at red buoy EA22. Turning to port again, all three boats tied up at the long dock by the crane. I walked to the office to get the winch handle, which was used to turn the gears on the crane. I gave it to Jim, climbed onto *Yankee Lady*, and backed her into the narrow slot by the crane. Some say that backing a sailboat is almost impossible, but *Yankee Lady* is exceptional because of the configuration of the rudder and the propeller and because she has a fin keel. Not only that, Jim and I have had lots of practice. We were required to back into our slips at Offshore East Marina for the six years we kept *Yankee Lady* and *Albatross* there. In fact, when some of the male captains complained to Rich, the marina owner, about having to back in, he would respond, "Judy does it," which was a boost to my ego and, I guess, a challenge to theirs. I had practiced the technique a lot in the open water before I felt comfortable at the dock. On the other hand, Barbara said that backing up *Misty* "was not a pretty picture." Nevertheless, she was able to get *Misty* into position by the crane.

The process was much the same for all three boats: take out the cotter pins on the shrouds, tie the shrouds to the mast, lift the mast out with the crane, and lay it on the supports we built. Everything went without a hitch.

I operated the hand crank on the crane, which raised and lowered the masts. This was not easy for me. I could sail *Yankee Lady* anywhere, but I had no confidence in my ability to do unfamiliar mechanical tasks. It's difficult for me to process what someone is telling me to do. From the time I was young, I used to say that if there was a wrong way to figure out some mechanical task, that's what I would do. If my schools had been teaching mechanical tasks instead of traditional academics, I would have been considered to have a learning disability. Fortunately for me, schools focus on teaching language, math, and writing. I excelled at these. I think one of the main reasons I chose a career in special education, particularly the field of learning disabilities, was that I understood the panic and frustration of not being able to understand something when everyone else could.

Our next stop was the city of St. Jean. We found ourselves in French territory where some people spoke no English. St. Jean is the largest city on the Richelieu River. During the 1840s, it was considered the busiest inland port in eastern Canada. Now it seemed a little shabby and quiet. It is located near the southern entrance to the Chambly Canal at lock number 9, which we would be transiting on our way to the St. Lawrence River. We tied up at the long, floating Federal dock in the heart of town. A strip of park lined the waterfront; benches were provided for folks who wanted to watch the boats and people. There were metered diagonal parking spaces next to the park. Across the street were restaurants and ice cream stores (we always find them). The rest of the city was laid out in blocks leading up from the water. Buildings were attached to each other and no more than three stories high. Signs were in French only, except on federal land or buildings. The Pont Gouin was less than a block away. Even with our masts down, it would need to open for us tomorrow.

Jim and I strolled through the city, stopping in a few stores, but all we bought was one croissant. Many of the buildings were empty and for rent. The other four explored more of the historic spots and were given a tour through the Saint Jean L'Evangeliste Church, which was originally built in 1828. Barbara spent a good deal of time sketching the first of many delightful watercolors she would paint on this trip.

We found the restaurant recommended to us by some French Canadian sailors back in Mechanicville on the Champlain Canal—FABI bistro. The waitress spoke a little English, but ordering from our first French menu was a challenge. We were all asking for translations at the same time. Barbara and I were encouraged because we could recognize a few items. The waitress took it all good naturedly. At one point, when we asked about desserts, she used the word "chou" and could not translate it. Finally, she went back to the kitchen and brought the item out to show us. "Oh, a cream puff," I said.

She went back to the cook and enlightened him. "Cream puff." I ordered two things I had learned about way back in high school French class—Coquille St. Jacques and crêpes au chocolats. They were delicious. We were able to tell the waitress, who translated to the other staff, a little about our journey, including the recommendation from the French Canadian sailors. They were pleased and interested.

Another diner took a picture of the restaurant, which included us. I thought he might like to know about us and our journey, so I went over and started speaking in my hesitant French, "Nous avons navigué de Connecticut…" After about two sentences, he said, "I'm from Dallas." Feeling a little foolish, I started talking to him in English.

After dinner, the other four stopped at the ice cream store. Jim and I spent the rest of the evening sitting on *Yankee Lady*, planning the next day's trip on the Chambly Canal. During the course of this voyage, we worked together to plan and chart courses. Jim was more familiar with the GPS at first, but I soon got the hang of it. Jim was better at reading a chart to pick out potential anchorages; I preferred to consult a guidebook. We ended up doing both. We both used parallel rulers and dividers to calculate longitude and latitude positions from the charts. We needed these numbers to enter as waypoints into the GPS. For backup, we compared our calculations with the others. We had no fancy computer programs that could give us latitude/longitude readings with an instant click of a mouse.

There was occasional friction, particularly between Tom Frasca and Jim as to the best courses to plot, but generally, we agreed on destinations if not the exact routes to get to them. Jim felt very much the leader and would get frustrated and sometimes angry if we didn't stay together. He told me that since he had initiated the trip and invited the others to join us, they should accompany us. I had a hard time with his attitude about this but didn't know what to say that would make sense to him. It was a subtle undercurrent that would create tension between us now and again, but it was not sufficient to ruin the trip. There were too many positive things for that to happen.

The Chambly Canal begins at St. Jean and runs parallel to the Richelieu River for ten miles to Chambly Basin. This stretch of the river is shallow and full of rapids. Before the construction of the canal, it was necessary for travelers to portage around the rapids, which necessarily limited the size of the boats, the number of passengers, and the freight carried.

I had not realized the historic importance of this waterway. The canal was built in the mid-1800s. There are nine locks: one at the beginning of the canal and the last eight at the farther end. During construction, up to a thousand men, Irish immigrants and French Canadians, labored with picks and shovels. A towpath, now a bicycle path, was built along the side. Canal boat captains not only had to pay to pass through the canal, they had to pay the haulers who used horses on the towpath to pull the heavily loaded barges. The completion of this canal, the adjacent St. Ours Canal to the north, and the Champlain Canal in New York State created a waterway that became a "moving road" linking the cities on the St. Lawrence River to New York City by way of these canals, Lake Champlain, and the Hudson River. It was the creation of this waterway system that explained the prosperity of St. Jean during the mid-nineteenth century.

The locks are twenty-one feet wide and a hundred feet long. We locked through together with three small powerboats, all lined up against the lock wall. We paid by the length we took in the lock, which included the boat and the overhang of the mast. *Yankee Lady* was thirty-three feet long. We were last in at each lock and had to squeeze in close behind *2nd Wind*. We needed to make sure the end of the mast was clear of the closed lock gate, so we tied the dinghy across the back of the transom as close as possible. The back of the dinghy was under the end of the mast. We figured if the dinghy was clear of everything, so was the mast. Heading north, all the locks descended. We held onto lines, bow, and stern, gradually releasing them as we descended.

Each lock site was neat, clean, and well kept with green lawns, flower borders, and freshly painted buildings. The lockmasters were friendly and helpful. They all spoke English and French. All the locks were hand operated, which made me feel as if we had gone back in time. Each gate had two cranks: one to open the valve to let the water in or out and, one to open the gate.

Traveling through the canals felt very European. The canals varied in width between twenty feet and a half mile. At times, we were so close to the road we thought we should stop when the streetlight turned red. Part of the time we could see the broad, rocky Richelieu River to our starboard. We watched bicyclists, walkers, and people on Rollerblades pass by on the towpath. They returned our waves as we cruised along. One little boy in front of a mobile home blew us a kiss, which Jim returned. We passed by open farmland, colorful wild flowers, and settlements of neat, brightly painted houses.

The lasts three locks were like stairsteps. Lock number 3 opened into lock number 2, which opened into lock number 1. After we left lock number 1, *Misty* and *Yankee Lady* turned to port and found an anchorage in seven feet of water. *2nd Wind* turned to starboard and entered a small marina where Tom bought gas. Then he motored *2nd Wind* over to our anchorage also. Aside from the Jet Skiers buzzing around like giant, watery mosquitoes, it was a comfortable spot. After dark, it was quiet.

Our anchorage remained peaceful although it poured for a short time during the night. There was one light-up-the-sky strike of lightning and one boom of thunder but no wind.

In the morning, we left Chambly and the fort to guard the rapids, as they have since the 1600s. We crossed the lakelike Chambly Basin, careful to avoid the shallows by following the buoys through the middle. Mont St. Hilaire rose from the flat terrain on the starboard side. It was a gray, overcast day. After all the heat, the cool was welcome. It sprinkled a little rain off and on as we continued along the north-flowing Richelieu River, now deep enough for our boats, to Saint-Charles-sur-Richelieu.

The river was wide here and used for a variety of activities. It was calm except for a few passing powerboat wakes. We saw a seaplane practicing takeoffs and landings over against the shore. At the town of Otterman, there was a canoe race in progress. A police boat motored by to tell us this was a no-wake zone. I always chuckle at being asked to slow down in a sailboat, but we did anyway, leaving only ripples. Even on this gray day, we could see a crowd of brightly clothed people at the finish line.

The channel turned left at Ile aux Cerfs, a private, woodsy island. There was a sheltered anchorage between Ile aux Cerfs and Ile de Jeannotte, but it was too soon to stop. The chart indicated several public docks along the way. Most of them did not look inviting as we passed by, large cement bulkheads with no floating docks. The guidebook indicated a municipal dock at St. Charles, which we chose as our destination. It was just before a small cable-guided ferry.

The cable for the ferry was strung across the river, secured at either end. The cable ran through pulleys on the ferry; a diesel engine and a propeller push the ferry through the water. There was no way to manually steer the boat; it followed the cable. Boat captains are warned not to pass in front of the ferry; their boats could snag the rising cable. Instead, it is customary to radio the ferry captain and ask for permission to cross behind the ferry where the cable is sinking again. We would be doing that tomorrow. However, this day, we radioed the ferry captain to ask for information about docking. We saw floating docks, which looked inviting, but the captain said they now belonged to the restaurant, not the municipality. He suggested that the owner might let us stay.

We docked at three in the afternoon and found that the restaurant opened at four. Even though it was early, Jim and I saw lights in the kitchen, which was in the back of the building. I knocked on the door and, between a few French words and the use of sign language, indicated we wanted to eat there and stay overnight. The cook thought it would be no problem. His boss would speak to us.

St. Charles is a charming rural town. Buildings date back to the early 1800s. There was a monument to the French volunteers and soldiers who fought the British in 1837 and lost. A small merchant convenience-type store faced the Restaurant du Quai where we were docked. The ferry silently crossed the river when there was traffic for it. The streets were tree lined and quiet, and many houses had beautiful flower gardens. The town started at the river and extended four blocks toward a wide expanse of farmland. Tom, Barbara, Tom, and Rosie went to the local Catholic Church, which was nearby. It was a short service, in French.

We ate at the restaurant and talked to the owner about docking overnight. He gave us permission but said there would be a ten-dollar charge per boat, which we agreed to pay. He assigned us an English-speaking waiter. We did fairly well with the menu. Some words, like spaghetti, are the same in both languages. The restaurant was crowded, the waiter was busy, and my meal came five minutes after the others, but we had a good time.

We left the docks at St. Charles at 9:30 the next morning in light rain and a south wind. I was getting excited. We were heading for Sorel on the St. Lawrence River. It was hard to believe that I would be on *the* St. Lawrence River aboard *Yankee Lady*. We motored along the Richelieu River passing through more small towns and rural farmland. Each bend of the river produced a different view. At one point, we rounded a curve, leaving a small group of uninhabited wooded islands to starboard. Ahead, through the mist, lay two towns, one on either side of the river, each with a cluster of houses and church spires reaching skyward. The haze softened the outlines of the buildings framing the river; the muted green silhouettes of the trees on the islands provided a foreground accent. The scene was right out of an Impressionist painting.

We called the St. Ours Lock, twelve miles before Sorel, to see whether we should tie our fenders on the port or starboard side. The lockmaster replied, "Put your fenders and lines on either side." This was the first time any lock had told us to use our own lines or choose which side to put them on. What kind of lock was this? We all prepared fenders and lines on the port side. The mystery was solved when we entered the lock. There were floating docks on either side of the lock walls. Instead of holding onto a line to guide us down the wall of the lock, we tied to one of these long floating docks. The whole dock descended five feet inside the lock. We stood on the floating dock talking to each other and hardly knew we were going down. This was a lot easier than balancing lines and boat hooks. When the lock opened, I thought, *At last, after all these miles from Troy, New York, we are at sea level once again.*

After the St. Ours Lock, the river banks became steeper. As we approached Sorel, there were more and more houses perched on top of the banks. Colorful flower gardens and green lawns descended to the shore. We crossed latitude 46 at 1:26; we were more than halfway to the North Pole from the equator.

We motored under a highway bridge and passed through an open railroad swing bridge and under another highway bridge. I could see the broad St. Lawrence River ahead. A few minutes more and we reached it. We had followed the watery highway from New York City to this mighty river, which flows from the Great Lakes to the northern Atlantic Ocean. It was an awesome moment.

THE MIGHTY
ST. LAWRENCE—
FRENCH COUNTRY

We would be voyaging over the mighty St. Lawrence, the river that helped open up a continent. The St. Lawrence is Canada's second largest river. It flows approximately 744 miles from Lake Ontario to the Atlantic Ocean. The entire waterway system encompasses the Great Lakes whose headwaters are found in the North River of the Mesabi Range of Minnesota, which is almost 2,000 miles into the center of the continent. Its drainage area also includes Lake Champlain, which flows north into the Richelieu River and then into the St. Lawrence.

In 1759, Captain James Cook and two others charted the river approaches to Quebec City. Using these surveys and charts, a British Armada of over two hundred ships navigated the river and ferried troops to the fortified city where they attacked and defeated the French at the Battle of the Plains of Abraham. Many of Cook's charts remained standard navigational references for over one hundred years. In fact, we would be using a chart based on one of Cook's surveys later in this voyage.

We headed east from the junction of the Richelieu River and the St. Lawrence toward Sorel. There were two marinas in Sorel: Marina de Saurel and Parc Nautique Federal. We found the two sets of red and green buoys that would guide us through a channel toward Marina de Saurel. From there, we would need to double back and find more buoys closer to shore that would lead us to the Federal dock, which had a crane for stepping masts. The young lady on the radio at Marina de Saurel told us it was too shallow for a boat with a five-foot draft to get to the Federal dock; we would get stuck. But we needed to get in there if we were going to step our masts. Barbara and Tom aboard shallow-draft *Misty* said they would go on in. Jim asked them to let us know what their depth sounder read. They reported less than four feet, which was too shallow for us. It looked as if *2nd Wind* and *Yankee Lady* would have to go to Trois-Rivières, thirty-one miles to the east, to get their masts stepped.

After *Misty* radioed the depth at four feet, we tied up at Marina de Saurel where *2nd Wind* joined us. Later, Tom and Barbara walked over to Marina de Saurel to join us for dinner at the marina restaurant. Should we try to get into the Federal dock or shouldn't we? We talked it over while the six of us ate dinner. We decided to try in the morning.

We had been told that navigating the river between Sorel and Quebec City was straightforward; we could follow the main shipping channel buoys. Consequently, we didn't have charts for this area, but we found we weren't comfortable with this. The marina did not have the charts in stock, but Tom Isele's dock neighbor did have them. He kindly sold them to Tom since he said he had just finished using them and wouldn't need them again until he had time to replace them. This was one example of how, time and again, we found unique and creative ways to find the information we needed.

Jim woke early the next morning thinking about stepping the mast. He decided we should try to get to the Federal dock. We turned in the bathroom key, got our ten-dollar deposit back, and left Marina de Saurel. Parc Nautique Federal was only one-eight mile away but with perils unchallenged. I was at the helm steering close to a green and red buoy. Green should have been the favored side, so I motored close, leaving it to port. We dug into the mud with a squishy thud. *Yankee Lady's* bow went down, and then we stopped. It was time to use our Florida techniques for getting out of the mud. We have had more practice at this than I would wish for. Jim took the dinghy to the bow, pushed against the side of the boat, and pivoted the boat around 180 degrees to aim us back toward the deeper water. I used full power at the helm and spun the wheel back and forth, which caused the fin keel to zigzag through the mud and make a little trench for itself. This was accomplished with lots of body English on my part. Jim, using the inflatable dinghy like a tugboat, went around to the stern and pushed. We moved by inches at first but then gained speed rapidly as the mud released us and we reached the deep water. At that moment of release, *Yankee Lady* seemed to glide weightlessly across the surface, free at last.

I found out later that there was a channel on either side of the buoy; it was just close to the buoy that was shallow. We touched two or three more times on our way to the gas dock but plowed through without stopping. *2nd Wind* followed us to the dock.

The dock boy told us there was only three feet of water at the crane, but we were determined to get there. Jim took the dinghy over and measured the depth with our six-foot boat hook. He found about four feet ending in soft mud. It was time to try. I climbed ashore to join Tom Frasca. Tom Isele joined Jim on *Yankee Lady*. They motored her toward the dock as far as possible and then threw bow and stern lines to us on shore. Jim manned the throttle. With motor pushing and Tom and me pulling, *Yankee Lady* made it to the crane. We followed our, by now, familiar procedures for stepping the mast. Tom Frasca picked up the mast with the crane; Tom Isele and Jim stepped the mast and adjusted the rigging.

2nd Wind was next and, having a deeper draft, took more persuading. Jim returned to the dinghy and pushed *2nd Wind* toward the dock while Tom used full power. After several maneuvers, Jim and Tom concluded that they were as close as they were going to get, about two feet too far out. Since the boat was aground and already tipped, they decided to put the mast on with the boat heeled slightly. This was not an orthodox procedure, but they were successful. Getting out of the hole *2nd Wind* had dug into became more of a challenge. Finally, Tom and Jim tied one end of a line to an adjacent floating dock and the other end to *2nd Wind*'s winch. As they turned the winch and used the motor, *2nd Wind* began to move. They worried that the strain might detach the dock from the wall it was fastened to, but fortunately, it didn't. *2nd Wind* floated free, and at last, we were all sailboats again.

Sorel was the end of cruising guide territory for us. From here to Quebec City, we would have to rely on the *Sailing Directions* published by the Canadian government and the charts that Tom Isele had purchased from his neighbor at the dock. We hoped to find more information when we reached the marina at Quebec City. The *Sailing Directions* manual was written primarily for large ships, but there was some information that could apply to smaller boats. We planned to anchor for the night at Batiscan, forty-eight miles downriver from Sorel.

We left the marina in a foggy haze; the soft outlines of trees and buildings along the nearby shore appeared muted and gray. *2nd Wind* led the way since Tom had the original copy of the charts. We all turned on our radar equipment. Radar screens are not that easy to read. When Jim and Carol first bought a radar for *Albatross*, Jim had approached this with his usual problem-solving style. They anchored at the mouth of the Connecticut River on a sunny day, turned on the radar, and compared what they saw on the river with what they saw on the radar screen. Since then, he has had lots of practice. Even though I was sailing in Maine, I never had radar for *Yankee Lady* until I married Jim. At that time, he asked me whether I would rather have an engagement ring or radar. That was not a difficult choice; I instantly replied radar. He bought it and installed it on *Yankee Lady*. I have always thought that was a good choice, but I still think he's better at reading it than I am.

The river and the buoys spread out before us on the screen, a very comforting view in the limited visibility outside of the boat.

Our first racon loomed brightly on the screen like some huge ship. This type of buoy transmits a radar signal, which is visible on every radar screen as a big square dot. I felt as if it were shouting its location at us. Ordinary buoys appear as small dots on the screen. There was, however, enough visibility to see a large ship approaching us and the two freighters which overtook us heading downriver. We passed the large ship port to port.

I reflected that it was comforting to know the international rules of the road that apply to these types of encounters. I learned these when I studied for my six-pack captain's license in 1996. I was living in Maine when I decided to prepare for this license by enrolling in an eight-week evening course at a nearby vocational-technical school. I was the only woman in the class and the oldest person there. At the end of the class, I drove to the Coast Guard headquarters in Boston to take an all day test, which included sections on "Navigation," "Rules of the Road," "Boat Handling and Safety." Getting that license was one of the most exciting things I have ever done. It ranks up there with other personal landmarks, which include earning my PhD degree and buying my first cruising boat.

Other cruisers had told us to watch out for big wakes produced by the big ocean-going ships. We did not find this to be the case. I thought, *This isn't much different than sailing on Long Island Sound or cruising on the Hudson River where we have encountered tugs and barges and occasional freighters.* We entered Lac (Lake) St. Pierre which is really a ten-mile wide section of the river. We easily followed the shipping channel buoys. Just before Trois-Rivières, the river narrowed again. In general, we kept to the starboard side of the channel leaving the red buoys to port and the green buoys to starboard. We motored under the suspension bridge at Trois Rivières four hours after leaving Sorel. There would be no more cities until we reached Quebec City one hundred miles from Sorel. At last, the mist cleared, and the day brightened under a sunny blue sky. The river was a mile wide, broad and calm. A few farmhouses, small villages, and an occasional silver-roofed church with a "conspicuous spire" lined the shores. Later, over coffee and dessert, we all chuckled over the frequency of "conspicuous church spires" described in the *Sailing Directions*. With one exception, they all had silver-colored roofs. We would need more than conspicuous spires to use as landmarks.

We made good time to our anchorage at Batiscan. The current was in our favor the whole way, giving us an extra knot of over-the-ground speed. We left Sorel at 8:00 a.m. and arrived at Batiscan forty-eight miles later at 3:30 p.m. The public wharf was visible from the channel as were the yellow buoys marking the large ship anchorage. We continued toward shore, past this anchorage, until we reached a depth of eight feet. In perfect teamwork, Jim and I anchored *Yankee Lady*. I headed the boat into the wind and eased the throttle until we almost stopped. Jim released the anchor line and let the anchor drop into the water. After the anchor rested on the bottom for a moment, I put the boat in reverse. Jim let the line pay out for about fifty feet and then secured it around the cleat. He held the line and signaled me to increase reverse power; the line remained taut. With a wave of his hand, he indicated that we were set. The others anchored nearby. We felt safe from river traffic; no big ship will come in this far.

Jim and I climbed into the dinghy and sped at full throttle across the calm water. It was exhilarating skimming over the mighty St. Lawrence River in a small air-filled, rubber dinghy with the breeze blowing over our heads. We slowed down as we approached the beach, the bow of the dinghy grated across the pebbly beach and brought us to a stop. We stepped ashore near the wharf and were joined by the others.

Batiscan is a small village with a population of 875 people. It has a long history dating back to 1639. As with most cities and villages in Quebec, the silver-tipped church spire is a prominent landmark. We walked along the sidewalk of the main street, which paralleled the river and was almost the only street in town. Neat, freshly painted houses faced the river from the landward side of the road. Almost every house had a welcoming, colorful flower garden in front of it. Just behind this row of houses and shops, flat, prosperous-looking farmland spread into the countryside. We stopped at an art gallery featuring works of Canadian artists. The lady in the store knew a little English; I know a little French. Wonder of wonders, with her help, I actually carried on a small conversation with her in French.

We were back in tidal water. Jim and I had spent some time studying the tide book to make sure we had not anchored in water that would be too shallow at low tide. I've done that before. When I was sailing by myself in Maine, one of my first "down east" cruises was to Trafton Island in Pleasant Bay. According to one cruising guide, any destination east of the Schoodic Peninsula required self-sufficiency. There were a few public docks but no marinas; I was on my own. With a small knot in my stomach, I sailed past tall Petit Manan Lighthouse and turned into Pleasant Bay. I had plotted my courses before leaving my mooring in Winter Harbor, and I carefully followed the chart to identify the several islands that I passed until I found Trafton Island in late afternoon. The guidebook described the island and the shelter to be found behind it. It stated that one should not anchor too close to shore as the water shoaled rapidly. It was close to high tide; I motored toward shore as far as I dared to a depth of eight feet where I anchored.

Yankee Lady was the only boat around. The scenery was glorious. Tall, sweet-smelling pine trees pointed toward the sky and granite cliffs and a small, sandy beach formed the shore. An osprey glided and circled overhead. I was feeling very proud of myself until I looked at the fathometer as the tide went out. It read six and one-half feet, and it wasn't low tide yet. I needed five feet. I didn't know the range of the tide, and I didn't know the exact time of low tide. Just before dark, I decided that I better move. I started the engine, leaving it in neutral, and hurried to the bow. The anchor was between *Yankee Lady* and the shore. I needed to pull the anchor line in until I was over the anchor. I hoped that the water had not already shoaled to less than five feet there. It hadn't. I pulled the anchor onto the boat and motored out to a depth of ten feet to anchor again. I spent an uneasy night but managed to sleep. I learned an important lesson that evening: always know the range of the tide and the time of high and low tide before you anchor. It was so beautiful and calm that I stayed another day to enjoy the peace. I read, knitted, and looked at the view: Pleasant Bay dotted with pine-clad islands, the mainland not too far away, and puffy white cumulus clouds overhead constantly moving and changing shape. I listened to the hoo hooing trill of a loon somewhere out of sight and watched the gulls and an osprey circle overhead. I walked my dog, Skipper, on the island, treading on the soft carpet of fragrant pine needles as the sun filtered through the branches above. My passion for boating was alive and well.

Here on the St. Lawrence, after one rolling wake from a passing freighter, *Misty* decided to move into deeper water so as to not touch bottom in the trough of a wave. However, the wake from river traffic was nowhere near what others had predicted. After supper in *Yankee Lady's* cockpit and dessert with the others aboard *2nd Wind*, Jim and I returned to *Yankee Lady* to sit in the cockpit and watch the soft colors of evening. A cool breeze rippled the water. The light from the almost full moon formed a silver path on the water to our west, while the lights of the town illumined the river bank to our east. The dinghy slapped against the wavelets, obediently tied behind our stern. Evenings like these are one of the reasons I have gone cruising, and now I had someone I cared about to share these moments with me.

2nd Wind's anchor had wrapped around her keel during the night, so she did not face into the wind and current. Instead, she faced out toward the main channel of the river. This actually gave

Tom and Rosie a better night's sleep because they faced bow into the waves created by passing freighters. It is always more comfortable to rock up and down than to roll from side to side. The rest of us met the waves sideways, which meant we rolled with each wave. There were probably five or six freighters during the night, just enough to remind us where we were but not enough to keep us from sleeping. However, this was a mild foretaste of things to come later.

In the morning, Jim pushed *2nd Wind* backward with the dinghy to take the strain off the anchor line. I think he really likes to play tugboat. Rosie released the line from the cleat and let it drop ten feet into the water. The line passed freely under the keel; Tom hauled it in and raised the anchor. Jim returned to *Yankee Lady*. We left at 8:15 a.m.

Just off Cape Charles, we met a large freighter heading upstream toward Montreal or beyond. Suddenly, loud, patriotic music boomed over the water from a building high on a hill. We looked up to see a series of flags flying on a flagpole. These included Canada's national flag with red maple leaf on a white background and, I guessed, the national flag of the freighter's country of origin. As we beat time to the music, the freighter signaled two long and one short blast from its deep, very-big-ship-sounding horn. The music appeared to be a planned salute from shore. It continued all the while the freighter steamed by us. After the freighter passed, the music stopped; all the flags on shore except the Canadian one were lowered. Hopefully, I removed our American flag from its holder on the transom and waved it vigorously. We waited patiently for the "Star Spangled Banner" to boom out, but apparently, our three little sloops were not large enough or from the right place. Perhaps the freighter had called ahead.

The deep part of the river narrowed at the Richelieu rapids, the outbound current increased dramatically. At one point, Tom Isele recorded a speed of ten knots over the ground on his GPS.

The riverbanks became steeper. Small settlements of cottages nestled on the shore beneath the high cliffs. I could see no visible road from the top to the bottom. I wondered, *How did they get there?* Perhaps, it was by water. Farms and houses, probably with civilized roads, also sat on top of the cliffs.

As we approached Cape Rouge, we saw heavy black clouds to our northwest, a squall line, rapidly heading our way. Lightning flickered and thunder rumbled. Jim and I quickly closed all ports and the front hatch and put on our rain gear. The others prepared also; some put on life jackets. The water ahead of us was a strange, eerie yellow-green.

The wind came first. It whipped the water into white caps and blew the tops off the waves. We heeled over ten degrees even without sails. We increased our power to provide better control. Thankfully, our autopilot held the course, and we did not have to leave the shelter of the dodger to steer behind the open wheel. Before the rain obstructed our vision, we noted the compass heading to the upcoming bridge, which was just before Quebec City. Then the bridge disappeared. It poured torrents and kept blowing for about twenty minutes. We huddled under the dodger, grateful for its protection. Gradually, it cleared from north to south in time for us to see the bridge before passing under it. Just after motoring under the bridge, we saw a large red freighter coming our way. We moved to the right side of the channel and were silently thankful that we hadn't met this large vessel during the height of the storm.

There is a lock just before the marina basin near Old Quebec. I called the Marina du Port de Quebec from inside the lock, and we received dock assignments. Shortly after, all three boats were settled. It was 4:00 p.m.

After relaxing for a while, the six of us crossed the walkway over the lock and went in search of a restaurant in Port Royal, the oldest part of Quebec City. Port Royal was founded in the early seventeenth century by the French explorer, Samuel de

Champlain. A natural fortress, it became the capital of New France and fended off numerous attacks until the British captured it at the battle of the Plains of Abraham in 1759. It is the only fortified city north of Mexico whose walls are still standing. It remained a British colony until confederation in 1867 when it became part of Canada.

The friction between French Canadians and English Canadians that has long been part of their history still exists today. In many ways, French Canadians have a separate culture from the English Canadians. The most obvious manifestation of this is the difference in language. We met many French Canadians who spoke little or no English. Quebecers are proud of their heritage, and many see themselves as a separate political entity. On this trip, we experienced no animosity. Everyone we met was friendly, courteous, and willing to help. I think too that the French were pleased that we tried to speak their language. At least I had a basic knowledge of grammar and some limited vocabulary.

After dinner and sightseeing we returned to our boats. The full moon hung over the lighted city. The illuminated green gothic roof of the Chateau Frontenac and the silhouette of the Parliament building dominated the skyline. Both were visible for miles from the river and the surrounding countryside. Jim and I sat in the cockpit, enjoying the view on this calm, clear night.

After breakfast the next morning, the six of us met on *Yankee Lady* to discuss the next segment of our voyage. We planned to continue along the St. Lawrence River toward Tadoussac, a small town at the mouth of the Saguenay River. We decided to stop the first night at L'Isle-aux-Coudres, an island about halfway between Quebec and Tadoussac. We learned later that it was so well protected from storms that it was considered a harbor of refuge. We reviewed the charts and the tide/current tables and decided to leave in the morning at 7:30, a half hour before high tide at Quebec.

We all went our separate ways for the day. Jim's ear was hurting. The marina clerk gave us a map of the city and marked the locations we needed. She told us to walk through the mall, come out on the other side, and walk four blocks to the clinic.

The people at the clinic weren't quite sure what to do with us. Beside the language difference here in Quebec, Canadians have a socialized medical system, which entitles them to free medical care. We were neither French nor Canadian. Some of the staff could speak enough English to help us. From the waiting room, Jim was first directed to an office where a clerk took his name, address, and birth date. She sent him back to the waiting room. Then he was taken to another room where a nurse took his temperature and blood pressure. She took him back to the waiting room again and then to the doctor who looked in his ear and who said it was infected. The doctor wrote a prescription for an antibiotic and eardrops. This whole process took about one-half hour and was very efficient. We asked the doctor how much we owed. The doctor said she didn't know and asked a lady across the hall. She said she didn't think we owed anything. The lady who took our address came out and said we didn't owe anything. All this was done with lots of hand gestures and shrugging of shoulders. We were most impressed with our snapshot of the Canadian health care system, the courtesy of the staff, and the efficiency of the process. The price was certainly right.

On the way back to the boat, we stopped for an ice cream cone and went to the grocery store. It was late afternoon. We enjoyed a free hot dog at the grocery store which we called part of dinner. We ate cold cereal later. We sat on the boat for the rest of the evening talking to the others.

Several sailboats entered through the lock, including one which docked next to us. We have always found that local boaters could provide us with valuable local knowledge. At this point, we had charts of the river but no guidebooks. So we asked our new neighbor for information about sailing to L'Isle-aux-Coudres and

Tadoussac. He and his friends had just returned from Tadoussac. Since tidal currents will be a factor during this portion of the trip, we were particularly concerned to time our departure to take advantage of a favorable tide. We did not find our tide table/current book helpful. Because of his limited English, he found someone else from his group to help us. We walked across the dock to a boat named *Geronimo*.

We looked at the charts again with *Geronimo's* captain. His advice was quite different from what we had planned. We wouldn't need to leave until ten the next morning to catch the proper tide. He showed us a cruising magazine and two cruising guides, all written in French. He also told us about a bookstore where we might find better guides for the area. We decided to meet again in the morning. Jim and I spent a restless night with the change of plans on our mind. We decided that Barbara and I should go to the bookstore while everyone else talked to the Canadians.

At 8:00 a.m., I walked over to *Geronimo* to ask for help translating the magazine guide I had borrowed. He and the captain next to him had been talking about us. As a gift, they handed me two small tide books that explained the hours of current change relative to high and low tide. They also showed me a current book that displayed the currents hour by hour between Quebec and Tadoussac, similar to what Eldridge shows for Long Island Sound. We knew that the currents ebbed in this area at five or six knots and flooded between three and four knots. The tide book also stated that at the entrance to the Saguenay River, the current ebbed at seven knots. This caused us some anxiety because anything over four or five knots is just about impossible for most sailboats to motor through although with a few white knuckles, we three boats have been able to inch through six knot currents. This is why we felt we needed more information. The sailors showed me a nautical guide to the St. Lawrence River published by the Province of Quebec, which was in French and English. I borrowed it to make a copy.

Armed with the books, Barbara and I set out at 8:15 a.m. to find the bookstore Libraire du Nouveau Monde across the lock and a few blocks into old Quebec. We waited a few minutes until the store opened at 9:00 a.m. Barbara bought the French magazine guide and the current/tide book. The Nautical Guide was unavailable, probably out of print. On the way back, we checked at the nautical store near the marina. No luck there either. I picked out some key pages from the book we had borrowed from *Geronimo* and asked the marina to make copies so that all three boats would have the same information.

Meanwhile, Jim, Tom, and Tom had talked to the Canadians. The second captain was most common-sense helpful. He recognized our experience and said motoring through these currents wasn't much different than planning to motor through Hell Gate in New York or Woods Hole in Massachusetts. That was comforting, but I remembered inching against the current in Woods Hole aboard my O'Day 23 with the outboard at full throttle. I thought I would never get by the green buoy that was lying on its side at the dogleg turn. I thought, *It's all in the planning.*

The captain said, "Watch the buoys when you get to the Saguenay entrance. When they are straight up, go on in. You can watch the whales until then."

Everyone said, "Don't go in the fog."

We left the lock at 10:45 a.m., a little late, to motor to L'Isle-aux-Coudres fifty-two miles away. We chose the northernmost Channel de L'Ile St. Orleans in order to see the northern shore, which included the spectacular Montmorency Falls. They are 240 feet tall, which is higher than Niagara Falls. After we successfully passed through this channel and saw the falls, we read the *Sailing Directions* book, which recommended local knowledge for this passage. Oh well. We passed the large Gothic church and shrine, Sainte-Anne-de-Beaupré, and noted Mont-Sainte-Anne, which rose behind the village where its many bare ski trails were clearly visible.

We've noticed that every Catholic church, since way back on the Richelieu River, had silvery, aluminum sheeted roofs and steeples. There was a church in every town and city. The cruising guides and *Sailing Directions* mentioned conspicuous church spires as landmarks for every town. Today, we passed a town with two churches. One had a blue roof, the other, the standard silver. We all must have been looking at the same time and wondering about the denomination of the blue roof because over the radio came this question from Tom Frasca, "Do you think they're color coded?"

We joined the main shipping channel, which was clearly marked with large buoys. The towns, nestled in the slightly rolling hills on the north shore, faded behind us. Ahead, we saw a spectacular ridge of mountains. Steep cliffs and green wooded hillsides dropped sharply to the water. Across the ever widening river, we noted a few islands, their dark shapes accented against the rolling hills, which appeared blue in the distance.

This was a rugged coast. There were no harbors to duck into for protection nor were there any safe anchorages. Depending on weather conditions, it could seem awesomely beautiful or threatening and foreboding. Today had the potential for either. We were zooming along under a blue sky and white clouds; the current was with us, and the wind was behind us. Using all available power, we had our jibs flying and our motors running. But the weather radio indicated thunderstorms to the west and east of us although there was nothing in our area. Nevertheless, this time, we prepared for them. Jim and I unplugged the dinghy so excess water would drain out and we brought out our rain coats. However, for the rest of the day, the thunderstorms remained only a nagging threat. Every now and then though, as we continued east, we would feel a cold blast of air, as if someone had just opened the refrigerator door. We guessed this was a preview of what was to come as everyone said it was cold on the Saguenay River.

We lost the favorable current just as we made out the faint blue outline of L'Isle-aux-Coudres, about ten miles away. We had been flying along recording our speed over the ground between eight and nine knots. Now the three of us came to an abrupt halt. We dropped to one knot and then zero. It was too deep to anchor; we motored at full throttle just to keep from going backward.

We stayed at zero for about ten minutes at a time, and then we would pick up a little. I can't think of anywhere where I have gone nowhere to somewhere for so long. With the flood current opposing the wind, the waves built into an uncomfortable following sea. We rocked and rolled and measured our progress in tenths of miles. We were thankful there was no severe weather. The wind finally died, and the seas calmed. At 6:00 p.m., I checked the little current book, which said that the flood current stops at high tide. High tide was at 6:40 p.m. We noticed an increase in speed shortly after.

By 7:30, we were near the entrance to the marina at L'Isle-aux-Coudres. I called on the radio to see if there were three slips available. The dockmaster who could speak English said, "Yes, you can come in now, but you know there is no water at low tide." We figured that we might have trouble getting out at low tide, our keels might touch bottom, but this has happened to us before. No problem. The current was running out swiftly as we entered; Jim, who was at the wheel, had to judge his entrance so as to not drift toward the ferry at the dock a few feet down current. We passed between red and green lobster-pot-type buoys and into the marina.

Several friendly people, including the marina owner/harbormaster, helped us tie up. One heavyset gentleman, Pierre Laliberty, spoke to us in English and told us he would be glad to translate for us if we needed it. He laughingly recommended "cholesterol-free" poutines, French fries with beef gravy, and mozzarella cheese, to be found at the restaurant/marina office at the top of the docks. Since our supper had consisted of peanut butter and crackers plus three Chips Ahoy cookies, Jim and I decided to continue our healthy diet and try the poutines. It was delicious.

We met the others at the restaurant and sat on the outside deck to debrief and look at the view. The sunset was a feast for the eyes. Among multishaped clouds, which were turning gray, the sky provided a palette of colors: blue, turquoise, mauve, purple, and pink. As night arrived, tiny, sparkling candles of light appeared from the sparse settlements on the mountains across the river. A freighter passed by on the river, its dark shape also lit by points of light. Returning to *Yankee Lady*, Jim and I slept through the night unaware of the dropping tide.

In the morning, five of us decided to rent bikes and ride around the island. Rosie chose to relax on *2nd Wind*. The rental shop owner gave us a free ride up the steep hill to his shop. We rented multispeed mountain bikes. Jim and I have ridden our bikes for several winters while we cruised in Florida aboard *Albatross*. However, Florida was flat. Here we encountered several hills.

We approached these hills from very different athletic backgrounds. Jim is a very active person; he has excellent endurance. Tom Isele is also an active person. He and Rosie walk a lot all year, and Tom skiis in the winter. Barbara is an early morning runner. She plays basketball and competes in the senior Olympics. Tom, Barbara, and Jim rode up the hills with relative ease. Tom Frasca was a little slower, but I lagged behind everyone on some of the hills. I have always loved competitive sports; I was a good athlete in school, and I love to be outdoors, but I did not like to exercise just for the sake of exercise. If there was a reason for it, I would do it. Consequently, I was not in tip-top shape. I walked up more hills than anyone else. However, we all enjoyed and finished the sixteen-mile trip.

The island was geared to tourists. Road signs indicated that the roads were for bicycles as well as cars. Jim and Tom Isele decided to show off by riding with no hands. Tom noted that as a kid with a newspaper route, he could ride with no hands and fold newspapers at the same time I couldn't be left out, so I tried the no hands approach also and rode successfully for a few feet. However, I saw some wild raspberries by the side of the road and promptly stopped to pick them, a small taste of summer. My family knows that I am almost fanatical about picking raspberries. I've been stung by bees and was once bitten by a snake when I stepped in a hole next to a tree on Mount Abraham in Vermont while reaching through the thicket of prickly vines for just one more berry. Fortunately, there were not many poisonous snakes in Vermont. Every summer, I make at least one batch of raspberry freezer jam.

Many of the houses on this island were made of stone and had steep, colorful metal roofs. Most of them had well-tended, beautiful flower gardens. The fields were filled with wild flowers including my favorite blue chicory. The river flowed on our right, offering landward views of the mountains we had passed yesterday on the water. The outgoing tide revealed salty smelling mud flats. Yesterday, we had noticed these on the chart and had taken special care to stay away from them. We stopped at a gift shop and ate lunch about four miles from the end of our route.

The hills on this last part of the island were not really steep, but at the end of this ride, they looked formidable. I walked them. We all made it back to the bike shop satisfied with our day's adventure. The bike shop owner drove us to the marina. When we stepped out of the truck, we looked at the boats, shocked. Although the dockmaster had said, "You know there is no water at low tide," we didn't think he meant *no water*. The entire harbor was mudflats. The boats just sat there, keels deep in the mud, masts upright, waiting for the return of the water. The buoys we had passed at high tide rested on the ground. We walked to our boats. What a strange feeling to walk on a floating dock that isn't floating. I thought, *It's a good thing we didn't pump water into the toilet in the middle of the night last night. We would have been pumping in mud, which would not have been a good thing for our sanitary system.*

We relaxed and did chores for the rest of the afternoon. Jim and I took showers in hot, sometimes cold water. We ate dinner on the boat. As promised, after dinner, we met with Pierre Laliberty. He said he would talk to us about his trip to the Gaspé and across the Baie des Chaleurs. All six of us sat on the deck in front of the restaurant while he shared a wealth of local knowledge about ports between here and there. With his twinkling eyes, his laughing, turned up mouth, and round shape, he could have been a stand-in for Santa Claus without the red suit and beard. We thanked him enthusiastically. He replied, "Sailors are made to give and help each other. The only thing you cannot give is your wife and your money."

We left L'Isle-aux-Coudres the next morning at high tide in fourteen feet of water. We planned to stop at Cap-a-l'Aigle twenty miles away. We picked up a favorable current about an hour later. Although we have asked and received advice from local sailors, the six of us decided that we needed to figure the current for ourselves, which would not be easy until we could figure out the local current schedules.

We rolled uncomfortably on the first part of the trip, but the scenery more than compensated for the discomfort. After we passed Cap L'Oies lighthouse we motored past villages, which seemed folded into the flat spaces between the hills. Occasionally, we would see a lonely-looking house perched high above one of the villages. A few campers occupied a sliver of beach next to the river. I wondered how they got there.

The wind to the north, and the seas calmed down for a while. However, as we approached Cap-a-l'Aigle, the wind came whistling from the hills straight at us, which created a bouncy chop. I radioed the marina and, in my best French/English said, "Nous sommes trois bateaux, thirty feet, avec le profondeur of five feet. Avez-vous trois slips?" I thought I was getting better at nautical terms. There was room for us. This harbor was also well protected and considered a harbor of refuge. However, it was not so easy to enter. Tom and Barbara led us in, at first hesitantly, because the entrance was partially hidden by the breakwater and didn't come into view until they were quite close to it. We all motored in, keeping the town wharf on the left and the end of the breakwater on the right. Straight ahead was a long ramp. Following directions, we passed by the wharf, turned sharp right, and then left to pass down a row of floating docks. At the end of this small channel, we turned left and tied up to our slips. We arrived at 11:00 a.m., a short time for twenty miles, thanks to the current.

The floating docks of the marina were located in a basin created by the massive breakwater. We would find that there were only a few natural harbors on this river system; most harbors have been created by government-funded breakwaters. We were assigned spots close to the shore. As I sat there at low tide, I watched the ends of the floating docks sway back and forth in the wind, taking their attached boats with them. That seemed like a lot of pressure to me, but the docks were securely fastened to the shore and the basin bottom by chains and anchors. Later, at high tide, Jim and Tom Isele motored *2nd Wind* to the dock to get fuel. On *Yankee Lady*, I watched a large seal poke his head out of the water, dive again, and swim out of the harbor. Jim and Tom saw him (or her) from the fuel dock.

Sunday afternoon at this marina was typical of a weekend at any marina in the States. Sailboats and crews glided into their slips returning from weekend or vacation trips. People visited back and forth, laughing and talking about their experiences. Our docks were part of the walkway to shore. All who passed by noticed our American flags flying from our transoms. Some said bonjour, some, hello, and some just passed by. A few people stopped to talk to us in English.

We met Charley, retired from thirty-five years in the merchant marine, who said he sailed as a substitute first mate on the

Grande Fleuve, one of the whale watching boats at the Saguenay River. We knew that whales fed at the mouth of this river, and we told him we were excited about seeing them. He told us where to look and how to approach them. He said it was illegal to approach closer than four hundred meters (about twelve hundred feet). However, if they come toward you, that's different. You can't stop them from going where they want. Whales are sensitive to the vibrations of our engines and to the echo signals produced by our depth sounders. He told us to always keep our engines running and our depth sounders on so the whales could easily know where we were.

Around suppertime, we walked across the long ramp, which extended from the docks to the shore, wharf, and restaurant. I paused halfway across to look over the railing at the restless water below and listen to the sound of the wavelets splash against the granite boulders, which is music to my ears. Barbara, who had already run six miles round-trip, up and down the hills almost to Malbaie, recommended we take the short walk up the 16 percent grade to the first guard rail above the restaurant. This would give us a bird's eye view of the marina and the river. We climbed this before stopping at the restaurant for supper. What an expansive view! The marina, harbor, and adjacent coastline spread out below us. How different to see what the birds see. We could easily have figured out the entrance and path to our slips if we had seen this overview first.

The small restaurant on the second floor of the office building had a pool table, bar, and dining area. The kitchen, behind the open counter, looked like an ordinary house kitchen. One lady did all the cooking. There was much laughter between us, the non-English speaking cook, and the few customers as we tried to figure out "Pate au viandes." One fellow sailor kept saying, "Meat *PEE*."

Finally, it dawned on me. "Oh, meat pie." Tom Isele played bartender to get our necessary drinks, Rosie played waitress to pick up our orders, and we all enjoyed eating in this home-like atmosphere.

After breakfast, we left Cap-a-L'Aigle at 8:30 a.m., an hour after high tide, bound for the mouth of the Saguenay River where we hoped to see whales. We soon picked up the favorable current, at times achieving a speed of ten or eleven knots over the ground. We passed two lighthouses, both with white buildings and red roofs, which made them a little confusing as landmarks—which was which? After the second one, we saw three white forms rising and diving in the water close to shore. This was our first glimpse of beluga whales, but they were too far away to get a good look.

The wind was slightly gusty from the northwest. Jim raised the mainsail, unfurled the jib, and we sailed for a short while. It was such a good feeling to hear the wind in the sails and the water slapping against the hull. While a diesel engine is certainly quieter than an outboard engine, to a sailor, nothing can improve upon the sounds and feeling of pure sailing. I've wondered what it must have been like in the days before engines. Adventurers like Joshua Slocum relied on the wind, tide, currents, and on their ability to interpret them correctly—and Slocum sailed around the world. But for Jim and me, I must admit it was comforting to have a reliable engine. Tom and Barbara reported problems with *Misty's* engine; it wasn't putting out enough water. They were able to keep going, but the problem created a long, anxious day for them.

We arrived off the mouth of the Saguenay River at 1:00 p.m. and passed the red and white candy-striped lighthouse that looked like a spinning top. As planned, we were a little early to enter the river. The Saguenay is famous for its currents. At maximum ebb, it can flow as fast as seven knots. We had been warned by others that the waves in the rip currents could be as high as twenty feet, which we found hard to believe. As with other dire warnings, we knew we had to see for ourselves. We arrived at almost slack tide. There were eddies and rips, but nothing worse than anything we have experienced in our home waters of Long Island Sound at Plum Gut or the Race on a good day.

It was time to look for whales. We saw several small boats, past Ile aux Rouge and near buoy K51. Then we saw the spouts of the whales, right where Charley had told us to go. These giants were in the rip currents, which stir up the krill they feed on. We motored over remembering Charley's warning not to get too close. The other boats were commercial whale-watching boats, and I didn't think they were too happy to see us. We entered the frothing rips, slowed down, and circled. There were huge forty- to fifty-foot finback whales everywhere. We were right in the middle of them. We throttled back to neutral and sat there in wonder. They surfaced within ten feet of *Yankee Lady*. We could see their dark shapes before and after they surfaced, hear the whoosh, and smell their fishy breath as they spouted and then dove under the water again. Their brown shapes glistened as they rose and dived. It was humbling to watch forty feet of whale close by our twenty-eight-foot boat, but we were too excited to be scared. I thought to myself, *Whales are intelligent creatures*, and I wanted to believe that they knew we were there. Just then, Jim saw one surface practically next to us. He said it looked at us, and then not taking time to blow, it dove under the boat.

Jim, mentally addressing that whale, said to himself, "I hope you go deeper than five feet." Fortunately, it did. I was looking elsewhere, but Jim took a picture just before the whale dove under the boat to prove it. Then it was time to enter the river. Reluctantly, we left this awesome spot.

The Saguenay River is a deep fjord carved by the glaciers during the last ice age. Depths range from three hundred to over five hundred feet. For the first fifty miles of its ninety-three-mile length, it flows between steep granite mountains that rise abruptly from the shore to a height of one thousand feet or more. The width of the river varies from six-tenths of a mile to two miles.

When we told people we planned to cruise to the Saguenay, almost everyone who had been there shivered and said, "It's cold." We found out it was. This day in August, Jim and I wore sweaters, foul weather coats, hats, and gloves as we huddled beneath the dodger to keep as warm as possible.

The river did not let us in easily. We passed through choppy rips at the mouth. We thought the waves would calm down after we passed the rips. Instead, we faced twenty-knot headwinds, waves with white caps, and a bouncy, uncomfortable slow ride in what seemed to be an ebbing current against us. *What happened*, Jim and I wondered, *to the favorable current indicated in the tide book?* As I sat shivering behind *Yankee Lady's* dodger, I wondered how Tom and Barbara were doing. Fortunately, *Misty's* ailing engine kept chugging along. The gray, cloudy skies made the circumstances seem more dramatic. Despite the drama, we marveled at the magnificent views of mountains, cliffs, bays, and capes.

After four hours and fourteen miles of coping with the weather, we rounded Cap de l'Anse au Cheval and found a haven behind Île Saint-Louis where we anchored in twenty-five feet of water. We had marked this spot on the chart as a potential anchorage, but you never know what it will be like until you get there. After facing wind, cold, and waves, there is no way to adequately describe the peace of a quiet anchorage. It was calm behind Île Saint-Louis's two high, pine-covered, granite hills. *Yankee Lady* rocked gently in the water securely anchored to the bottom. We settled in for the late afternoon and evening. For a while, we sat in our sheltered cockpit and enjoyed the majestic scenery.

It was calm in the morning; the water was flat. Tom, Rosie, Jim, and I circumnavigated Île Saint-Louis in our dinghies. Tom Frasca fixed his engine and cleaned *Misty's* cabin. Jim and I beached our dinghy at a small, pebbly beach, an indentation between the cliffs. We climbed across slippery granite rocks to some piles of driftwood. We selected a few pieces plus some sweet fern and red berries to share with *Misty* and *2nd Wind*. We climbed higher, boulder after boulder, to gain a bird's eye view (a not too high-flying one) of the fjord northward. It was worth the climb.

We ate lunch at anchor and then left, motoring between Île Saint-Louis and the shore in over sixty feet of water. *Misty* purred along with the rest of us. Six miles later, we entered L'Anse-St-Jean thinking to anchor there for the night. The bay was beautiful. A cluster of houses, a town wharf, and a marina occupied the southeast end. On the opposite side, we saw green hills and cultivated fields, punctuated by a waterfall. The lower end of the bay dried out at low tide. We looked for a place to anchor where we would be protected from the wind. We found eight feet of water west of a tree-topped islet near the bay entrance, but we decided that we did not want to sit at anchor watching the ominous, lurking rocks nearby.

We continued toward Baie Éternité. We looked and felt like three toy boats set against the immensity of the cliffs and mountains. After following the steep mountain-sided river, we abruptly arrived at the bay on our port. The two capes on either side of it were the highest points on the river, fifteen hundred feet high. Their glacier-scoured cliffs dropped hundreds of feet straight down. When seen from the river, Cap Trinité on the northwest side resembled three giant steps. A thirty-two-foot-high statue of the Virgin Mary, Notre Dame du Saguenay, was located on the first step four hundred feet above the river; a cross was located on the second step at seven hundred feet above the river. We turned to port and entered the bay. Steep cliffs towered over us on either side as we motored toward the end of the bay. Ahead, a lush, grassy meadow filled a small valley. The meadow was divided by a sparkling, meandering river. "It was a sight," as one of our French Canadian fellow sailors had said, "to fill the eyes." I decided that Baie Éternité must be one of the definitions of the word spectacular.

There were eight moorings, provided by the provincial park service, available for cruising boaters. *Yankee Lady* narrowly lost the race for the last empty mooring to the catamaran who motored in just in front of us. It was just as well; the others needed to anchor anyway, and we wanted to stay with them. Anchoring was not so easy. The end of the bay shelved sharply from ten feet or less to one hundred feet or more. Jim and I tried three times before the anchor set. We figured that the first two times the anchor caught on the shallow edge of the shelf and just slid down it into deep water. Only *Misty's* anchor held on the first try. Of course, in the middle of all this, big gusts of wind swept down from the mountains, making our efforts that much more diffi-cult. Tom Isele, on *2nd Wind*, had the most trouble. Finally, even though he was in deep water, his anchor seemed to hold, so he stayed there for the night. *Misty* and *Yankee Lady* put out second anchors to keep us from swinging too close to shore.

During an evening rain shower, we were treated to a double rainbow. Its palette of colors arched over the harbor, the moored and anchored boats, and the mountains on the south side of the harbor. As far as I'm concerned, no man-made effort can beat Mother Nature's beauty. We gathered on *2nd Wind* for dessert and coffee.

In the morning, three moorings near the provincial park's dock became available. Even though these moorings were only twenty feet from shore, the water was sixty feet deep. Tom and Barbara raised their two anchors and motored over to one of the mooring balls. Then Tom motored his dinghy over to tell *2nd Wind* about the second mooring. Tom Isele took his dinghy to the second mooring and tied it onto the mooring painter, a nautical way to secure a mooring reservation. Tom Frasca ferried him back to *2nd Wind*. After the third mooring became free, Jim and I raised our two anchors and motored *Yankee Lady* over to it.

Between sailing *Albatross* in Florida and *Yankee Lady* in the north, Jim and I have developed a variety of techniques for getting our anchors up. This time, Jim tied a fender on the second anchor line and dropped it in the water. That anchor was now free of the boat. Then, he hauled in the first anchor. I motored *Yankee Lady* in a slow circle while Jim stowed the first anchor. I next approached the floating fender as if I were approaching a mooring, pointing *Yankee Lady's* bow into the wind. Jim picked up the fender with the boat hook as *Yankee Lady* slowed to a stop. The line for this anchor needed to be stored by winding it around a large spool. It was a nylon line that tended to get tangled; I always had trouble with it when I was single-handing. But Jim was in charge of the situation. He slid the spool onto the boat hook pole. He tied the pole across the bow pulpit with the spool in the middle. As he pulled the anchor in, I placed the line onto the drum and wound the line by spinning the drum around the pole. There was nothing to it. As usual, I continued to marvel at the way Jim could make difficult things look easy. I motored over to the third available mooring. I thought to myself that sometimes it's comforting to gain the security of something more permanent than an anchor.

Our plans were to go ashore at 10:00 a.m. and hike to Cap Trinité, a one-and-one-half-mile climb. However, *2nd Wind* had other plans. Tom Isele could not raise his anchor. He called Jim and Tom Frasca over to help. To get more pulling power, they wrapped the anchor line around the jib sheet winch on the side of the boat. All three of them tried to crank up the anchor. *2nd Wind* heeled over. They winched again; *2nd Wind* heeled over more. Finally, when the anchor was within thirty feet of the boat (as marked on the anchor line), it would budge no farther. There was *2nd Wind*, heeling over on her side, firmly attached to a taut anchor line. What was the matter?

This was not the first (or the last) time that Tom has had anchoring dilemmas. Jim recalled another time in Great Salt Pond on Block Island when Tom's anchor was caught on something. Someone had told Tom to use a winch. Unfortunately, Tom had taken his main halyard off the sail and tied it to the anchor line. He then started winching just as if he were raising the sail, but since the halyard was attached to the top of the mast, the pressure from the anchor succeeded in pulling the mast toward the water. When Jim saw him, *2nd Wind* was heeled over almost to the gunwale. At this point, the anchor was within reach. It was firmly attached to the main water hose that supplied water from the town to the Coast Guard station! Tom tied another line around the hose to hold it in place, released the halyard enough to take pressure off the anchor, and then disentangled the anchor. With the anchor stowed on *2nd Wind*, Tom untied the hose and let it drop to the bottom. Then *2nd Wind* popped to an upright position.

Jim took the dinghy ashore and explained the problem to a park ranger who could speak some English. The ranger found three carpenters, two men and a woman, who were building a tent platform in the park. These three left their project and boarded a raft meant for pulling moorings. They were carpenters, not boat people, so Jim had to start the outboard motor for them. They putted over to *2nd Wind* while Jim followed in our dinghy. Then he and Tom Isele climbed aboard the raft. Tom tied *2nd Wind* to the raft and transferred her anchor line to a small winch on the raft. For almost two hours, this little group tried valiantly to winch the anchor up the remaining thirty feet. They succeeded in raising it to within ten feet of the chain but could get it no farther. Since the raft was now attached to the anchor, *2nd Wind* was free to leave. Tom Frasca and Rosie untied *2nd Wind* from the raft and motored over to the mooring. Leaving the raft attached to *2nd Wind*'s anchor, Jim ferried the carpenters to shore, gave Tom Isele a ride to *2nd Wind*, and returned to *Yankee Lady* in our dinghy. Everyone stopped for lunch.

After lunch, the ranger motored over to *Yankee Lady* in the park's workboat to talk over the situation and think about alternatives. He realized that Tom Isele didn't want to cut the anchor line and lose his anchor, but no one could see what the anchor was attached to or figure out how to get it up. The young ranger was most sympathetic. With a big grin, he gestured toward the river and said, "How you say, like a bath tub, I could go pull the plug?"

The ranger and Tom returned to the raft with a crowbar and a rope. This time, they winched the anchor line until the end of the chain just touched the raft, but they could get it no further. The raft was tilted so far over that one edge of it was in the water. They deduced that whatever the anchor was attached to, it was huge. One end of the mystery object was still on the bottom, ninety feet below. We never did find out what it was. Finally, with Tom's permission and Canadian ingenuity, the ranger attached his own line, shackled it to the chain, put a mooring ball on it, cut Tom's line, and declared it a new mooring for the harbor. He told Tom he had a free mooring anytime he comes to Baie Éternité. Four boats rafted on it that night. We wonder if it is still there.

During the afternoon, we walked to the Visitor Center and toured the exhibits using English audio tapes for guides. At last, we found out why the current was always ebbing. The cold water from the Atlantic, the Labrador Current, sweeps into the depths of the fjord. The warm water from Lac Saint-Jean at the head of the river overlays it and flows out, causing a circulation pattern that continually refreshes the fjord with nutrients. It is the same system, which attracts the whales for their summer feeding. Since the warm water continually flows out, there is never a favorable current for entering the river.

We spent the evening on *2nd Wind*, laughing (even Tom Isele) about the activities of the day, eating dessert, and playing cards. We enjoyed a secure night on our moorings.

It was cool in the early morning; the mountaintops were covered with clouds. By 9:00 a.m., they were clear. We walked to the Visitor Center to leave certificates of appreciation for Dominic, the park ranger, and the others who had worked on the anchor.

They were freshly created on my laptop computer and printed on my portable printer. Then it was time to tackle the mountain, a little over a three-mile hike round-trip. Not bad, you say? Ha, sometimes, it felt like straight up or straight down. The four others went on ahead of us. Jim and I started up a moderately steep trail and passed under a massive boulder jutting out over the path. Three picnic tables, a fire ring, and an oven-like chimney fit underneath. It was an interesting place for a picnic, and I supposed that hikers could use it as a rain shelter, if necessary. Then we came to the first set of stairs. From then on, it was stairs, rocky path, strategically placed seats to rest on, more rocky path, and more stairs. I think there were supposed to be twelve hundred stairs, but I didn't count them. There was a small shelter part way up and a large log cabin near the summit.

We stopped at an observation platform where the sign said we were twelve hundred feet above the river. We could see the entire bay, the Éternité River Delta, part of the Saguenay River, and our boats, tiny below us. The view was a just reward for our effort. Continuing along, we crossed inland and slightly upward to the log cabin shelter. But this was not the end. The path to the statue, Notre Dame du Saguenay, trailed down to the first level of the mountain—four hundred feet above the river. This involved more stairs and more rocky and dirt paths. I was a bit daunted when I saw all the steep steps going down. My knee hurt, and I thought, *Oh no, I have to climb these steps on the way back. Should I go?* The answer was yes. As we walked down the steep trail, we passed through pine and maple trees which were sweet smelling and beautiful. At last, we joined the others on the ledge near the statue.

Two tour boats passed by, one paused and saluted the statue by playing Ave Maria over the loudspeaker. Jim and I found a compatible seating arrangement on two boulders, which were at right angles to each other. They were as comfortable as two flat rocks could be. Our ledge ended at the top of a steep cliff. There was a small wire fence that marked the edge of the cliff. I had no desire to walk over to it for a better view of the water below.

We lingered after the others left, enjoying the view and the day. But then it turned colder and started to rain. As we started back, the paths became slippery and muddy. We had one raincoat and one poncho, which more or less kept us dry and warm. I found those twelve hundred steps down more challenging. My knees hurt, and I became frustrated with the rain and the slippery going. Almost in tears, I asked myself, "Am I ever going to get off this mountain?" It was slow going, and several times, I used Jim for balance. He was very patient, but my pride and my confidence took a beating. Finally, we reached the dinghy. I was very glad to get back to warm, dry *Yankee Lady*.

Everyone came over to *Yankee Lady* to talk about the day and to eat dessert and play cards. Dominic came by to collect mooring fees from *Misty* and *Yankee Lady*, but *2nd Wind* still stayed for free. We gave him a small dinghy size North Cove Yacht Club burgee, made by Jim, who asked him to put it on the mooring. We don't know what he'll do with it.

We dropped our moorings at 9:00 a.m. and motored out of this magnificent bay. As we approached Cap Trinité, we looked up to see segments of the path, the twelve hundred stairs, and the observation platform. The sight was more meaningful since we had been there the day before. We rounded the cape and headed north until we were abeam of the statue. We gave her a mental salute as she stood guard over the Saguenay River. Was she blessing it? We felt blessed to have experienced its grandeur. We turned south to leave, motoring in calm water and warm sunshine.

Jim wanted to see for himself that this fjord was deep right up to its steep cliffs. We motored to within three feet of one cliff; I could almost touch the rough granite. The depth sounder read thirteen feet. Jim wanted to go closer, but I wouldn't let him. *Yankee Lady's* sides were too tender for that granite wall. *Misty* took a picture of us dwarfed against the mountain. Heading downriver, we motored behind two islands on our port side, just before Île Saint-Louis. A meandering creek and a small, green valley begged to be explored by dinghy. We identified an excellent anchorage, just off the creek, but there was no time. We couldn't even say, "Next year."

I think St. Margaret's Bay more than made up for that lost stop. As we approached the bay, we saw little slivers of pure white rising and falling in the water. These were the beluga whales. We motored into the bay, stopping well before we reached the whales. We idled there, motors running. They came closer to us, spouting and blowing bubbles. Four swam over to *Misty*, staying briefly beside her or under the boat. One nosed up to *Misty's* rudder, as if nibbling it. Tom was pacing on the deck, watching and saying, "I can't believe it. I ran out of film." Then they came over to *Yankee Lady* and swam all around our boat. Four of them, appearing to be a family, stayed for a moment under the boat. Then one, about fifteen feet long, swam up to our rudder. We leaned over the stern rail as far as we could. We hardly dared to breathe. We could see the entire whale, head to tail, poised under us for a brief minute. Its white skin appeared light brown because of the tannic acid in the water. He (or she) turned sideways, and one black eye looked up at us. We looked back, making eye contact. It was a spiritual moment—two of God's creations in silent communion with each other. Although I guess aquariums, which proudly display their captured whales and dolphins, will enrapture and educate some visitors, seeing them in the wild like this will forever spoil us. We reluctantly left this enchanting place.

The wind and waves picked up and were against us until we left the river and turned to port to enter the marina area at Tadoussac. Although there was an anchorage nearby, which would have been secure in any wind but south, we decided to enjoy the security and convenience of the docks at the marina. I radioed Club Nautique de Tadoussac to obtain dock space for our three boats. We rounded the high public pier (quai) and followed the directions of the young man who motioned us to our three spaces at a long finger dock. The dock was connected to a central walkway, which led to a clubhouse containing the office, showers, and laundry facilities. By evening, the finger docks had filled up with mostly transient boats.

Tadoussac is definitely a tourist town in the summer, and I think the whales should get extra credit for the influx of people who come to see them. Cruise and whale-watching boats of all sizes were docked at the quai or at nearby floating docks. These were the boats we had seen when we were whale-watching before we cruised up the Saguenay River. Other boats, including one graceful old schooner, took passengers for tour rides. Some rounded the point to cruise up the Saguenay River.

In the winter, about five hundred people live here. During the summer, the streets are busy with people. The sidewalks were lined with gift shops, restaurants, and boutiques. A large hotel, three stories high with a red roof, cupola, and rooster weather vane, dominated the waterfront. It overlooked a small crescent beach. I observed that the size and shape of the beach increased or diminished according to the tide. At low tide, I noticed several people walking the beach and two very happy black and white dogs, running, splashing in the water, and running again.

It blew twenty-five to thirty knots for the better part of the next day. We decided to stay put. I was still a little stiff from the mountain and was happy to rest, read, and relax. Jim fixed the hot water tank, helped Tom Isele fix his macerator pump, and did the laundry. All six of us walked to one of the hotel restaurants, the one in the back, not the fancy one in front, for dinner. Later, Tom, Rosie, Tom, and Barbara went to church while Jim and I walked back to *Yankee Lady*. I made coffee and fixed the strawberries Rosie had bought for dessert. When the others returned, we ate strawberry shortcake and discussed plans for the next day. The weather still sounded iffy.

We continued to meet friendly, helpful people. A sailor from the Coast Guard boat helped Jim find a three-fourths inch plug to fix our hot water heater. While I was sitting in the cockpit, a man named Jacques stopped to comment on our voyage. He offered to lend us two cruising books: the one we had tried to buy in Quebec and a French one. He put his name and address in the book and said, "Return it this winter." I could never get tired of this kind of Canadian hospitality. The French navigation guide *En suivant le Saint-Laurent: De Montréal* à *la Baie des Chaleurs* became our most valuable guide for this area. I was grateful for my high school French and successful guess work that enabled me to translate the information we needed for this unfamiliar cruising ground. It became the victim of several coffee emergencies in *Yankee Lady's* cockpit, so at the end of the voyage, I ordered a new one to return to him.

The next morning, the weather forecast had not improved. In fact, we faced gale warnings, so here, we stayed. The six of us, together or separately, went for walks, viewed a video on beluga whales at the Visitors Center, ate at various restaurants, and shopped. I thought, *We are beginning to get bored. It's time to move on.*

At last, we had favorable weather to leave—blue sky and a light wind from the southwest. We left at 8:00 a.m. on an ebb tide. Leaving was easier than entering had been because the light wind did not stir up many waves in the tide rips.

We set course down the coast for the Bergeronnes, hoping to see whales. We were not disappointed. A small pod of finbacks headed our way. Again, we slowed down and tried to steer parallel to their course. One seemed about to cross *Yankee Lady's* bow; we stopped, and the whale turned. We knew that this whale was an intelligent creature, but we were relieved to see it turn just the same. Two others surfaced just to the starboard and behind us, blowing so loudly that we jumped; we hadn't seen them coming. Another surfaced beside *Misty*, too close for their comfort.

Then another surfaced upwind of us, so close we could smell its fishy breath. We were so impressed every time we encountered these magnificent beings. To think that they cruise thousands of miles north and south during their annual migrations is one of the wonders of creation.

It was time to head across the St. Lawrence River to the south shore. We planned to pass Île du Bic and enter L'Anse à l'Orignal (Moose Bay), forty-three miles from Tadoussac. We still hadn't seen the biggest whale of all, the largest living mammal, the blue whale, which was known to feed in this area. Halfway across the river, we saw more spouts. Then *2nd Wind* spotted a gray-colored whale with large flippers. Jim and I didn't see that one, but shortly, there was another spout nearer to us. Yes, it had a gray shape, a smooth back with no fin showing, and it was rolling over so that its large flipper extended above the water. The flipper was so huge Jim and I figured that this had to be a blue whale. It was too far away to get pictures.

The coast of the south shore consisted of narrow ridges of hills, which ran parallel to the shore divided by deep valleys. We could see other hills through the valleys, giving everything a three-dimensional effect. One mountain, Pic Champlain, had a conspicuous line of cliffs that took the U shape of a California mudslide, except that it was granite. It hung ominously over the few houses on the beach, several hundred feet below.

We passed our charted waypoint, red and yellow cardinal buoy "Roche Alcide" (Alcide Rock). The buoy had two black triangles on top of it pointing up. Neither Jim nor I had encountered many cardinal buoys on our voyages, and we needed to check the chart and *Sailing Directions* to figure out that we should stay north of it. The cruising guide indicated that the rock was situated on top of a shoal three-tenths of a mile long. It was a small rock with a depth of four feet over it. Small or not, we didn't want to hit it. The buoy was located just north of the reef.

Actually, we always refer to local charts when navigating unfamiliar waters. There are international rules governing aids to navigation, which are standard for North American shipping traffic. These define the shapes and colors of buoys and other navigational markers and the procedures for vessels, which pass them. Almost all boaters know the mnemonic, "Red on right returning," which refers to the lateral buoy system and is a handy way of remembering that when returning from sea or entering a harbor, red buoys are kept to starboard. When cruising offshore, the lateral system rules state that red buoys should be kept to starboard when traveling in a clockwise direction around land masses. An easy way for me to apply this is to remember that the red buoys are always closest to the continental land mass, whichever direction I am traveling. I think my favorite lateral buoy is the red and white vertically striped "safe water" buoy. It is used to mark landfalls, channel entrances, or channel centers. It may be passed on either side but should be left to port when proceeding in either direction. To me, it says, "All is well. It is safe to come over here." After a stormy or foggy passage, it signals a safe arrival to me. I've thought, *We've made it this far. Now we have to follow the other buoys into the harbor.*

After passing north of Alcide Rock, we left low-lying Île du Bic to port. It was a green wooded island, about two miles long. Drying ledges of slate fringed the shore. We needed to avoid the reef and pass by a small island at the entrance to Anse à l'Orignal (Moose Bay). We carefully entered the bay between Cap à l'Orignal, 238 feet high, and Cap Enragé, 250 feet high. In these parts, it is important to pay attention to the tidal range. Here, it was about twelve feet. Twelve plus our five-foot draft is seventeen. To be safe, we anchored in twenty-three feet of water near Cap Enragé. Here, we would get the best protection from the forecast east or southeast winds.

I absorbed the northern, salty view: rolling hills, cliffs dropping into the water, beaches spotted with driftwood, and rocks covered with seaweed. At low tide, the inner part of the harbor dried out, leaving small mounds of sand and rocks. At high tide, these turned into several small, puffy islands. Jim and I dinghied around these and across the bay to the visitor's center. This area is a provincial park, and we observed many hikers on the beaches and a few kayakers paddling nearby. We landed on a rock and walked through a very large raspberry patch. Unfortunately, a very large number of people had also picked them. I found and ate two ripe ones.

Before returning to *Yankee Lady*, we took the dinghy to the small island at the entrance of the bay and landed on a rock ledge. I hoped to find raspberries, but the woods were too thick to walk through. However, it was pleasant to sit together on a sun-warmed rock and look at the beautiful harbor. These islands were much like the ones in Maine, but we wondered if the seals spoke French.

The wind blew all night, but it obliged us by staying to the southeast where we had the protection of land. Behind us lay the wide St. Lawrence River. A north wind would have created uncomfortable waves.

It was cloudy in the morning when we left the harbor. Isolated rays of sun highlighted clusters of seaweed, which glistened green and yellow against the gray, rocky shore. We passed the small village of Havre du Bic. There, we noted the usual groups of houses and a gleaming silver church steeple. The bay was shallow here but would have been accessible with local knowledge.

Twelve miles later as we approached Rimouski, we were careful to keep to the outside of Ile Saint-Barnabé, which lies about two miles off the city. At low tide, it is connected to the mainland by mudflats, no way for us to go. The island was uninhabited, topped by pines, and fringed by a gravel beach.

There was a picture of the harbor in our French guidebook, which made finding the entrance to the marina easier. We kept buoy H2 to starboard, headed straight for a large wharf with a green buoy just before it, rounded the buoy, and turned left, following the wharf and breakwater in front of it. The entrance appeared at the end of the breakwater. There was also a breakwater on the other side of the entrance, which protected the marina. From offshore, it was frequently difficult to pick out the openings between breakwaters like these; we usually motored slowly until the entrance appeared. Then we would see with relief that everything made sense.

Rimouski is a commercial port, considered to have the best shopping in the area for marine and hardware supplies. After we docked and were settled, we walked by the freighter and ferry docks one-half mile to a Canadian Tire store, passing a small shopping center and an assortment of stores. Jim was able to obtain stove alcohol, an electric heater to plug in at the dock on cold nights, and an alternator belt. He couldn't get the raw water pump belt or the impeller for the water pump.

Barbara and I had discussed the need for the next small scale chart, number 4026, after number 1236 ran out. When the six of us gathered in the evening, she showed us another example of Canadian helpfulness. The marina did not have this chart in stock, but there was one on the wall. The person in the office took it down and made copies of it piece by piece on the office copier. Tom and Barbara taped it together, and voila, the necessary chart of the area. Later that night, Tom made copies for each boat.

At 5:00 a.m. the next morning, Barbara walked to the marina office to use the ladies room. There was a picture of a little girl on the door; the men's room, obviously, had a picture of a little boy on the door. At 5:30 a.m., Tom Frasca, half asleep, walked to the marina to take a shower. After he was thoroughly wet, he looked around and thought, *This shower is a single shower and a lot cleaner than I remember seeing last night. I wonder if I'm in the ladies room.* Someone opened the door but didn't enter. He anxiously finished. When he was through, he checked the entrance door. There was the picture of the little boy! Someone, this early in the morning, had switched the pictures, and Tom, indeed, was in the official ladies room—thankfully alone.

As planned, we left at 8:00 a.m. bound for the port of Matane forty-five miles away and the beginning of the Gaspé Peninsula. This peninsula is a popular tourist destination, famous for its French Canadian culture and for hunting and fishing in its forests and waterways. It lies between the estuary of the St. Lawrence River and the Baie des Chaleurs and extends 150 miles into the Gulf of St. Lawrence. It marks the southeastern point of the province of Quebec. The interior is a mountainous wilderness, completely forested and punctuated by numerous streams and lakes. This mountain chain, called the Chic Chocs, is an extension of the Appalachian Mountains. Above the forest at the highest peaks lies the tundra, home to the last herd of caribou outside the arctic. The forests also have the highest density of moose outside of Alaska. Settlements are almost wholly confined to the coast and are composed of picturesque fishing villages and a few small cities. It was this coastline and some of these villages and cities that we would be exploring during our voyage.

We motored in a slightly lumpy, following sea under a mackerel sky. I am wary of a mackerel sky. I had learned when I taught sixth-grade science that a mackerel sky meant a warm front was approaching with wind and possible rain showers. *Ignore these clouds at your peril*, I thought. I had ignored them once before when Jim and I were sailing *Albatross* from Bimini in the Bahamas to Fort Lauderdale, Florida, and we had been caught in the Gulf Stream in the middle of eight thunderstorms followed by ten-foot waves.

The scenery changed from views of mountains, hills, and beaches to views of low, flat ridges of cultivated land, villages, and small settlements. A little less than halfway between Rimouski and Matane, we passed the one and only anchoring spot, Anse du Petit-Metits. It was marked on the west side by a lighthouse and two buildings, which were white on the bottom and red on top.

A reef extended one-half mile out into the river. Since we did not plan to anchor there, we stayed more than a mile off shore. Just before Matane, we passed a small forest of modern windmills, all motionless on this calm, gray day. I knew they were good for the environment, but they were ugly to us.

We arrived at Matane and passed the end of the large breakwater where a red flashing light signaled the entrance to the new commercial port. The entrance to the old port and the Club du Yacht de Matane was one and one-half miles farther toward the city. This entrance was marked by a private red/white buoy. The water was shallow on either side of the entrance. Two long breakwaters extended out from the basin where the yacht club was located. The waters of the Rivière Matane flowed between these breakwaters, which provided a relatively deep channel, but we didn't think at low water there would be enough depth for us to enter. As instructed by the French guidebook, I called the yacht club on channel 68 before entering the channel. The operator told us it was high tide and that there was twelve feet of water in the channel; there would be no problem. He also told us that the basin was dredged and never had less than six feet of water in it. We were assigned slips over the radio and adjusted our fenders and lines accordingly. There was a charge of one dollar per foot for each boat. We motored through the breakwaters, turned left into the basin, and found our slips.

The yacht club building contained a sitting/dining area, a kitchen, and an office. There were free showers and a laundry in a separate building. As was traditional at yacht clubs, the rafters were lined with burgees from other yacht clubs. We were sorry we didn't have a North Cove Yacht Club burgee to add to their collection, especially because the members we met were very interested in our journey.

As we were registering, someone ran in and said there was a seal on the boat ramp. We hurried over and stood behind the fence. Sure enough, a little guy, probably young, was three-fourths of the way up the ramp, definitely unhappy to be surrounded by people. Two men approached him. He growled at them, showing his teeth, a spunky little critter who was very frightened. His big brown eyes made your heart melt. One of the men took a long oar and prodded him toward the water. After more growling at the oar, he turned and humped toward the water, stopping once more to argue with the oar. At last, he entered the water, took a few strokes with his flippers and tail, and dove out of sight into safety.

All six of us needed to eat dinner and buy groceries. The yacht club maintained a dinghy dock across the channel next to a shopping center. We left our three dinghies at this small dock and walked through the shopping center to a pub/restaurant. Matane is famous for its locally caught shrimp. Five of us ordered shrimp dinners, which were delicious. Jim doesn't like shrimp, so he ordered fish and chips, also delicious.

Buying groceries for our three boats could be a delicate balance. We didn't have refrigerators, so we relied on ice to keep our food cold. It was not much of a problem for Barbara since she is a vegetarian and cooks accordingly, but Rosie and I needed to figure out how much perishable food we could buy and use before it spoiled. This was a challenge because we didn't know when we would find the next grocery store. We kept thinking we would be venturing into the wilderness and would need lots of food on hand. Instead, we would find more towns with restaurants. Rosie and I were never ones to pass up a good restaurant, so therein lay the challenge—lots of food on hand and a good restaurant nearby. What to do!

The mackerel sky was right. It was dark and starting to rain when we returned to our boats. The weather forecasts for tonight and tomorrow morning were not good. Rain and high winds were predicted, calming by afternoon. We met on *Yankee Lady* to discuss the next harbor possibilities, near or far. We decided to see what the weather was like in the morning.

It rained and blew most of the night and early morning. We had tentatively agreed to meet for breakfast at the yacht club at 7:00 a.m. Four of us made it, but Tom and Rosie thought that if it was raining, we would meet later. It was certainly a go-back-to-bed morning. They showed up at 9:00 a.m. The waitress didn't speak English, which added to our already confusing morning. Jim ordered toast; the waitress brought him two eggs, bacon, home fries, toast, and coffee. That's also what I ordered; now we had two big breakfasts. Jean, a young man we met yesterday, was sitting nearby, so we invited him to share one of our breakfasts, which I thought was a creative way to solve the surplus food problem. Since he was bilingual, we could converse with him easily while we dined together. As we talked about our plans, he supplied us with the names of some people in Shediac, New Brunswick, who may be helpful when we haul our boats there for the winter.

We all decided to stay put for the day. We shopped, napped, and visited in the yacht club. In the evening after church, Tom, Barbara, Tom, and Rosie joined us in *Yankee Lady's* warm cabin for dessert: sponge cake layered with Cool Whip and Canadian blueberry sauce. Eating dessert aboard *Yankee Lady* after church was becoming a tradition.

Over dessert, we reviewed our planning strategies. How far should we travel in a day? There were many variables to consider including the weather, available harbors or anchorages, facilities ashore, and sights of interest. We decided that short twenty- to thirty-mile trips were better when possible because we would have more time to go ashore and see the countryside. That was part of the purpose of this voyage. We planned to leave in the morning no later than 9:30 in order to have enough water to get through the breakwaters before low tide. It would be twenty-seven miles to Les Méchins.

Jim spent an uncomfortable night because his tooth, the one that will eventually need a root canal, was hurting. In the morning, his jaw was swollen. We needed to do something *now*. I checked at the marina office at 7:00 a.m. The clerk called a few numbers; there was nothing open, which was no surprise on Sunday morning. There were no dentists and no clinics available. The only option was to go to the hospital to get a prescription for the infection and for a painkiller. By 8:00 a.m., we took a taxi to the hospital. It was quiet in the lobby. Since we didn't have a Canadian medical card, the admissions clerk, who spoke about two words in English, showed us the price—$286.00. We both looked dismayed, gasped, and said, "Wow." She evidently felt compassionate because she gestured for us to follow her; she did not officially admit Jim. We followed her down the hall to the triage nurse. Again, Jim pointed at his jaw and said he just needed a prescription. The nurse told us to sit down (*asseyez-vous*) and disappeared. A short while later, we were ushered into an examining room where we met a young doctor who spoke a little English. He examined Jim's mouth and wrote a prescription for the necessary medicine. He said Jim shouldn't drive a car, and we explained our voyage. He was very interested in our adventures. We asked, "How much do we pay?"

He replied, "Ten dollars." With great relief, Jim offered him twenty. He would only take the ten. I guess to the hospital, Jim didn't exist; we were very grateful for the kindness of the nurses and doctor. We called another taxi (the same driver) and were back at the marina at 8:40 a.m.

We told *Misty* and *2nd Wind*, who had figured we wouldn't be able to leave on the morning tide, that if we left right away, we could still get out the channel. We thought the drugstore in the shopping mall opened at 9:00 a.m. I said I could wait on *Yankee Lady* outside of the breakwater while Jim took the dinghy back to the yacht club's dock near the stores. We all made it out with no problem. Jim took the portable radio ashore with him. After finding the drug store, he called me to say it didn't open until noon. We forgot that in Quebec, nothing opens before noon on

Sunday. We changed plans. *Misty* and *2nd Wind* headed for Les Méchins. Jim returned to the boat, and we anchored in fourteen feet of water, waiting for noon, two and one-half hours away. We made the best of it. The wind was calm; we rocked gently in the water. The sky was beautifully blue. We napped and relaxed. Jim went ashore at 11:30 a.m. At 11:45 a.m., I put the minestrone soup on to heat. He called just after noon as he was leaving the dock. I started the engine, pulled up the anchor, motored toward the breakwater, and met him. He tied up the dinghy and climbed aboard. We ate lunch underway.

The pain pills helped, but they made Jim sleepy. Autopilot and I motored through a calm sea while he slept. I woke him to see a whale, but it was too far away and disappeared. He went back to sleep. We were two miles offshore. I was daydreaming along when I looked toward the horizon across the river, which was over forty-five miles wide at this point. I thought I saw a boat with a mast and dark hull. But it disappeared. Then I saw rising mist and looked again. There was a whale under that mist. This one was closer and huge, a finback. I called Jim. We could see its big head come out of the water, followed by a glistening, brown, fifty-foot body rolling out of the sea until the fin appeared and then a brown back. Just as quickly, it dove and was gone.

There was more wildlife to see. We noticed a number of gannets sitting in the water. They took off before we got very close, but their white wings with black tips reminded us of the white pelicans we had seen in Florida. These birds, however, were smaller. At various times, two or three seals kept track of our progress through the water. Their puppy-like faces would pop out of the water, watch us briefly, and then disappear under the water again. About a quarter of a mile before the harbor, another small whale, probably a minke, provided us a brief escort.

Les Méchins village, population about fifteen hundred, is located at the head of a wide bay, not much more than an indentation of the St. Lawrence River. The village is nestled on a flat plain beneath a ridge of wooded hills. Two massive breakwater/ wharves form and shelter the harbor. We rounded the end of the eastern wharf and anchored in the middle of the harbor near *Misty* and *2nd Wind*. Two tugs were tied to the wharf, buffered by clusters of used black car tires. A smaller breakwater inshore sheltered several smaller fishing boats. A floating dock extended inside the harbor from this breakwater. You can usually tell something about the depth of the water by the size of the boats tied to a dock. Here, the water appeared shallow because only small runabout powerboats were tied to it. From the cockpit, we could see the small shipyard and dry dock located on the east side of the harbor. The dry dock was a big enclosed space with a sturdy gate at the opening. The concept is very simple. Workers take a boat into the dock at high tide, wait for the tide to go out at low, and then close the doors to keep the tide from coming in again. It was Sunday, so all was quiet. There was a small ferry boat in the dry dock waiting for the workers to return on Monday. On shore, the crescent-shaped gravel beach gave way to a strip of grass. Behind these were two layers of simple, white, wood houses. Framing the picture was the ridge of wooded hills, three to four hundred feet high. It was a very northern fishing village scene.

In the evening, Jim's tooth still hurt, so we declined the invitation for dessert on *2nd Wind*. Not to be put off, Tom and Rosie came over in the dinghy; Rosie, ever the provider, was holding two bowls of strawberry shortcake.

We left at eight the next morning under blue skies with a light wind rippling over the water. We planned to stop for the night at Sainte-Anne-des-Monts. Our first landmark was Cap Chat. From a distance, it looked like an island, but as we motored closer, we could see that it was a peninsula. There was another forest of windmills turning slowly in the ten-knot wind. One looked like a giant egg beater; we read that it is the largest wind turbine in the world. The lighthouse, 120 feet above sea level, sat on a small plateau on top of a steep cliff about one-third of the way up the mountain. It looked like a miniature, dwarfed by the five hundred feet of mountain above it. Behind the town of Cap Chat, as we looked through the valley, we could see part of the Chic Chocs mountain range rising to four thousand feet and blue in the distance.

The wind increased behind us. We unfurled the jib and, oh joy, were actually able to sail at speeds over five knots for the last six miles. Sainte-Anne-des-Monts is located along the shore of a wide bay. The harbor was formed by yet another configuration of public wharves and rock breakwaters. We passed between the two rock jetties, turned left, and were directed to a small marina, which had floating docks, electricity, and water. Jean, our breakfast buddy from Matane, helped us tie up *Yankee Lady* and *2nd Wind*. He said he was leaving shortly, which would make a third space available for *Misty*. I thought how fortunate we have been this whole trip to find space for all three boats. The long public wharf formed the third wall of the harbor. We were totally protected from wind and waves in a small enclave of pleasure and fishing boats. It seemed that everyone on the dock stopped to talk to us. We managed with our little French and their little English. As we have so often found, we were in a very friendly place.

Sainte-Anne-des-Monts, population six thousand, is a town with a hospital, police station, post office, and various stores and restaurants. We walked a few blocks along the bay, turned left, and found the post office near the main road through town. At the visitor's center, we learned that this area is part of the Gaspé Peninsula. The Chic Chocs Mountains are its back bone. Arctic, tundra-like vegetation is found at the top of the highest mountains, one of which is named Jacques Cartier after the explorer. We read a flyer, which invited us to rent a car, drive to this mountain, and then hike four or five hours to the top. The reward would be sighting a herd of caribou in their most southerly habitat. In this area, moose, deer, and caribou coexist and survive. All six of us decided against this adventure.

Jim and I and Tom and Rosie ate supper at a local seafood restaurant near the dock. It was a no frills, fresh fish only, delicious feast. Back at *Yankee Lady*, Jim and I spent a warm evening with the electric heater on, enjoying the convenience of a plug-in dock.

In the morning as we were preparing to leave for the thirty-mile trip to Mont-Louis, a gentleman about our age hurried onto the dock asking if anyone had left a wallet in the men's room. No one had. His name was Reinhard Zollitsh; he was hurrying to leave in his ocean-going canoe, which, he explained, looks like a kayak but has a different paddle. He wanted to take advantage of the favorable current. He had paddled here from Whitehall, New York (where we put up our masts prior to sailing on Lake Champlain). He said he paddles about twenty-five miles a day and then camps somewhere on the shore in his small green tent. We were impressed. He was heading for Campbellton, New Brunswick, in the Bay of Chaleur. In the winter, he teaches modern languages at the University of Maine in Orono. We would get to know him better as we played hopscotch along the shore with him for the next few days.

A front went through last night. We listened to the roaring wind and felt snug and secure tied to the dock in a protected harbor. We left in what we thought were diminishing southwest winds. The wind was predicted to be light and variable by afternoon.

We passed another lighthouse sentinel, Sainte-Marthe-de-Gaspé, a dark-red, conical pillar with a vertical white stripe. The associated buildings were painted dark-red also. Some lighthouses stand out by themselves on rocky cliffs. This one was not so easy to see. It was situated on a point with a small village behind it. A small stream ran through the middle of the village creating a small valley. Higher mountains rose behind the village.

The coast had become rocky again, with cliffs, steep slopes, and wooded hills rising to fifteen hundred feet close to shore.

Mont Louis Bay, our next destination, was one of four coves, which were evenly distributed along this section of shoreline at intervals of three and one-half miles. Each cove was in a valley and had a small village clinging to the shore. As usual, there was a conspicuous church spire in each small village. As we passed each cove and valley, we glimpsed again the high mountains deeper in the peninsula.

The predicted diminishing winds didn't. Instead, they increased to at least twenty knots from behind us, which gave us a sloppy following sea. *Misty* and *2nd Wind* unfurled their jibs. Jim raised the mainsail on *Yankee Lady*. He thought the mainsail would provide stability and a knot or two of extra speed. I was nervous about this. I didn't say anything because I wanted to avoid an argument, but I knew that it's much easier to furl a jib when sailing in strong downwind conditions than it is to take down a mainsail. With the main, there is no way to slow the boat unless you turn into the wind so that the sail can luff and lose power. In a strong wind, the boat can heel over dangerously in the turn into the wind. I felt the boat was overpowered; neither of us would be able to control it at all times. We accidentally jibed as the wind and waves increased. When that kind of jibe happens, the boom travels suddenly across the cockpit from one side of the boat to the other side with a loud crash, shaking the whole rigging of the boat. It isn't very pleasant, and it can be dangerous. I tried to stay calm and didn't talk about it, but I was angry inside. I couldn't imagine what I would have felt like if I hadn't had ten years of experience sailing *Yankee Lady* by myself. For better or worse, it's not in my nature to put all my faith and trust in someone else. Under better circumstances, I would have acknowledged that our combined experience was strength; that Jim and I could rely on each other. I knew that he was a good sailor and that he would push *Yankee Lady* more than I would, but today, it just caused more tension. The dinghy was also a problem. It slewed around behind *Yankee Lady* until Jim pulled it close to the transom. It was a tense day between Jim and me and between *Yankee Lady* and the wind, but we slogged on. The autopilot actually held out and steered for all but the last mile or so when Jim took over.

Anse de Mont-Louis was the third cove in the sequence. All three boats entered the harbor rocking and bucking in the rollers, but it was worse for *Yankee Lady* because we still had the mainsail up and didn't have as much control as I would have liked. For a few moments, it was hang on and surge ahead.

The planned anchorage behind the east wharf was impossible; there were too many waves. There was space to tie up at the west wharf, which was sheltered from the twenty-five knot winds and higher gusts, but there were down drafts from the mountains to contend with. The end of the wharf was in disrepair, and there were ruins of an old dock 250 feet to the south. However, we really had no choice at this point. *Misty* tied up to the wharf in the midst of one of the down drafts. She was more or less glued to the wharf where her shrouds caught between two pilings. Tom and Barbara managed to push off enough to free the shrouds; they put two small fenders on them to keep them off the wharf.

Meanwhile, now in the calmer water of the harbor, I headed *Yankee Lady* into the screaming wind while Jim went forward to the mast to take down the mainsail. With the sail flapping wildly, he released the main halyard, and because of the pressure of the wind, he had to manually pull the luff of the sail down the mast. Then starting at the mast and working toward the stern, he rolled each noisily flapping section of sail around the boom and tied it securely. At last it was quiet; we were under control and could relax a little. Safe in the harbor, my emotions calmed down also, and I was ready to get on with the journey. I motored *Yankee Lady* in a circle while Jim prepared the fenders and dock lines. There was enough room to circle, but I needed to watch out for the sunken dock. *2nd Wind* circled also. We nosed into the wharf just in front of *Misty*, and then to make it easier for Tom and Rosie to dock, both *Yankee Lady* and *Misty* moved forward so *2nd Wind* could pull in behind us. At last, we were all settled. Then it rained all night. That solid wharf felt very secure. We lit our alcohol heater and spent a warm evening reading and relaxing.

The next day, the weather forecast predicted fifteen-to twenty-knot winds out of the northeast backing to northwest. We figured the northeast wind would blow against the outgoing Gaspé current and create an uncomfortable chop. We decided to stay another day and move the boats toward the shore end of the wharf to avoid the swell and to find ladders where we could get off the boats easily.

There was a small fish processing plant situated near the inner end of the wharf, which sold fresh fish. Jim and I checked with the clerk to see if any fishing boats would be coming into the dock this day. He sent us to the Federal Bureau next door. We were told that it would be all right to dock anywhere from the little gray building seaward. We also found that there was a charge for the wharf, ten dollars for two nights.

It took about an hour for us all to move and adjust our dock lines. All secure, we climbed the ladders and walked around the town behind the crescent beach and bay. It was a cold, gray day. Jim and I stopped at a store that specialized in smoked salmon. He snacked on that while we continued walking. All six of us met in the small local restaurant. The menu provided for all our appetites: pizza for some, breakfast for others, and hamburger (sandwich and/or dinner) for others.

Later, when Jim and I were relaxing in the cockpit, a small white sea canoe entered the harbor and paddled over to the ramp next to the fish store. Tom and Barbara were just returning from town, so they stopped to help Reinhard pull his canoe above the high watermark and unload his tent and belongings. He thinks we're courageous to do this trip. We think he takes the prize.

After a night of being pushed against the wharf by the wind and listening to the fenders squeak against it, the wind changed direction to southwest. It was easy to leave. Jim untied the bow and stern lines while he stood on the wharf. I pulled the boat in by the spring lines; he climbed down, untied the spring lines, and we were blown away from the wharf. Our destination was Grande-Vallée, twenty-seven miles away.

It was cool in the shade, but the sun was delightfully warm in the cockpit on this downwind day. On land, the road continued to skirt the shore. Each little dip in the mountains contained at least a few houses. Today, in the sun and shadows, the mountains stood out in three-dimensional shades of light and dark green. The brown twisted layers of sedimentary rocks gave evidence of long ago geological forces.

At 10:18 a.m., we passed the point of Gros Morne, a conspicuous promontory three hundred feet high. This was a milestone for us because it is the most northerly point of the south shore of the St. Lawrence. Since we intended to follow the shore around the Gaspé Peninsula, we would go no farther north—this was the most northerly part of the journey and as far north as any of us have been in our boats. *Misty* recorded their position at 49N 16' 597" and 65 W 32' 522". A little later, Jim and I saw the spout of a whale, its brown body and graceful tail rising and diving into the water. It was a humpback. We detoured north to try to get closer. The whale dove and disappeared, but our whale detour put us at 49N 16' 86", 65 W 29' 27", our most northerly point. We took a picture of our GPS screen. From here on, we would be heading in a southerly direction. It has also been fun to notice the position of the North Star above the horizon. At forty-nine degrees it was more than halfway between the horizon and the zenith, which, of course, also meant we were more than halfway to the North Pole from the equator. I would have loved to reach fifty degrees of north latitude, but that was about sixty nautical miles from our current position. We weren't going there.

We motored on toward Grande-Vallée. The road swerved inland for a bit, leaving the cliffs and hills to meet the shore unobstructed. Grande-Vallée, population 1,500, was another small village at the head of a small cove. We entered this cove and turned right to the public wharf, which juts out from the west side.

The wharves we have found along this coast are massive structures, protected by large rock fills. They were usually three hundred to five hundred feet long and could be twenty feet high at low tide. The tops were wide enough for fishermen or for sight seers to drive out and/or walk on. All had ladders spaced at intervals along the walls. At the top of each ladder, there was a grab rail, shaped like an upside-down U, securely fastened to the surface of the wharf. It was comforting to be able to hold onto something solid at the top of the ladder. All six of us retired sailors were becoming adept at climbing and descending fifteen feet or more of a vertical ladder fastened to the side of a wharf. I never would have thought I could do it when I started this trip.

We were all refining our docking techniques. Each boat crew would claim a space next to a ladder. On *Yankee Lady,* Jim tied all lines, bow, stern, and spring to any niche he could find in the wall of the wharf, halfway between the low and high tide marks. He left enough slack to allow for the shift in the tide. Usually, the ladders were accessible from the middle of the boat, but sometimes, we had to climb out from the bow or the stern. We have noticed with interest (and gratitude) that the wharves and the ladders were not slimy or covered with seaweed. Winter ice and cold year-round water temperatures prevented anything from growing.

This was a beautiful spot. There was a small, rocky hill extending from the wharf's approach road to the water, covered with my favorite pointy pine trees. Trees and wild flowers lined the road. It seemed quiet and deserted until all the fishermen parked their vehicles and proceeded to fish from the wharf all evening, accompanied by local gawkers who had come to view the three sailboats from the States. No problem. It quieted down at night.

Jim and I walked toward the small beach at the head of the wharf. There, almost hidden among some bushes, was Reinhard's green tent and white ocean canoe. We stopped to visit. He told us he always tried to protect his privacy by being as inconspicuous as possible. There really wasn't much space for him to be out of sight from the public inside a small green pup tent. As we talked about our various travel experiences, he said that during the winter, he had paddled the ninety-nine miles of the wilderness waterway in Everglades National Park, Florida.

The Everglades are one of our favorite places. We have seen some of that wilderness aboard *Albatross*. In fact, we have taken her to places most thirty-two-foot sailboats don't go. One winter, we cruised twelve miles up the Little Shark River and Shark River to Tarpon Bay in the heart of the mangrove wilderness where we anchored and spent a few days. Both Jim and I wanted to see if we could explore with the dinghy far enough to find the beginning of the saw grass. One morning, we packed the dinghy with peanut butter sandwiches and sodas, which were wrapped in a towel to keep them cold (*Albatross* had a refrigerator and a wind generator) and started exploring. We never found the saw grass, but it was fun trying. At the eastern end of Tarpon Bay, we entered Avocado Creek, narrow and shallow. We proceeded slowly under a canopy of mangrove branches until we came to a small pond. Several alligators watched our progress from the muddy shore. At the far end of the pond, we saw a small dock, a chemical outhouse, and a sign that said Canepatch. We landed at the dock under the watchful, enigmatic gaze of the resident alligator who was lazily floating nearby. We followed a path to a small clearing surrounded by lush tropical trees and bushes. At one time, settlers tried to harvest sugar cane in this area without success. There was not much solid ground here. This clearing was a tiny oasis surrounded by water and mangrove forest, far from civilization. I thought, *Between possible encounters with snakes, alligators, and mosquitoes, there is no way I would camp on the ground here.* But Reinhard did. Here we were, talking about this faraway wilderness while we stood on the banks of the St. Lawrence River.

Jim and I walked to the town, which was really just a few houses and one small restaurant named Chez Denise. We joined the others for coffee. I don't think anyone spoke English except the six of us. We got along with lots of gestures and my elementary French.

There was a conspicuous church and spire situated high on a slate cliff on the east side of the cove. Jim and I crossed a bridge over the small river and noticed a small white boat, which had the pink word "excursions" painted on it. Later, we saw it heading out into the cove. I guess excursion boats come in all sizes and shapes. There were other small fishing boats tied against the old wooden docks, which lined the entrance and part of the river. Jim continued up the hill while I explored the base of the slate cliff. Pieces of slate and chunks of a limestone intrusion were strewn over the ground. I picked up several pieces of slate to take home for the grandchildren. They could play "old fashioned" school and use chalk to write on the slate. I rejoined Jim, and we returned to Chez Denise where we ate supper. In the evening, we played cards on *2nd Wind* while the local people fished from the dock.

In the morning, we left for Rivière-au-Renard, thirty miles away. The town was nestled in a small valley, which opened into the bay. A large breakwater and a public wharf extended from opposite shores to form a man-made harbor. The entrance between them was easy to find; it was four hundred feet wide. Inside, toward the head of the harbor, there was a second breakwater, which protected a public wharf and a set of floating docks. The marina, Club Nautique Forillon Inc., was at the west end of the wharf. According to the *Sailing Directions*, Rivière-au-Renard is the most important fishing port on the northern coast of the Gaspé Peninsula. The large public wharf was lined with big, no-nonsense fishing boats. There were a variety of services available including a fish plant, a large marine hardware store, medical clinic, post office, and assorted stores. There was also a Canadian Coast Guard Search and Rescue Station.

We proceeded toward the floating docks at the head of the harbor. There were several small boats and two cruising sailboats at the floating docks, but no one to direct us anywhere. We eased into a slip next to *Winds Away*, Jean's boat. He had told us back in Saint-Anne-des-Monts that he was going to leave his boat here while he went to Quebec to visit his girlfriend. *Misty* and *2nd Wind* found two other spaces near *Gypsy Soul*, an old wooden boat sailed by a young couple whom, with Ernie, their golden Labrador, we had briefly met in Saint-Anne-des-Monts. Every sailor has a dream. Theirs was to cruise to the Caribbean if they could fix their malfunctioning engine. They told us that someone would eventually come to collect a fee for the dock. The fee was thirty dollars for up to three people and included a key to the showers and laundry. I had been looking forward to a little civilization: well-kept docks, showers, and laundry. In actual fact, the docks were rundown, and we didn't have high expectations for either the shower or the laundry. We thought that thirty dollars was a lot, given the location and state of the docks.

Jim and I walked halfway down the dusty fishing wharf in search of a phone. We didn't find one, but Jim went across the street to the marine parts store to look for the extra belts and impeller that we needed. The store didn't have them. We returned to the boat just in time to meet the lady who collected the fee. Between French and English, we bargained with her. If we didn't use the shower, we could stay for twenty dollars. We figured we could use the sun shower on the boat.

We walked to the main road, met the others, and told them about our bargain. The town appeared to be a strictly commercial place, geared to the fishermen. There was no discernible downtown except for maybe the bank and the grocery store two blocks away. We talked about walking to a restaurant around the bay but decided it was too far. The only other eating-out possibility would have been one of three mobile canteens on the fish dock. Each offered three or four picnic tables for customers. This did not seem appealing either.

Jim and Tom Frasca took their old belts and impellers with them to another parts store, hoping to find replacements there. That store didn't have them either, so the parts man drove Jim and Tom to two other hardware stores. I need to say a word here about, at least, some of the Quebec drivers. Jim described it like this: "We got in the car, and zing, we careened around this corner, and then zing, we zoomed down this street, zing, zing, zing."

Rosie, Barbara, and I waited awhile at the picnic table above the marina and then walked to the small country grocery store. I asked one clerk for sour cream, but he didn't know what I meant, and the language barrier was a problem. I couldn't remember the French name for sour cream. I asked another lady for ice. She disappeared out back and, about five minutes later, came back with a frozen gallon jug of water. I asked for another one for Rosie. She disappeared again. Finally, when I reached the checkout counter, she reappeared with more ice and so did the man who had found the sour cream. Since I was in French Quebec, I figured I needed the proper gestures. But of course, I threw my hands out in surprise and said, "Merci." With all our bags of groceries and the ice, I decided to ask for a ride back to the marina. Between gestures and my hesitant French, I succeeded in communicating with a man who, I think, was the manager. He didn't say anything; he just disappeared and returned with his van, which had no backseats. Rosie and I sat on the floor in back. Barbara sat in front. We too experienced the zing, zing, zing as we careened around a corner and down the road to the marina clutching our grocery bags and holding on.

We ate aboard our own boats because we decided the restaurant was too far away and the road was too busy, especially after our experiences with local drivers. While Jim and I were eating in *Yankee Lady's* cockpit, I managed to withstand the pleas from Ernie, the golden retriever, who stood hopefully on the dock.

We left Riviere-au-Renard on a sea unrippled by wind although we rocked up and down slightly on swells originating from the open water. We were planning to sail around the end of the Gaspé Peninsula and into the Baie de Gaspé. *Yankee Lady* got a late start. *Misty* and *2nd Wind* were about an hour ahead of us. I was anticipating another significant passage. In my mind, we would be sailing around the very tip of a continent and the end of the Appalachian Mountain range where the mountains dropped into the sea. We planned to stop in the city of Gaspé at the head of the bay.

Mountains rose steeply from the shore. Small settlements of houses were nestled in the valleys. Every now and then, we saw a whale spout or the dark shape of a finback rising and falling. *Misty* and *2nd Wind* reported passing through a pod of small whales. To port, we could see the long, low line of Anticosti Island. It sits in the middle of the Gulf of St. Lawrence about forty miles away; for us, it was an unexplored horizon.

We passed Cap-des-Rosiers light. Built in 1858, it is now a national historic monument. Its white ninety-foot tower is the highest lighthouse in Canada and would have been a welcoming or warning beacon to ships entering the St. Lawrence River. The long point of land leading to the lighthouse ended in short, rocky cliffs, twenty-five feet above the water. We could see clearly and didn't need the guidance of its beacon light nor did we need to hear its warning fog horns, but it was worth a shiver to think of the shipwrecks from the past near this treacherous shore. The sloping surface of the land behind the light was flat, topped by green grass, a solitary road, and several houses. Ahead of us were the mountains and cliffs of Presqu'île de Forillon peninsula, the approach to land's end.

According to the Royal Proclamation of 1763 and by decision of the Geographic Board of Canada, the line constituting the division of the St. Lawrence River from the Gulf of St. Lawrence starts at Cap-des-Rosiers. It crosses the island of Anticosti and extends to the north shore of the river, which is seventy miles wide at this point.

As we passed this cape, we officially left the river and entered the estuary of the Gulf of St. Lawrence. It is considered to be the world's largest estuary and is the outlet for the Great Lakes and the St. Lawrence River into the Atlantic Ocean. It opens into the ocean through the Cabot Strait and the Strait of Belle Isle. We would be spending the next segment of our voyage on its waters.

As we left Cap-des-Rosiers, the wind picked up to between ten and fifteen knots. It was cold but beautiful. We noticed a small harbor at the mouth of a creek in a small bay just before the Presqu'île de Forillon peninsula. The *Sailing Directions* noted that there was an interpretation center there, part of Forillon National Park. This was of no particular interest to us until we talked to Reinhard a few days later.

The Presqu'île de Forillon peninsula is a long, narrow ridge of land, which extends five miles out to sea where it ends—suddenly. Sitting in *Yankee Lady's* cockpit, we motored slowly by gazing up in awe at a series of five-hundred-foot-high limestone cliffs rising abruptly out of the water. The chalk-gray cliffs were topped by a green forest of pine trees silhouetted against the blue-gray sky. Three small sandy beaches, little footholds from the sea, were spaced at intervals along the base of the cliffs.

We had been warned of currents that might push us closer to shore, but we observed an excursion boat passing practically at water's edge. It appeared tiny against the sheer rise of the cliffs. Visibility was excellent, and we saw no discernible tide rip, so we set course for the six fathom spot off Flowerpot Rock, about three hundred feet off the tip of the peninsula.

We were looking at the continental end of one of the oldest mountain ranges on earth. The Appalachian mountains (locally known as the Chic Chocs) abruptly seemed to have fallen into the ocean here. They were formed three hundred million years ago, and they extend almost two thousand miles from the state of Alabama to this point we were sailing around. They have been built up, worn down, twisted, layered, and folded. Glaciers have shaped plateaus and gouged out deep U-shaped valleys. The turmoil of these past geological forces had produced the magnificent landscape we saw before us.

Here was the picture as we rounded the cape. Two massive gray and tan cliffs rose to a height of six hundred feet. Their layers of limestone had been tipped so that they slanted from their summits down to the southwest where they met the water. A glacier-carved green valley lay between the two cliffs. A white lighthouse with a red roof was perched almost on the edge of the taller cliff, a man-made afterthought to the grander view. Four white gannets soared almost effortlessly in the air currents between *Yankee Lady* and the cliffs adding a three-dimensional quality to the view. I admired their freedom, and then I thought, *Yankee Lady, my beloved boat, was giving us a kind of freedom too, freedom to experience sublime beauty such as this.* It was an awe-inspiring, emotional experience. We were all touched in some profound way by the beauty, power, and majesty of the scene we saw before us. It touched the very spiritual core of my being.

FIRST YEAR COMPLETED: AROUND THE GASPÉ TO SHEDIAC, NEW BRUNSWICK

We would be spending the rest of this season and part of next in the Gulf of St. Lawrence. The gulf is so large that it is thought of as a semi-enclosed sea. It is also the world's largest estuary. It is surrounded by Labrador, Newfoundland, and Nova Scotia, including Cape Breton, the Gaspé Peninsula, and New Brunswick. The gulf flows into the Atlantic Ocean through the Strait of Belle Isle, the Cabot Strait, and the Strait of Canso although the Canso Causeway, built in 1955, does not allow water to flow freely between the Atlantic and the gulf. We would be traversing the Strait of Canso and the Cabot Strait during our voyage. Because of my love for adventure and my desire to always go farther, I also wanted to go north through the Strait of Belle Isle between Labrador and Newfoundland, but it was too far out of our way so my iceberg detour had to be given up. For the rest of this summer, we would be cruising along the southwestern edge of the gulf, which included the Baie de Gaspé, Percé, the Bay of Chaleur, and Northumberland Strait.

Directly after rounding Cap Gaspé, we turned into the Baie de Gaspé, a small sliver of a bay about four miles wide and eleven miles long. We were bound for the town of Gaspé at the head of the bay. The St. Lawrence River was now a memory. With the wind behind us, it became instant summer. Looking at the landscape, we would never have known we were passing by the same mountain ridge. A soft layer of green trees sloped down to gentle meadows—light-green, yellow, and purple in the colors of late summer. People were hiking on paths through the meadows and out to the lighthouse. Scallop-shaped formations of thinly layered rocks connected the meadows to the shore. We passed the small harbor of Grand Greve where there was a campground belonging to the national park. This was where Reinhard landed his canoe after a harrowing passage around the tip of the peninsula. The rangers at the interpretation center had forbidden him to camp in the small bay at the beginning of the peninsula, although he had explained that because of the increasing wind and waves it would be dangerous for him to round the point that afternoon. Nevertheless, he had to do it. There was no other place for him to pull out between that bay and the point. It required all his strength and skill to keep from capsizing or being blown against the rocks. Here, campers sheltered him and helped him hide his canoe from the rangers. As we cruised past two sandy beaches, we noticed people actually swimming and staying in the water for more than a quick dip. Other campers were picnicking on top of a small cliff.

We passed between the red and green buoys at Sandy Beach, a long spit of sandy land that extends out from the west side of the bay. It forms a protective barrier for Gaspé Harbor. We motored two more miles to the town. Shortly before the bridge, we turned left between two small breakwaters into Gaspé Marina. The city was across the bridge to the right, about a five-minute walk.

The marina was not bustling with activity this Saturday in August. In fact, it was rather quiet and laid-back. There was no one to direct us to dock space, so *2nd Wind* and *Misty* tied up to the fuel dock while we waited on the long side of another dock. The manager was nowhere to be found until Tom and Jim walked to the other end of the marina where he was talking to some boaters. While they walked back to the fuel dock, Tom told him we needed diesel and gas. The manager told Tom that another boat had purchased all the gasoline from the shoreside tank at the marina, so he agreed to drive Tom and his jerry cans to a gas station. When they returned, Tom had to carry both of the heavy cans to *2nd Wind*, not quite so convenient as pulling up to the gas dock. There was plenty of diesel fuel, so *Misty* and then *Yankee Lady* filled up their tanks.

This was our first fuel stop since Matane. Contrary to some predictions, finding fuel has not been a real problem. *Misty* and *2nd Wind* filled jerry cans at a gas station near the dock in Mont Louis. We poured our extra six gallons of diesel fuel into *Yankee Lady* at Rivière-au-Renard and arrived at Gaspé with well over one-fourth of the tank left.

While we waited, a fisherman across the marina shouted over to ask us if would like some fresh-caught and filleted mackerel. We gladly took enough for the six of us. Dinner was a gourmet affair aboard *Yankee Lady*, but it required ingenuity to bring it about. Since using the propane grill was forbidden at the dock, it took a little thought to figure out how to cook a fancy dinner on *Yankee Lady's* two alcohol stove burners. I gained another burner by setting up the Origo alcohol heater and turning the top grid upside down so it fit more closely over the heat canister. I made coffee and cooked a combination of wax beans and carrots on the stove. They stayed hot while I browned the hash brown potatoes over the converted heater. Then Jim cooked the fish using two frying pans on the now free stove. Barbara and Rosie brought salads. I didn't think I was a fan of mackerel, but I discovered it was delicious. I decided that expensive restaurants had nothing over the ambience, camaraderie, and tasty food we shared on *Yankee Lady*. Dinner over, we discussed the next segment of our journey. We decided to leave for the next harbor L'Anse-à-Brillant the next day. It would be a short twelve-mile trip along the western shore of the Baie de Gaspé.

We spent a lazy morning relaxing and doing laundry. The others went to breakfast and to church, which was in English for a change. We walked up the hill to a small grocery store. Unsure of our next grocery stop, I again stocked up on food and other necessities.

We left our dock slips at 1:00 p.m., bound for L'Anse-à-Brillant. As we motored toward the bay, we looked out to see, uh-oh, that three-letter F word—*fog*. To complicate matters, this was the day they were adjusting the GPS system to factor in the year 2000. We could not get any satellite readings. Sometimes, I think fog is fun. In home territory, when the GPS waypoints are familiar and the radar is working, there is a certain mystery to it. Gliding along in my own small space surrounded by curtains of fog, I would feel that *Yankee Lady* was the center of the universe. Not so in this situation. We considered anchoring behind Sandy Beach.

Then *Misty* nosed over to the buoys at the end of the beach. Tom reported that the western shore was clear of fog. *Misty* and *2nd Wind* still had their LORAN receivers and could use them for direction. We also had all plotted dead reckoning courses to the red and white buoy off L'Anse-à-Brillant. Tom Frasca turned on his LORAN, and we decided to go for it. The fog hovered nearby but never reached us. As we approached the harbor, we worried slightly about the depth of the water inside. One person had told Tom Frasca that someone told him it was too shallow (we are always skeptical about this kind of local knowledge and want to see for ourselves). On the way across, Tom Isele said someone had told him the harbor was now dredged. We found out later that the harbor had been dredged last week. I thought, *How's that for good timing?*

From the bay, the entrance appeared to be a small dent between two tall cliffs. I don't think I would even have noticed it if I hadn't been looking for the harbor. As we motored closer, we saw two rock jetties, one on either side of the entrance. They seemed to punctuate it like two parenthetical markers. As we entered the channel, we noticed a pair of range markers on shore, one behind the other with the taller one at the back. I knew that by keeping them lined up, we would be in the center of the channel and on course, *but* it took a lot of faith to keep going because it looked like we were going straight into land. We couldn't see the ninety-degree-right-hand turn until we were almost upon it. There lay a small, calm harbor about one hundred feet wide and eight hundred feet long, lined by short cement and/or wooden docks. Four small fishing boats with powerful outboard motors were tied up on the shoreside. *Misty* and *2nd Wind* found spots behind them. We tied to an old wooden dock on the opposite side, across a small boat ramp from two more fishing boats. We could go no farther because the water shoaled quickly as it reached the head of the harbor. There the water narrowed to a small stream, which flowed from the top of the nearby hill. A small bridge spanned the glistening cobbles and stones underneath and provided passage for walkers and cars.

There were four buildings: one Quonset hut, one closed fish processing plant, one closed ice-making plant, and a shutdown house/business-type building across the harbor, not a very prosperous scene. Between two small hills and the Quonset hut on our bay side lay several old fishing and sailboats that will never go to sea again. Nestled between two of the boats was a small green tent. Reinhard's ocean canoe was near it. I looked up to see him sitting cross-legged in front the tent waving a greeting— our welcoming committee. This is the third time we have met him. We greeted him like an old friend. He was really glad to see us, especially after his traumatic experience rounding the Gaspé Peninsula. I think he needed the sight of our familiar faces and our adventure-bound attitudes.

We walked across the planked dock and around one of the sandy hills covered with poplar and pine trees until we came to a small crescent-shaped beach. It was framed by one of the stone jetties and a high, steep cliff. A young teenage girl appeared, calling a dog, "Here, Sam." The dog bounced over from exploring the bushes. He looked and acted like my dog, Skipper, my traveling companion and crew for more than ten years. He passed away four years ago, and I have designated him as crew emeritus for *Yankee Lady*. Sam and I became instant friends. The girl is visiting her aunt who lives up the hill.

Aunt Judy appeared on a four-wheeler. She told us that she and her husband, Reed, own over a mile of this beautiful wooded land. They live up the hill on the dirt road that connects to the bridge. She and her niece left for home on the four-wheeler. She was excited to tell her husband about us. Sam bounded along behind.

Shortly, Reed and his brother-in-law appeared in an old pickup truck. Reed has been a fisherman, a mechanic, and a general jack of all trades. He has even quarried gravel from one of his hills. He and Jim established quick rapport; they spoke the same mechanical language. We decided he is also a salesman because he tried to sell us the brown house next to his or a piece of his property or a variety of junk/antiques from his old barn, which he is going to tear down sometime. At the moment, he collects unemployment from the government, cuts wood from his property, and works at a variety of odd jobs. Like many other Canadians, he is eager to obtain American dollars, which at this time have a very favorable exchange rate. He is strongly pro-American and talked for several minutes about the role played by the United States in keeping Canada and other parts of the world free. On this trip, I have always been conscious that we were traveling in another country where there is a different government and a different national culture. While there are many close ties between the United States and Canada, I had not expected to hear such enthusiastic praise from a local citizen. I appreciated it. Aunt Judy, her niece, and dogs (Sam and a Pomeranian) returned to invite us to stop at their house.

In the evening, Jim and I walked over the bridge to *2nd Wind* for dessert and cards. The smells and sounds of the north woods accompanied our footsteps. The six of us decided to leave tomorrow and possibly get as far as Bonaventure Island.

The next morning, Jim's tooth started bothering him again. At 8:00 a.m. we walked up the hill to seek information from Judy about dentists. We walked by the brown house (that Reed tried to sell us) and the barn. Behind the brown house, we could see a mowed field that sloped uphill to the edge of the cliff overlooking the blue water of the bay. Judy's house was just beyond the field. She invited us in, and we explained the problem. She called a dentist she knew in the town of Gaspé. He was in the office this day planning to do paperwork, but he said he would see Jim at 9:00 a.m. Judy agreed to take us and wait, but she would have to charge us the usual rate of $20 for the trip. We, of course, agreed. The dentist told Jim that he needed two root canals, which would take a series of appointments over two weeks. Yuk. Obviously, this was not possible. As an alternative, the dentist gave Jim a prescription for two weeks of antibiotics and recommended that he get the work done when he arrived home. Judy gave us the scenic ride back so we could see where we had been in the boat. We gave her an American twenty-dollar bill, which pleased her very much.

When we started this trip, friends asked us (and we wondered ourselves) how we would deal with medical emergencies. So far, Jim's experiences in Quebec City, Matane, and Gaspé have been adventures in Canadian kindness and ingenuity.

By 10:30 a.m., we motored out of L'Anse-à-Brillant into Gaspé Bay. The water was calm as we passed cliffs, farms, and a waterfall. As we reached the western tip of the bay, Pointe Sainte-Pierre, we entered open water. We motored between the point and flat Île Pâté, covered with nesting sea birds, four-tenths of a mile offshore. We stayed in the middle of the passage to avoid the reefs that reached out from both pieces of land. The water became more turbulent and choppy as we encountered a brisk southwest wind.

While we were rocking up and down, we watched the fog cover Bonaventure Island and then Percé Rock, six miles away. Our plan had been to motor over to Percé Rock (as close as we dared), then anchor off Bonaventure Island to go ashore, and circle the island to see the birds nesting. We decided there was no point in going there if we couldn't see. Jim suggested that we choose nearby Mal Bay Harbor instead. We turned our radar on just in case the fog moved in. Although we had decent visibility, we watched the outline of the nearby land on radar for practice. We rounded another small point of land to the right and finally saw a pile of rocks that protected a government wharf. This was Mal Bay Harbor. We rocked and rolled around the end of the wharf until, again, we were in man-made calm. The seaward end of the wharf was occupied by several small open fishing boats rafted together. There was just enough room behind them for the three of us to tie up one by one facing forward using our, by now, routine techniques for attaching ourselves to tall wharfs.

Jim and I were relaxing and napping in the cabin when I heard the revving of a powerful engine. I looked out to see a large white wooden presence next to us about to raft onto us. We most definitely did not want to be sandwiched between the wharf and a big fishing boat. We popped out of the cabin and talked to the fisher people (two men and a woman). We said they could have the berth next to the dock; we would raft next to them. We undid our lines and circled while they docked, then proceeded to tie up to them. Someone told *Misty* who was at the outside end of the dock that a scallop boat frequently tied up there at night. They decided to move and raft up to *2nd Wind*. Sure enough, the boat returned in the evening, gunning it into the open space. *How wonderful*, I thought again, *that throughout this trip, we have always been able to find secure spaces at night for our three boats.* Each harbor has been different, but moving around and trading places with fishing boats was something I could never have imagined doing, let alone taken for granted.

In the early evening, a young man, dressed in jeans and a T-shirt, stopped at *Yankee Lady* to collect some money. He said the fishermen had appointed him to collect a fee from visiting boaters. We wondered at first if he was legitimate, but somehow in this setting, we figured that he was. Not knowing what to expect, Jim asked, "How much?"

He replied, "Two dollars," hardly an exorbitant amount. We found out that the Federal government has stopped subsidizing the maintenance of the wharfs and has turned that responsibility over to the fishermen or to the local town. For most of this trip, we were not charged a fee except at the marinas where we secured slip space.

I must say it gave us a welcome feeling every time we pulled up to a wharf and a fisherman said, "Pull up anywhere there's room, no charge." I guess that two-dollar fee was a harbinger of things to come. On a more recent trip to Brier Island, Nova Scotia, the charge for the space inside the breakwater was $20 a day.

At 5:30 in the morning, I heard voices on the dock and then the vroom of an engine. The fishing boat crew was back. Yes, they were leaving (yesterday they said they weren't leaving in the morning). Oh well, we're the guests here. I woke Jim up from a sound sleep. He crawled onto the deck to untie our lines while I took the helm and then circled *Yankee Lady* past the end of the dock while we waited for them to leave. I don't think Jim's eyes were open, but it was a beautiful sight. The rosy glow of sunrise cast a soft light over Bonaventure Island, Percé Rock, and its adjacent peninsula six miles away from us. We tied back up to the dock, and I cooked breakfast. The coffee tasted especially good at this time of day. "We're up," I said. "We might as well leave early." This was no problem for the others; all of them were early risers.

By 7:45 a.m., the three boats from Connecticut filed out of the harbor, an impressive sight in the morning light. The wind was from the northwest behind us. We unfurled our jibs and motorsailed across the Baie de Malbaie. Jim also put up the mainsail on *Yankee Lady*. We were going to try for photo opportunities near the large hole in Percé Rock and then explore Bonaventure Island. We hurried on ahead to get on the other side of the Rock so we could take pictures of each other through the massive arch.

What an impressive sight. Rounded mountains clad in green velvety trees sloped down to the tourist town at the shore. Percé Rock lies about two hundred feet offshore. It is the massive remnant of an ancient limestone cliff, 1,400 feet long, 296 feet wide, and 289 feet tall at its highest point. It is considered by many to be one of the ten most amazing rock formations around the world. Its steep sides were like a giant solid wall which descended straight into the water from top to bottom. The wind and water have worn a large opening through a section of the base two-thirds of the way out from the land side.

This giant arch is fifty feet tall, which makes it one of the largest rock arches in the world. At low tide, it is possible to walk out to it, and at high tide, it is possible to take a kayak through. The chart indicated deep enough water for us to motor to within at least a hundred feet of the rock. We noticed excursion boats passing much closer than we were. Jim and I very briefly considered anchoring and going through it in the dinghy, but we decided we were not that adventurous. We found out later that Reinhard was braver. He went through it in his sea canoe. That rock was massive, especially when seen through the binoculars. Passing by it gave me the same feeling I had when we sailed by the skyscrapers of New York City. How small we were! We took pictures of *Misty* and *2nd Wind* with the telephoto lens as we looked at them through the arch.

When dreaming of visiting faraway places, I had read about Bonaventure Island and thought that it would be an exciting place to visit. Now here I was on my own boat. We motored toward the anchorage on the shoreward side of the island. We saw paths through the woods but no information building to find out about the birds. *Misty* and *2nd Wind* had decided to circle the island, so we headed into the wind and waves to join them. Suddenly, *Yankee Lady's* engine began to lose rpms. This required a change of plan. We called the others to say we had engine problems and were moving toward a harbor. We consulted the charts and guidebooks to find a convenient spot. I was disappointed not to see more of Bonaventure, but I certainly didn't want to head farther out to sea with an ailing engine. Meanwhile, wouldn't you know, the engine picked up speed again. Jim then concluded that the fuel filters were dirty and needed changing, not an immediate threat, but a job to be done at the next harbor. We decided to continue on and find a harbor.

The forecast for tomorrow indicated winds out of the southwest—twenty to thirty knots. We would have to head right into it, a slow, bouncing, uncomfortable ride, not something we wanted to do. We needed to pick a harbor that was protected because we figured we would probably wait out the wind there. Our GPS was working once in a while; the others couldn't get any readings. Jim put in waypoints to clear the rough water off Cap d'Espoire and then for the buoys off both Chandler and Newport harbors. Chandler offered the least protection. After several radio discussions with the others, we chose Newport, which was also the farthest. We sailed while we waited for them to catch up. The wind and waves increased behind us. After turning the engine back on, we proceeded at top speed toward the red and white buoy off Newport and then passed between the red and green buoys and the two breakwaters into the fishing harbor.

We never knew what to expect as we rounded these tall breakwaters and public docks. Newport is an active fishing harbor. Large ocean-going fishing trawlers, as well as smaller boats of many colors, were rafted together at the docks. We saw no open spaces for us. We approached the dock to our starboard and asked a fisherman on shore if we could raft up to his boat. He replied, "Yes, but I will be leaving at *cinq heures* (5:00 a.m.)."

I thought, "Okay, we would move then and tie up to the next boat in." We tied up to the outermost boat and then walked across two boats to the dock. There, everyone was pointing and offering advice—in French. We finally figured out that two boats tied up across the harbor at another wharf were through for the season and would not be moving. So we moved. *Yankee Lady* tied up to one boat, and *2nd Wind* tied up to the other at a ninety-degree angle to us. *Misty* rafted to *2nd Wind*. Thus, we settled into this section of the harbor. Our sterns all pointed toward the corner, forming a conversational setting like a living room arrangement with a two-person couch and a chair at right angles to each other. You might say our dinghies were the end tables.

During the evening, several boats left to go fishing. Like the car drivers, it seems that fishing boats also have two speeds—stop and fast. Most of them left the harbor with engines on high. Nevertheless, the boats were skillfully moved around the harbor and in and out of docks.

We gathered on *Yankee Lady* for cookies and discussion about the rest of the trip. We plan to sail almost to the end of the Bay of Chaleur then travel on the opposite side of the bay to Shippagan Harbor, and then south along the New Brunswick coast to Shediac. We wondered about nighttime activity in Newport, but all was quiet, and we spent a peaceful night.

It was calm in the morning, but the wind was still predicted to blow around thirty knots by afternoon, so we decided to stay put. Jim and I needed a layover day anyway. He changed the two fuel filters and the air breather filter, adjusted the stuffing box, and, in general, inspected *Yankee Lady's* engine. The primary filter was dirty with a few drops of water in it. After all this motoring, this was our first problem (not a serious one) with fuel on the whole trip. We stopped at the *cantine* for a hamburger and then walked to the nearby convenience store for ice, eggs, film, and ice cream sandwiches.

The others read, napped, and went for walks. The two Toms tried to get their GPS instruments to work without much success. Tom Isele measured his mast to see if he could fit under the lift bridge at Shippagan. He concluded that it might be possible at low tide. By afternoon, the predicted wind arrived. We stayed deliciously comfortable and quiet. Jim and I decided to order out at the canteen. He brought two scallop dinners back to *Yankee Lady*. We decided to leave Newport and head for Paspébiac in the Bay of Chaleur, a distance of twenty-seven miles, in the morning.

The weather forecast was confusing. The English version was read by a basically French-speaking person. He talked so fast we had difficulty identifying our sector. We thought we heard him say that the winds were from the southwest at fifteen to twenty knots and would become variable in the afternoon. We decided to leave. We started out in calm weather at 8:00 a.m. By 10:00 a.m., the wind and waves picked up. Soon, we were playing rocking horse, the waves reducing our speed by as much as two knots. *Misty* was having a hard time of it, taking water over the dodger. *Yankee Lady*, with her higher freeboard, was dry. I have always been proud of how sturdy she is under rough weather conditions. We sat on our comfortable cushions, facing backward behind our dodger while the autopilot held us on course. Periodically, one of us turned around to make sure we were on course and that there were no boats heading for us. It was actually quite comfortable. Lunch, however, was our standard rough weather fare—peanut butter and crackers.

All six of us listened to another English forecast from New Brunswick. It didn't sound like the wind would die down until almost evening when it would switch to the northwest. There really was no good alternate harbor. Port Daniel, close by, was in a small, relatively unsheltered bay. It had an anchorage, but it was crowded with fish traps and not too sheltered. We all decided to continue to Paspébiac and the security of a harbor with a breakwater and a public dock.

Wouldn't you know, about a half hour before we arrived, the wind and the waves began to lessen. Jim saw the red buoy off Pointe Paspébiac through the binoculars about two and a half miles away. We made sure to leave it to starboard to avoid the long sandy Banque de Paspébiac, which extends from the nearby point. Yet again, we passed between a breakwater and a dock to find the harbor. There were two sections to it. To our starboard and straight ahead was a large dock built on pilings. This was used by the commercial fishing boats. There was a small marina with floating docks to our port.

We saw an empty space at the fishing dock, found the usual vertical ladder, and tied up to the dock with the ladder amidships. *2nd Wind* tied up in front of us, but then, they noticed an empty space at the marina's floating docks and hurried over to get it. I could understand why. It's a lot easier to attach your boat to a floating dock, step off, and climb a gently sloping ramp to shore. Oh well, there was only one empty space there. *Misty* found a space in front of us between two large fishing boats. Unlike the others we have found on this journey, this dock is not built over a solid bulkhead. Instead, it is built over a series of pilings. There is a big space between each piling so that the water continued under the dock to a bulkhead against the shore. The pilings were so wide apart that *Yankee Lady* would have fit between the pilings (bow first) if she didn't have a mast. Sounds of the water splashing under the dock were magnified and echoed back to us. It was not a very secure feeling.

Tom and Barbara were told that they would have to move by 8:30 in the morning because one of the fishing boats was going to be sand blasted. Speaking of sand blasting, the wind shifted to the northwest and blew gusts of excess sand from a nearby parking lot on to *Yankee Lady* and *Misty*. We've faced lots of things on this voyage including dragging anchors, low water, large waves from passing boats while we were attached to one dock or another, but sand blasting was a first.

This harbor is next to the sandy point. A beach extends out into the bay where people were at least sunbathing if not swimming. On the other side of the harbor is a grassy marsh and a small road, which leads to a museum at the top of the hill. We climbed our ladder, met the others, and walked to the museum.

This Paspébiac museum is composed of eleven buildings dating from the last half of the eighteenth century. They remain witnesses to the prosperity of this region when it was the hub of commercial activity. This was Quebec's first cod fishing port, and dried, salted cod was the mainstay of the economy. In particular, two families, originally from the island of Jersey, formed substantial financial empires by shipping the salted cod to ports throughout the world. The museum documents the evolution of this industry. Role players roam the buildings dramatizing the life and activities of the people who lived during this time.

We toured the buildings and then ate supper in the restaurant, which was slightly expensive but good. I ordered seafood vol-au-vent. The waitress who spoke little English couldn't describe vol-au-vent, but I decided to get it anyway. It turned out to be seafood in a patty shell. Throughout the meal, we listened to the taped background music. I particularly enjoyed the selections from *Les Miserables* and *Phantom of the Opera*, two of my favorite musical productions.

After supper, we met on *2nd Wind* to discuss the plans for the next day. We decided to cruise thirty-two miles to Carleton, which is close to the end of the Bay of Chaleur. After dark, Jim and I returned to *Yankee Lady*. The eight rungs of our ladder were clammy, moist, and slippery as we descended at low tide. I was eerily conscious of the cavern-like watery underground below the dock, felt the damp, and sensed the inky black water. I could almost hear the phantom's diabolical laugh.

Since we were uncertain about the weather in the afternoon, we left early to try to stay ahead of any nastiness. I cooked breakfast underway, before any significant waves developed. Jim unfurled the jib. It billowed out in front of us to give us more stability and an extra push through the following sea. It was a hazy day; the shoreline was dimly visible. About seven miles from Carleton, I looked ahead and saw a large dark shape next to the horizon. Is that a big black cloud or a mountain? We checked the chart. Carleton lies at the bottom of the majestic Appalachian mountain range; it wasn't a cloud I saw. Shortly, the shapes of the mountains became better defined.

We motored to our GPS spot just past Pointe Tracadigache and turned north into the harbor keeping the lighthouse, which flashed a red light every five seconds, to our right. The harbor was filled with docks. We motored toward the public dock, which was less open to the west or southwest wind, but it looked like it belonged to the fishermen, and it was crowded. Since the prevailing wind is from the west or southwest, I would have liked this extra protection, but it has been my experience that the fishermen always have the choice spots. Probably rightly so, they work hard, and fishing is their livelihood. We turned to the privately owned floating docks. All three boats found slips at this marina for $15 a night.

Carleton was settled around 1756 by exiled Acadians fleeing a brutal deportation by the English from Nova Scotia. In 1787, a group of American Loyalists joined them. French is the primary language spoken here.

There is no fuel dock in the harbor, and we all needed fuel. The dockmaster spoke French with a little English thrown in. After confusing French/English conversations and a lot of gesturing, he agreed to take the following to the gas station in his van: three marina jerry jugs and one of Tom Isele's containers for gasoline, one jerry jug for diesel for *Yankee Lady*, one jerry jug plus two gallon jugs for diesel for *Misty*. You can see why this was confusing. After this was negotiated, we met Roger who was bilingual. He would have made our negotiations a lot easier. Oh well.

Roger was most interested in the tales of our adventurous voyage. I think he sort of adopted us during our stay in Carleton. One of the first things he did was offer us the use of his car. He said, "You must need groceries. Here are the keys to my Chrysler. It's that white one over there." Rosie, Barbara, and I took advantage of the offer. As the driver, I felt very responsible. I hadn't driven a car in over two months, and it felt slightly strange. I drove carefully.

We all ate on our boats. The grocery store had fresh strawberries, so I replenished our supply of strawberry jam. Just in time, we were out. We met on *2nd Wind* for dessert and cards.

Since none of us had really had time to explore Carleton, we decided to stay another day. The others went to a restaurant for breakfast while we enjoyed a leisurely breakfast in the cockpit. As we sat there, Roger and his wife stopped by. Their thirty-two-foot Carver powerboat is around the dock corner from us. We invited them aboard. They shared some local knowledge with us, and we talked to them about the Intracoastal Waterway trip to Florida. They invited all of us to drive to the top of Mount Carleton in the afternoon.

Jim and I walked into town. We stopped at the town hall information center but gained no new insights from what other local people had told us. We ate lunch at the Blue Heron and then stopped to talk to Tom and Barbara who were at a phone booth talking to Barbara's cousin Hector. A car pulled up beside us. It was Roger's wife. She told us Roger was too busy to be with us, so they had decided to let us use her car. She brought an English pamphlet about Miguasha Park, twelve miles away, which is the site of a large group of fossils. I have always loved geology, so this was an exciting prospect for me. Twelve miles would have seemed like an impossible distance without a car. As she started to walk home, Jim said, "At least you could let me drive you home." She did. We accepted their offer, as usual touched by the kindness of the people we meet.

Tom and Rosie had left to go on a tour, so Jim and I and Tom and Barbara decided to drive up the mountain and then go see the fossils.

Miguasha National Park has been designated a UNESCO World Heritage Site. It is famous for the fossils of fish that lived 370 million years ago, during the Devonian period or age of fish. For more than a century, the fossils of Miguasha have been recognized as unique and have been studied by scientists from Europe and America. The staff is continually finding more fossils in the cliffs and on the beach. It is possible also for visitors to tour the beach area and find fossils. However, visitors have to give what they find to the museum. We couldn't go down there for two reasons: it was late and it was high tide.

The wind was blowing hard (ten to fifteen knots) from the west when we returned to the marina. This meant that the waves were entering the basin and setting docks and boats in constant, undulating motion. Roger and his wife were on their Carver. Walking on the dock to return their car keys was like walking on the deck of a tossing small boat without any handrails or taking a trip through a carnival fun house. We accomplished the trip, visited for a while, and then returned to *Yankee Lady*. Later in the evening, the wind calmed down, and we spent a peaceful night.

In the morning, all six of us listened to the weather three or four times. Predictions were for west to northwest winds fifteen to twenty knots. This meant that the wind would either be coming from the side (a broad reach) or from behind (downwind). In either case, *Yankee Lady* could handle stronger winds from these directions than she could if she were heading nearly into the wind. It also meant we would rock and roll in the waves as they pushed us from behind toward Shippagan, thirty miles away. We have all sailed in these conditions before and didn't feel threatened by them. We decided to do it.

Jim and I put up both sails and, for about two hours and ten miles, enjoyed an exhilarating sail. But the wind increased, and we were having difficulty controlling the boat, overpowered by the wind and waves. First, we furled the jib. This was not enough. We started the motor to make as much speed as possible in order to keep up with the waves. It was still too much with the mainsail up. One big wave lifted the stern and turned us broadside to the waves; a gust of wind filled the sail and laid us on our side, nearly putting the rail in the water. Everything not secured on the starboard side fell to the port side of the boat, including crew. We needed to take the mainsail down. In order to do this, I had to turn the boat halfway around so that the bow would point into the waves and the sail would luff into the wind. This meant heeling over again as we turned broadside to the wind and waves before the bow finally swung into the short, choppy, four-to-five-foot waves. I needed full power to keep forward motion. Holding onto whatever he could, Jim struggled to the mast to pull the mainsail down. With the sail flapping wildly, I released the main halyard cleat (which is in the cockpit). Jim grabbed the edge of the sail along the mast and pulled it down. How quiet it became. We had enough. We turned around and headed for the nearest port, Belledune, about five miles away. Back in Carleton, local sailors had said, "Don't go in there. It's a large commercial port." Meanwhile, the others were having similar problems. In spite of the warning, we all decided to enter this man-made harbor to regroup out of the waves. We really felt we had no choice. It gave new meaning to the phrase, "Any port in a storm."

The Port of Belledune is indeed a deepwater harbor for large commercial ships. I thought, *Most commercial ports are surrounded by big cities. This one feels as if it were in the middle of nowhere.* As we entered, I noticed that it was surrounded by a few rocky outcrops and fields of scrubby grass and bushes. Yet it was the gateway for shipping to the arctic and European markets. As we circled inside the harbor, we saw ugly but functional commercial warehouses, large cranes, conveyer belts and smoke stacks. The bulkheads and docks were much too large for us. I think if

Yankee Lady could have talked, she would have said, "What's a little boat like me doing in a big ship harbor like this?" I would have reminded her that when she was new in 1986, she had anchored a few hundred feet from the Statue of Liberty in the middle of the Hudson River, surrounded by hundreds of other boats, all celebrating the one hundredth anniversary of that "lady."

We really didn't know what to do. *Misty* and *2nd Wind* anchored at the head of the harbor while Jim and I tried to call the port authority on the radio. There was no answer. Finally, Jim reached the Canadian Coast Guard. He told them that we were three small sailboats seeking refuge from the weather and asked if we could stay in the harbor. The Coast Guard called the port authority by phone. We received permission tie up next to a tugboat, which would be leaving at 5:00 p.m. to bring in a ship. Then we could tie to that dock. Meanwhile, Jim and I motored around the corner of the southern wharf. We saw a small cove, which was sheltered from the blowing west wind; it looked like a possible anchorage. We motored back into the harbor to check out the tugboat. Not possible. There was a small dinghy-like boat tied to the outside of it, the sides of the tug were too rounded, and the dock was too big. We called the Coast Guard back to ask if we could anchor in the harbor. We couldn't, but they said we could anchor around the corner in an anchorage where we would be safe: the cove we had just found. We motored over to the other two boats to tell them to move. We returned to the anchorage; *Misty* and *2nd Wind* pulled up their anchors and joined us. We anchored in about 24 feet of water, letting out 150 feet of anchor line. There was no need to put the engine in reverse to set the anchor. The wind did it for us.

Around 4:00 p.m., Atlantic Daylight Time, we saw a large freighter appear on the horizon. It grew bigger as it steamed closer. Sure enough, at 5:00 p.m., the tug emerged from the harbor. It nosed up to the south side of the freighter with its bow facing the stern of the freighter. As we watched them enter the harbor, I figured there would have been some anxious moments if we had been anchored there.

The wind continued to howl; sometimes, we think thirty knots or better, until just before we went to bed. It calmed down briefly and then whistled again. But we were not bouncing in waves, just swerving back and forth gently on our anchor lines.

I noticed a lighthouse on the small point, which defines one side of this basin. It glowed with a steady yellow light, which every few seconds increased in brightness and intensity. As I watched the almost full moon rise, golden on the horizon, the glow of the lighthouse paled next to the moon's grandeur. Although the wind howled, we slept peacefully all night.

Believe it or not, we all discussed the weather over our radios at 6:30 the next morning. We had listened to the forecast, which predicted winds from the northwest at fifteen to twenty knots. After yesterday, we were suspicious of twenty-knot forecasts and all agreed we should stay another day. Jim and I went back to sleep.

Our scenic view from *Yankee Lady* was a mixture of commercial/industrial and rural "middle of nowhere." We saw the rock breakwater, which consisted of giant boulders piled high to protect the harbor from the beating waves. Industry flourished around the edges of the harbor. There were two processing plants, a smelter plant, and a fertilizer plant, one of which belched white steam smoke that dissipated into the blue sky. Cranes poked up from the dock.

But we also looked at the lighthouse on the sandy point, a crescent sandy beach in shore, an old cemetery, and a few houses some distance across fields of scrub grass and bushes. Tom, Barbara, Tom, and Rosie at various times explored the beach and dirt roads. Jim and I dinghied over to the lighthouse and walked that beach. By midafternoon, the wind was probably blowing at twenty knots. We gathered on *Misty* to discuss navigation plans and then played cards.

More wind! Another day at anchor. How cozy *Yankee Lady* felt as we waited in this small, protected cove for better weather. Not having to go anywhere, we relaxed in our own little world of comfortable cushions surrounded by the warm wood tones of *Yankee Lady's* cabin. Sunshine, streaming through the ports and hatch, brightened the atmosphere of peace and contentment. We spent the day reading, napping, and doing various chores. But although this was a safe haven, we were ready to leave.

At last, the next morning, the winds were forecast to be from the west—ten to fifteen knots. We're going to Shippagan, fifty-five miles away. Jim and I listened to the forecast, with eyes not really open, at 6:00 a.m., but we figured that if the wind freshened in the afternoon, it would maybe go to twenty knots, but it wouldn't start screaming at twenty-five or thirty knots.

We were due to leave at 6:30 a.m. I put the coffee on and fixed breakfast, which was ready about 6:25 a.m. We decided to finish eating before leaving since *Yankee Lady* could motor a little faster than the others, and we could catch up. *Misty* and *2nd Wind* motored out into Chaleur Bay. After they cleared the protection of the breakwater, we watched them start to rock and roll. We were glad we waited and could eat breakfast without everything sliding around.

The wind probably stayed around fifteen knots from the west, but the following sea was really sloppy. The larger waves were four to five feet. All of us put our jibs out and started our fifty-five-mile trip. Given our experiences entering Belledune, we were all a little anxious. There was really no nearby stopping point with enough deep water on this segment of the trip. The autopilots on *2nd Wind* and *Yankee Lady* were behaving admirably in the following sea, but *Misty's* wasn't, so Barbara and Tom had to steer the whole way, which was very tiring and stressful. At twenty-two miles or so, we could have altered course for Paspébiac, but it was still six miles away. Around 11:00 a.m., I listened to the updated weather—west wind at ten knots with gusts to fifteen;

that made us all feel a little better. There was a positive side to all this. We arrived in Shippagan around 3:00 p.m.—eight and one-half hours later. That's an average speed of over six knots an hour—pretty impressive for sailboats our size.

While underway, Jim and I took turns resting below. I crawled into the aft berth, set myself against the inside wall, snuggled up to the extra pillow to buffer the rocking, and fell asleep—not bad at all. Jim takes the prize for lunches prepared under uncomfortable conditions. He tied a cooking pot handle around the cutting board, which was stored behind the stove. This kept the pot from falling off the stove in the wavy conditions. Then he prepared a macaroni and cheese lunch, which tasted delicious on this cool day.

Forty-three miles after leaving, we reached the red and white bell buoy that marked the entrance to Shippagan channel. The passage through this channel became more confusing than we had anticipated. We had planned to simply follow the red and green buoys into town, but we found that they were difficult to spot; we needed the security of the proper heading to each one.

There were several reasons why Jim and I had decided not to create GPS waypoints for these buoys. First, we thought we would have no trouble finding them visually. Second, there were a lot of them, and since we would not pass this way again, we saw no point in creating waypoints for them. Third, it required a lot of planning to manually calculate the latitude and longitude for each buoy on the chart and then enter the information into the GPS instrument. We had no navigation programs or computers to do this with the push of a computer key. Lastly, we figured that, if necessary, we could find the correct headings the old-fashioned way, by looking at the chart and using the parallel rulers to line up the correct information on the appropriate compass rose. This is what we now had to do.

I steered through a quartering sea, which still bounced us around while Jim went below to do the course plotting. He then relieved me at the wheel. Things became tense when we rounded red buoy EG14. The plotted course to the next buoy said 170 degrees, but Jim couldn't see another buoy in that direction. I went below to check the course on the chart. I was anxious because we weren't sure which way to steer. I needed to use the parallel rulers to check Jim's calculations. This was not an easy task since we were still bouncing in the waves. I wanted to hurry, but the rulers kept sliding around on the chart. Fumble, fumble, check, double-check. Oh no! Both of us had plotted on the compass circle, which gave the true heading instead of the magnetic one. (There are variations in the earth's magnetic field, which causes a compass to swing toward the magnetic field instead of to true north.) Oops, the magnetic heading was 192 degrees. This was why we always tried to double-check each other. Corrections made and anxiety reduced, we continued on course.

Now we motored through calm water sheltered by the land. We could see the public wharf and fleet of fishing boats, but where was the marina? I called the marina to ask for directions as instructed by my French guidebook. No one there spoke English. Someone interjected over the radio, in English, that I should call the Coast Guard. At the same time, a small powerboat arrived to escort us in. Between the Coast Guard and the captain of the powerboat, we were told that the marina was just before the public dock. The marina person told us to motor between the red and green sticks and go to the second dock. We did. There were two attractive young ladies standing on the dock waiting to take our lines. We called the other two boats who were behind us and gave them directions in English. Mission accomplished; we have landed.

We walked to the small office to register with the young ladies—$15 per night. With French, English, and body language, we asked about showers, laundry, and a place to eat. The showers and laundry were in the nearby building. They asked what kind of restaurant did we want. We tried to indicate a little bit of everything. Then, to illustrate "fish," Jim moved his hands back and forth to simulate a swimming fish, and to illustrate "steak," he did a talented rendition of a cow. "*Moo*." We were not disappointed in the restaurant, Pirate's Bistro, which was a five-block walk through town toward the bridge and causeway. We all ate too much.

After dinner, Tom Isele walked over to the bridge to talk to the bridge tender about the height of the bridge from the water. He was a little worried; he knew that even if he removed his radio antenna, he would still need forty-five and a half feet to clear the bridge. If he couldn't clear the bridge, he would have to retrace his way into the Bay of Chaleur and sail around Miscou Island. The bridge tender told him that at low water there would be a maximum clearance of forty-seven feet. I reflected that this would not be a worry-free passage for Tom. Given the variability of tide, wind, and waves, one and a half feet was not a lot of room to spare.

Jim and I returned to *Yankee Lady* while the others stopped at the grocery store in the shopping plaza in the middle of town. Since Tom and Rosie can never pass by a bargain, they returned with a half gallon of Baxter mocha fudge ice cream because it was on special for $1.99. Not only that, Rosie is a dessert person. So even though we were still full from dinner, the six of us had to eat it right away; it wouldn't keep without a freezer.

After listening to the weather, we decided to stay another day and explore the area. Shippagan seemed a pleasant town. The main road was busy with car and truck traffic, but the side streets were quiet and residential. The marina arranged a ride to the gas station for Jim who took *Misty's* and our jerry jugs to get diesel. The gentleman who took him would accept no money.

The marina was sheltered by fifteen-foot sandbanks topped with grass. There were two and one-half rows of floating docks, which extended from the town side of the shore. Smaller docks extending from these formed the individual slips for boats.

Counting the three of us, there were five sailboats. The rest were small runabouts or lobster-style fishing boats. Lobstering is not allowed during the summer here, so we didn't have to worry about dodging lobster pots. Fishing is primarily for cod although fishing areas and amounts are strictly controlled by the government.

This is Acadian country. Almost all of the people who live here speak French. They are descendents of the first French colonists who settled in the Maritimes during the 1600s. Separated by geography and culture from the French-speaking settlers of Quebec, each has different traditions, history, and French language dialects. Somehow, I have been able to communicate with both using my American high school variety French.

While the Acadians seek official government recognition, there is not the same move to separate from Canada as there is in Quebec. We found them to be friendly, fun-loving, and proud of their town.

The six of us have been discussing our next stop. We located Escuminac on the southern side of Miramichi Bay as a possibility, but we have received conflicting reports about the depth of the water at the entrance to the Escuminac public wharf. There are two harbors, inner and outer. Either one would provide enough protection for an overnight stop. Jim and I consulted the chart and the notices to mariners. The latest notice for that area is dated 1994 (we have them through 1998). The depths are shown at four feet or lower. That would not be deep enough for *Yankee Lady* and *2nd Wind*. We called the Canadian Coast Guard to see if they had any later information. The officer verified that 1994 was the latest charted information. Jim mentioned that we needed five feet of water. The officer said, "No problem. There's plenty of water. I live there, and I go in and out all the time." So who do you believe?

Meanwhile, we discussed ways for *2nd Wind* to get under the bridge. One idea was to attach *2nd Wind's* main halyard from the top of her mast to a winch on *Yankee Lady's* deck. By winching the halyard tighter, *2nd Wind* would tilt sideways. Given the fact that *2nd Wind* would have to go under the bridge at the same time and *Yankee Lady* would have to be nearby, this did not seem like a good idea. Tom decided to climb the mast and take down his radio antenna, which would give him a clearance of 45.6 feet. He would have to go under the bridge at decidedly low tide. Jim and Tom Frasca hoisted him up in a homemade bosun's chair. More power to Tom; he accomplished the task. There are some of us in this group who could not be paid enough to go up there (we know who we are).

Another day in Shippagan. We were going to leave near low tide at 4:00 p.m. so that *2nd Wind* would have the 45.6 feet of clearance he needed under the bridge. But the wind started howling at 2:30 p.m., and the weather looked uncertain again, so we decided to stay another day. We still had two or three weeks to cover the 120 miles to Shediac where we plan to leave the boats for the winter.

All along this trip, we have found creative or unexpected ways of getting information. It has not been possible to go to one store or source to get the charts, cruising guides, or any other information that we need. The best cruising guide from the St. Lawrence to Shippagan was in French, loaned to us by a cruiser in Tadoussac. I've really increased my nautical French vocabulary so that I can read that book. For New Brunswick, we have the government charts, *Sailing Directions*, and *Notices to Mariners* through 1998, but we do not have specific information on depths in harbors, peculiarities of the weather, etcetera. We hoped we might find more reliable information from local people here.

We were getting better at doing this. While it's okay to get advice from individuals who say their brother knows someone who fishes who goes in there (wherever) all the time, we don't know the level of experience or reliability of the person. As noted above, even the Coast Guard can give confusing information. However, here was how we put together more pieces of this puzzle.

Tom Isele decided to talk to someone at the university. Yesterday, he met Nicole who spent an hour or better searching for information for us. She learned that a gentleman who works for the Federal Department of Fisheries and Oceans would be here today and arranged a 10:30 a.m. meeting with him. Tom asked about the depth of the water at Escuminac. The official called the manager of the Escuminac wharves who said there are depths of five to six feet inside the basin and at the approach. He stated that the Coast Guard is not necessarily notified of dredging that takes place within the harbor basins. This explains the difference between the *Notices to Mariners* and local knowledge.

Later, Tom and Barbara were at the Coast Guard station asking numerous questions about the weather, tide, and currents for this area. Oh, they said, "Do you know about these two books? We only have them in French, but there is an English translation you can send for." Taking no chances that the books might be out of print, Tom and Barbara secured the French ones. Together, Barbara and I can read most of them. They contain local information about prevailing winds and currents.

All six of us planned to regroup at the marina and leave at 5:30 p.m. to walk back to Pirate's Bistro for dinner. At five, a lady dressed in white knocked on *Yankee Lady's* hull. In hesitant English, she asked for the couple in the yellow shirts (Tom and Barbara were wearing their yellow Lenny and Joe's T-shirts). We directed her to *Misty*. She invited us to take a ride around town to see the local sights. This would also give her a chance to practice her English (she wants to visit relatives in Massachusetts). She had first met Tom and Rosie and then Tom and Barbara while walking in town. They, of course, had explained our trip. She works for the retired nuns in the convent. Tom Isele was still in the aquarium, but the rest of us piled into her standard shift, compact car for what we thought would be a twenty-minute ride. Wrong.

She told us she was a beginner at driving with a stick shift, but we really didn't need to be told. *Vroom*, the engine revved up, out came the clutch, our heads snapped back to the seats, and away we went. When we came to a speed bump, the loaded car didn't have the momentum to get over it, so the car stopped and bounced back. *Vroom* went the engine again, out came the clutch, back went our heads, and over we went.

She drove us to the beach/campground at one end of town. Each campsite was surrounded by trees, separated from all others. Some had paths leading directly to the water. I mentally filed this information in case we ever decided to bring our camper here. Back through town, we crossed the bridge (the one *2nd Wind* has to fit under) to Lameque Island. Lameque and Miscou Islands are both connected to the mainland by bridges. Geographically, they separate Chaleur Bay from the Gulf of St. Lawrence. When we leave Shippagan, we will rejoin the Gulf.

We drove by miles of peat moss, brown and flat except for several piles of it shaped like pale Hershey Kisses. As we turned down another road, she told us we were going to the end of the world. It did seem a little that way as we drove through this sparsely populated area. She kept up a running commentary, "That big house over there has beautiful lights at Christmas. My brother lives over there, my sister over there, etcetera." She has thirteen brothers and sisters, most of who live on this island. Her three sons live nearby also. Her two-month-old twin granddaughters will be baptized this Sunday.

We drove along the beach road to her house, a small ranch. It is situated across the street from the ocean. I asked her if she ever saw any icebergs. She said she did see some in the winter.

Icebergs form in Greenland and drift with the current toward the coasts of Labrador and Newfoundland. At latitude 47.48 degrees north, the water here is far enough north for the odd iceberg to reach this area. I really wanted to see one, but it was not to be. I think Jim was just as happy not to, nine-tenths of a berg is underwater and couldn't be seen from a boat. It was spooky to me that the Titanic sank over 360 miles south and east of our present latitude during the month of April. Did that mean we could still see an iceberg? I didn't think so.

She (Leontine) said it was her prayer to live on this remote island. She went in the house to get her husband, James, who, she said, speaks better English than she does (he does). We all talked together for five or ten minutes. He works for a fishing company. She said she always has lobster to eat. She wanted to invite us in for coffee, but her three dogs were making too much commotion. We said we really had to get back; it's 6:00 p.m. She dropped us off at Pirate's Bistro while we looked for Tom Isele. Moments later, he came walking up. "Where the —— have you been?" We explained, thanked Leontine several times, and gave her *Misty* and *Yankee Lady* boat cards with our names on them. Shortly after, we ordered dinner; she appeared with her two-year-old grandson, just to show him to us. This trip continues to surprise us. How can you ever plan for events like these?

We enjoyed another delicious meal at the restaurant. The waitress remembered us from two days ago. During the course of our meal, as evening moved toward night, the lights were turned down...to make it more romantic? When the bill came, Jim kidded with the waitress, asking her how he was supposed to read it in this light. With a slight grin, she walked away and came back with a penlight, which she held over the bill in front of Jim's face.

At last, we had the weather window to leave. Since low tide was in the afternoon, this would be one of our shorter voyages. We planned to motor under the bridge and anchor on the other side, a distance of one-quarter mile. Jim and I made phone calls, did a little shopping, and ate lunch at Tim Hortons. We returned to the boat just before 2:00 p.m. Tom called the bridge; clearance was 46.6 feet. It was time to go. We filed through the narrow marina channel. *Misty* slowly motored under the bridge first. They have the lowest mast, *Yankee Lady* is next, and *2nd Wind* is the tallest. We passed through uneventfully (don't look up) and then watched *2nd Wind*. We think they had only inches clearance, but they made it.

We anchored alongside the causeway leading to the bridge in twelve feet of water. The others dinghied ashore to go to church and then out for pizza. They came back full of news. Leontine was in church (we thought it was she who honked her car horn at our anchored boats as she drove across the bridge). When she arrived home yesterday, she looked at our card and saw our last name—Silva. She told our group that their last name is Desylva. Both husbands are James. She was very excited to have that connection with us.

Meanwhile, back at the anchorage, a rugged, twenty-three-foot fishing boat with an enclosed cabin stopped by. The captain, a French Canadian who looked like a full-sized Danny DeVito of *Taxi*, asked if we wanted some fresh-filleted mackerel. Yes for Jim; no, for Judy—oh well, I'll have a little. He rafted to *Yankee Lady* while he filleted the fish. He gave us two pounds of fish. He is unquestionably an entrepreneur. He had been a fisherman, employing sixty people. When the government shut down the cod industry several years ago, he quit fishing and, together with his son, built a sales business on the Internet. Today, he sells trading cards (Harley Davidson, movie stars, etcetera) and also works for an Australian company marketing their product (we're not sure what it is) worldwide. Now he has six people working for him. He has also captained a forty-six-foot charter sailboat in the Caribbean. He's having too much fun to retire.

Jim cooked the fish on the grill. I ate about one-quarter pound; Jim finished the rest. I must admit it was delicious. We lit the kerosene lamp and relaxed for the evening until we went bump with *2nd Wind*. It was the turn of the tide; there was no wind. Not to panic. Jim pulled in ten feet of anchor line; I gave *2nd Wind* a push, and we separated.

At 6:30 the next morning, just as the sun was rising, Jim and I heard a knock on the hull. We were awake because several fishing boats had rocked us with their wakes on their way out the channel. It was Tom Frasca asking us to listen to the weather and then confer with the others. There were predictions of south to southwest winds fifteen to twenty-five knots, not getting much better toward evening. We needed to make a decision early while *2nd Wind* could still get under the bridge to go back to the marina. Since we were in unfamiliar territory, we did not relish the idea of coping with twenty-five-knot winds. The unanimous decision was to return to the marina. After removing pounds of sea grass from our anchor lines, we motored under the bridge with no problems back into the marina, another one-fourth-mile "voyage." This was not the direction we had planned on. Then, all morning, we sat around in a perfectly calm day. Where was the wind?

Looking for something to do, Jim changed the oil in *Yankee Lady's* engine. He discovered fuel leaking out of the air vent on the secondary fuel filter. He decided to replace the scarred copper washer, which acts as a gasket. But today is the Sunday of Labor Day weekend. We walked to the hardware store. The sign on the door said closed Sunday and Monday. No surprise. We needed the engine before then, so he took out his Leatherman, filed the washer smooth, and put the engine back together. I don't think Jim ever lacks for creativity when he is on the water.

We ate lunch at the local sub shop. People were talking and laughing in French, but of course, we were oblivious. We met Tom and Rosie outside of Dunkin Donuts. Tom told us the ice freezer at the marina was unlocked. Aha! I bought a half gallon of Baxter's Grape Nut ice cream and stored it in the freezer until after supper. We all needed to use up food from our ice boxes, so we decided to have a potluck supper on *Yankee Lady*. Pooling our resources, I cooked pork chops in mushroom soup, Rosie brought a salad and rice, and Barbara brought cooked peppers and onions—simple when everyone does a little. After supper, we six had to eat the whole half gallon of ice cream. It was easy, covered with the hot fudge sauce I had made before supper.

At last, the weather was favorable. Our destination was Escuminac, forty miles away. We planned to leave at 7:30 in the morning but at 7:00 a.m., Tom called the bridge to get the height of the bridge above the water. The bridge tender said the tide was rising and the clearance was dropping. Tom wanted to leave immediately. We did (within ten minutes more or less). After we cleared the bridge, we motored through a narrow, winding channel to reach open water. There were shallow sand flats on either side. I thought to myself, *you can always tell it's shallow when you see birds walking in the water.* It always makes me feel a little nervous. Three-fourths of the way through, the rpms on *Yankee Lady's* engine started to drop. I looked at the exhaust water coming out the pipe in the stern. It was black instead of clear (According to Jim, this means the engine is getting too much raw fuel.). I throttled back, and Jim went below to investigate. If there is anyone I want to be with on a boat with a sick engine, it is the master mechanic, Jim. If humanly possible, no engine has a chance to give up while he is around. One at a time, he opened the high-pressure fuel supply fittings at the injectors. This removed air and verified that the injectors were working. We returned to full speed and the engine purred. Deduction: there was probably some air in the fuel line.

Since the Caraquet/Shippagan area, the landscape has been flat and sandy, no more mountains and cliffs. This is not a friendly shore for cruising sailboats. The water is shallow and the currents are tricky close to shore. We motored forty miles to Escuminac, staying about five miles from land until we closed on that peninsula. It was a lumpy ride. Suddenly, about halfway, a voice on the radio (we monitor channel 78) burst forth with song, "I'm an old cow hand, from the Rio Grande…" It was Tom Isele in his best barbershop voice, referring to rolling in the saddle or on a boat. I remarked, "Yes, the scenery is great. One wave looks pretty much like the next."

Finally, we spotted the rotating green light on the end of Escuminac Wharf. At 3:00 p.m., close to high tide, Jim and I cautiously motored through the entrance to the inner harbor and then the outer harbor. We found six and seven feet (The tide drops as much as four feet, and six minus four does not equal the five feet that *Yankee Lady* needed.) Then *Yankee Lady* gently touched the bottom near the outer wharf. We didn't know what happened to "There's plenty of water," but this spot was not for us. We didn't have much choice on where to go. Jim had originally marked an island on the chart as a good place to anchor. It was now about five miles away. We could have gone there still, but the water outside the wharf was calm. We worried about the fishermen leaving or returning and creating big wakes with their boats, but all in all, we thought we would be okay to anchor there in nine or ten feet of water. All six of us agreed to stay. Wrong.

First, there was a mass exodus of fishing boats. To Barbara, it was like Jonah's whale spitting out fifty trawlers; to Jim, it was like a swarm of bees leaving the hive. What a parade! Just as we thought there can't be any more boats in that harbor, another one would nose through the opening. Some slowed down for us, some didn't. One slowly approached our stern and asked why we weren't in the harbor. We replied we needed five and one-half feet at low tide. There answer was, "Oh, there's plenty of water" and/ or, "There is about three feet of soft mud under the water."

Suddenly, I thought, *Maybe that's the answer to the mystery of "plenty of water." With their high-powered boats, all they had to do was plow through the mud and never notice the depth.* They asked if we needed anything. We thanked them and said no. It was nice of them to stop.

Jim and I wanted to make sure we could be seen after dark. We turned on the anchor light and the steaming light (which only works when the running lights are on). Jim covered the red and green bow lights with aluminum foil. That left us with an all-around light at the top of the mast, a white light facing forward halfway up the mast, and a white stern light. We looked at *Misty*. She had steaming lights on. We noticed that the green rotating light on the dock reflected against the hull, lighting it up every few seconds. We called to tell them not to worry; they would be seen.

Then the wind changed direction from southwest (where the land sheltered us) to northeast where there was no protection. It seemed as if the wind and ocean swells reached us all the way from Cabot Strait at the tip of Nova Scotia. It was a gentle wind, but with the long fetch, we got a variety of waves, not big, but uncomfortable. The wind was not sufficient to head us into the waves. We started to rock and roll. We rocked in the wind-created waves, and we rolled in the fishing-boat-created waves—all night. There was no pattern to them. Our bodies would almost get used to rolling, and then we would have to adjust to rocking. At one point, I laid down on the cabin sole, thinking I would be closer to the center of gravity and not feel the motion quite as much. It didn't matter. Besides, the floor was hard, and I didn't have enough blankets. Back to the bunk, rock, roll, rock, roll, no sleep. *Is it morning yet?* I have spent restless nights at home in my bed where I have tossed and turned all night. But this time, it was *Yankee Lady* who was tossing and turning, and there was no escape.

At 1:00 p.m., Jim and I discussed leaving for Richibucto, our next destination which was thirty-four miles away. We would arrive in the light. We also thought this might give us an extra edge on the weather. The winds were forecast to be from the southwest at fifteen to twenty knots (in our face) by Tuesday evening. We called the others on channel 78 (We had agreed to leave our radios on for the night.). They were also awake—how could they not be. Should we leave now? The consensus was that it would be difficult to set up the radars and GPS and leave in the dark. Even with the instruments, navigation would be tricky in these unfamiliar waters, especially as tired as we all were. We would leave at daylight. I think Escuminac will be etched in our memories as one of the worst nights we have ever spent at anchor.

Jim and I must have finally dozed off because Barbara, the early morning person, awoke us with, "North Cove, North Cove, it's 5:20 in the morning. Daylight should be at 6:00 a.m." *Groan— call us back at 5:45 if it's light.* We finally got up. It was cloudy and not really light enough to leave until 6:15 a.m. I couldn't make the coffee at anchor because the boat's motion was too unstable. We needed to wait for the regularity that comes with actually moving through the water.

As dawn progressed, the first part of the trip was pleasant enough. There was a light wind. Evenly spaced rollers caused us to ride up one swell and down another, sort of like driving on a slightly hilly road. We rounded Point Escuminac, staying well offshore to avoid the shoal water and reefs. We set course for Sapin Ledge and then for a buoy off the Richibucto River.

Shades of Maine, it seems lobstering is allowed in this section of New Brunswick waters for ten weeks during August and September. Just before Sapin Ledge, we encountered a nest of brightly colored lobster pot buoys. Some had flags attached to sticks, which made the buoys more visible. In retrospect, this would not have been easy at 1:00 a.m. in the dark. At the same time, the wind and waves increased. By 10:00 a.m., the wind was blowing at least twenty knots, maybe twenty-five, with higher gusts. So much for the weather forecast of fifteen to twenty by evening. The waves in front of us built into white caps, short, steep four-to-five-footers. Also, the rollers were still coming from behind us. This created a very disturbed sea. Thus, we bounced around in the wind and waves and dodged pot buoys until we were a mile off the entrance to the Richibucto River. Then we had three and one-half miles of wind, pot buoys, narrow, winding channel, and sand bars to navigate.

Shortly after Sapin Ledge, Barbara, who was steering *Misty*, called to say they were having difficulty making progress through the waves and the blowing wind. She said, "Our GPS is reading less than one knot over the ground." Also, *Misty*, with her low freeboard, was taking heavy spray over the dodger into the cockpit every time she went bow down into a wave. Barbara was at the tiller; Tom was sitting in the cockpit. They were wet and worried as they put on their life jackets. Barbara later told me that Tom didn't want to go on deck to put up the mainsail. He also didn't want to unfurl the jib. He was afraid the jib might get stuck and not roll up again if the wind became too much.

Jim and I were frustrated. We were cruising at one-half to three-fourths power, bouncing around in the waves, trying to go slow enough so that *Misty* could keep up. To Jim, it seemed obvious that they should put out a sail and fall off the wind a little. Over the radio, Jim strongly suggested to them that they put out a sail. Finally, Tom unrolled *Misty's* jib. Tom Isele, always preferring to sail than motor, did the same for *2nd Wind*. Both boats decided to fall off the course enough to take the waves at a more comfortable angle. Both boats picked up speed and continued on a course, which angled slightly away from *Yankee Lady*. We maintained our original course and arrived outside of Richibucto about a mile ahead of them.

As far as Jim and I are concerned, praises go to *Yankee Lady*. She is the shortest and the lightest boat, but with her double hull and two-cylinder Yanmar engine she is sturdy and powerful. We were able to continue motoring on course, seldom falling off for the waves. We stayed dry, warm, and comfortable because the controls for the autopilot are under the dodger on the companionway bulkhead. One of us sat comfortably on two stacked square flotation cushions at the companionway entrance, facing forward. The cushions made us high enough to look through the open dodger window while we pushed the buttons on the autopilot to keep us on course. We took turns steering or sitting below where it was dry.

In order to keep the boat warm on cool nights without bothering to slide in the hatch boards, Jim had fastened a towel to the companionway sliding hatch cover. At night, we shut the cover and left the towel hanging down over the opening. We rolled it up on top of the hatch when we were not using it. Today, every now and then, a wave broke over the bow and splashed the person steering through the open dodger window. Well, what's a towel for? We dried off the wet spots on ourselves and the boat. Thus, we arrived at the red and white buoy marking the beginning of the channel to the entrance of the Richibucto River. The entrance lies between two sandspits, each extending for several miles along the coast. The buoyed channel is narrow and shifts with the action of wind and waves. We soon found this out.

Where was the next buoy, the one we entered into the GPS? It wasn't where it was supposed to be. The sands and channels had shifted since our chart was published, and the buoys had been moved. We scanned the water around us with the binoculars and finally saw a red and then a green buoy off to the right. Cautiously, we motored over and identified them as 03 and 04, the correct ones to start entering the channel.

We watched a couple of lobster boats speed by to enter the harbor. They, however, cut the buoys. We didn't. We could see breaking waves over one sandbar to our right. At this point, we were running parallel to a long sandy spit of land, South Richibucto Beach. We rounded green buoy 025 and turned southwest toward Richibucto Harbor following the marked narrow channel, which passed between shallow water on either side of it.

We discovered a sandbar building out from red buoy 032 because we hit it and stopped. *Oh no, not aground again.* The wind was still blowing twenty to twenty-five knots. Jim made a little channel in the sand by turning the wheel back and forth while using almost full forward power. At last, the wind caught the bow, *Yankee Lady* moved, and we were off. We continued into the shallow Richibucto River. From here, Jim was able to use the range lights, located on shore, to guide him to the public dock. The others also found the buoys and used the range lights to approach the harbor.`We found the marina had been moved from its charted location on another branch of the river to a basin just before the fishing wharf. Jim and I cautiously entered the basin but thought it was too shallow. Two men working on a small raft at the end of the dock didn't know the depth—in French (*profondeur*) or English. We turned around and motored to the face of the dock where the lobster boats were unloading their catches. One captain told us we could tie up in front of him. We found a ladder and tied up, but this was not a good place. The wind blew wood shavings, dirt, and cigarette butts off the dock onto *Yankee Lady's* decks. Beside getting sprayed with dirt, we needed to make room for another lobster boat, which was attempting to squeeze in front of us. There were no places left for *Misty* and *2nd Wind*, which were now approaching.

We needed to reconsider the marina. Just as we were leaving the wharf, Tom Isele, about one thousand feet away in *2nd Wind*, radioed to say with anxiety, "My engine quit. I'm drifting, and I need help." The wind was still whistling.

Jim replied, "Put your anchor out. We're just leaving the wharf. I'll come and help with the dinghy after we get tied to a dock in the marina." Someone on the fishing dock told us to stay on the left side of the marina; it was the deepest. We did and tied up to a rickety, floating dock. *Misty* followed us in. Another boat owner showed them an open space.

Jim took the six-foot boat hook and walked about one hundred feet to an empty face dock. He stuck the pole into water and reached bottom at five and a half feet, just enough for *2nd Wind*. He returned to *Yankee Lady*, climbed into the dinghy, and sped out to *2nd Wind*, now anchored. Tom had been busy while he waited. He switched gas tanks and verified that there was fuel in the tank and that the valves were open.

When he arrived, mechanic Jim diagnosed and fixed the following:

- There was no fuel in the carburetor because the fuel pump wasn't working.
- He fixed the fuel pump.
- The engine flooded because the choke was stuck shut. He fixed the choke.
- He removed the spark plugs and found them full of carbon.
- He put in new spark plugs and adjusted the carburetor.
- He started the engine, but it would not idle below 1,600 rpm.
- He deduced that the carburetor was dirty and the engine would not run at idle speed until it was cleaned.

Jim asked Tom, "Do you want to take it into the dock this way, or do you want to get one of the fishing boats to tow you?" Tom decided to motor in. Jim walked up to the bow and raised the anchor, then stayed on deck to await the next turn of events. He left the anchor hanging over the bow in case he needed to let it down suddenly as an emergency brake.

Who do you know that can anchor to a dock? Remember what happened to Tom, the anchor man, at Eternity Bay? This time, Tom headed into the harbor like a local lobsterman, full speed ahead (Remember, he couldn't idle the engine.). He sped by the bows of the boats facing him at the finger piers. Just before the face dock, he made a sharp ninety-degree turn to the left and shifted into reverse with no difficulty because the engine had stalled. He hollered to Barbara, Tom, and me, the North Cove dock crew who stood on the dock watching with some anxiety. "Stop the boat." Jim quickly handed Tom Frasca a bow line. *2nd Wind* was inches from the boat in front of her when Tom wrapped the bow line around a dock stanchion, and *2nd Wind* stopped—immediately. The bow plunged down, the hanging anchor swung under the dock, and when the bow popped up, the anchor dug in. Since we felt that *2nd Wind* may run out of anchors, Tom Frasca spent five minutes prying it loose.

We gathered at the local pizza restaurant for supper. What a day! We were still functioning on little or no sleep, which made us slightly silly. I had forgotten my reading glasses, so I asked Tom Frasca if I could borrow his to read the menu. He passed them over. Quiet Rosie laughed and said, "It's a good thing we all have our own teeth."

It wouldn't have mattered what the weather prediction was—we were going to stay put. All of us slept soundly all night long. Barbara actually slept until 7:30 a.m. and *2nd Wind's* engine still needed fixing. Tom cleaned the carburetor. Jim planned to help later.

On the dock, we met a young man named Pete. He was proud to show us the old wooden Northumberland Strait fishing boat he had restored. He and his friends use the boat to dig quahaug clams. They dive for them wearing wet suits in this cold water. There followed a discussion between Pete and Jim, who grew up in Rhode Island, about the merits of various kinds of clams. These quahaugs are big and can be tough unless prepared correctly. Pete said he would give us some for supper

We decided to make clam chowder. Barbara and Rosie went to the grocery store for onions, potatoes, carrots, cream, and French bread. I borrowed Barbara's big pot to cook the chowder later.

Rosie and Tom went to Dixie Chicken for lunch. Rosie put her purse down and left the restaurant without it. When she went back, it wasn't there. Did someone take it? She never got it back, a discordant note in this adventurous trip.

It poured during the afternoon. Jim did not feel like getting drenched walking down the dock to *2nd Wind*. Besides, he and Tom would have had to work outside as well as inside. He called

Tom on channel 78 to cancel. He noted that since the weather did not look promising for tomorrow either, we would be staying another day. The engine could be fixed then. We also postponed the chowder supper. We stayed on the boat, napped, and read. It cleared by evening. Smells of frying chicken drifted toward *Yankee Lady*, so Jim and I decided to eat at Dixie Chicken, a short block upwind. The smell was better than the reality. What a disappointment, all those calories, and it wasn't really that good.

Meanwhile, Pete brought two pints of home-canned clams and broth to *Misty*. He visited with them for a while. He told them the lobster-fishing season is ten weeks long. Lobstermen can make as much as $50,000 during that time. For the rest of the year, they collect unemployment. In the winter, Pete works for a company that restores and repairs lobster boats.

The next morning, we ate a late breakfast. Barbara came over to consult about supper. Tom Isele, under Jim's direction, fixed the carburetor. The engine purred so smoothly that Tom was practically jumping up and down with pleasure.

While Jim and Tom had the engine in pieces all over the cockpit, Rosie sat with me on *Yankee Lady*. Suddenly, Barbara came over in tears. She and Tom had been fighting about things that had happened on the boat. She said she didn't know if Tom would continue the trip next year. Barbara very much wants to finish it. I listened and then talked to her about my experiences as a single sailor. I cautioned her that next year, we would be facing more open water and, potentially, more difficult weather conditions. It's not easy to find a capable, compatible crew member, and this is definitely not a trip to do alone. After awhile, Barbara calmed down and began to think of solutions for herself. Later, she told me, again, that she really wants to finish. Tom said he would let her know by January whether or not he will continue. That way, she would have time to look for another crew member before spring. I thought to myself, *Hopefully, this will all blow over. We all have disagreements and arguments from time to time, but we get over them. I know that neither Jim nor I would consider not finishing this voyage.*

Everyone regrouped. Supper was truly a joint effort and one of the most delicious meals of the trip. On *Yankee Lady*, Barbara peeled the potatoes, onions, and carrots; then she chopped the onions and sliced the carrots. Rosie brought the cream. Jim diced the bacon and potatoes. I lightly sauteed the onions and cut up bacon, added the clam liquid, and timed the cooking of the potatoes and onions so nothing would be mushy. Jim supervised the addition of the clams and heating thereof. We carried the hot chowder to *Misty*. There are those of us who believe clam chowder should be "Rhode Island" style using clam liquid only; there are those of us who believe in "New England" style, clam liquid with milk or cream. We won't even discuss "Manhattan" style with tomatoes. Jim and Barbara relished the clear chowder, and the rest of us enjoyed chowder with cream, both accompanied by crusty French bread. After that, we ate Rosie's salad. Tom F. did the dishes. After a brief shakedown walk, we gathered on *2nd Wind* for dessert: angel food cake, hot fudge sauce, lemon pie filling, and whipped cream—sort of a Boston cream pie feast. Believe it or not, we can all still fit into our clothes.

We're still here. Winds are forecast to be from the southwest fifteen to twenty-five knots, with gale warnings for after midnight and tomorrow. Jim took the dinghy to the gas dock to get diesel fuel and noticed that the wooden oars, the small manual bilge pump, and the tiller extension were gone. The oars had *Albatross II* (from our Florida boat) burned deeply into the paddle sections. We have met so many wonderful people on this trip it's too bad to have this happen. I resolved that it won't, however, dampen our enthusiasm for what has gone before or is yet to come.

We needed to report the theft to the police, so Jim asked someone in the parking lot how to get there. A man named Alcide, who started the ice cream restaurant years ago and is now retired, said, "It's too far. I'll take you." He did, and Jim reported it. Do you think Alcide brought Jim right back to the dock? You might have guessed it. He gave Jim a tour of the town: the camp ground, the school, ice arena, tennis courts, the tomato factory, and more.

We also asked two or three more people in the parking lot to keep an eye out for the oars. Then the six of us walked a half mile to the lunch buffet at the Chinese restaurant. On the way back, Jim and I stopped at the marine supply store, the Coop, and the sports store to try to buy replacement oars. There was nothing suitable and cheap enough. We told the clerks about the theft also. By the time Tom Frasca went to the barbershop, the barber knew about it. That's the way of small towns, word travels. Perhaps, the end of this story isn't written yet. (It was. We never got the oars back.)

Another day—the gale and the rain arrived. We spent the morning securely tied to the dock aboard *Yankee Lady*, reading and visiting with a boater from the marina. With nothing better to do on this stormy day, Barbara counted the number of lobster boats that went out to fish. There are thirty lobster boats in this harbor. Eighteen went out which was over half of them. She figured, then, that there was an over 50 percent probability that the weather wasn't really so horrible out on the water. I said that maybe this weather prediction method was related to the practice of forecasting the weather by counting the number of cows lying down in a field. The saying goes that the more cows that are lying down, the more probability of rain. Well, we all must amuse ourselves on rainy days.

Jim and I enjoyed the last of the clam chowder for lunch. Since I knew that it was an old New England custom to never return an empty pan or jar when someone has given you food, I decided to fill the pint jars from the clams with freezer strawberry jam. Barbara and Rosie walked to the store and bought the strawberries; I made the jam. We all signed a thank-you card when we gathered on *2nd Wind* for some afternoon cards. Just before supper, Pete walked by; we called him over and gave him the jam.

All six of us planned to meet in the morning at the local breakfast restaurant. I was looking forward to toasted homemade bread, eggs, and home fries; Jim would rather have had a bagel on the boat. We arrived at the restaurant only to find it closed on Sunday. What to do? Well, we agreed, there's always Tim Horton's near the main highway. So after hiking a mile, we ended up with muffins, doughnuts or croissants, and coffee; it's wasn't the same. We walked back by way of a nature path, which was more pleasant than the road.

The day was beautiful. We had thought to wait until the wind and waves calmed down, but the breeze was in the ten- to fifteen-knot category from the west, blowing from the land, which meant no big waves. It was time to leave for our next harbor. We saw Pete cleaning his boat, so we gave him our dock keys to return to the dockmaster. We thanked him again and shook hands good-bye. By 11:15 a.m., we raised our mainsails at the dock and left under sail, with motors in either low power or neutral, just in case. In these light winds, the narrow channel out of the harbor and river was not nearly as formidable. The lobster pot buoys were easy to see with the light behind them. The sand dunes were bathed in sunlight, and the water lapped quietly against their shores. We rounded our GPS waypoint and set course for flashing green buoy X17 thirteen miles away. We turned off our engines, let out the jibs, and *sailed* on a broad reach, with the wind coming over the side of the boat. Depending on the wind gusts, our speeds alternated between four and six knots. *Yankee Lady* moved gracefully through the water, bobbing slightly in the wavelets. The overhead sky was cloudless and blue; there were puffy cumulus clouds on the horizon where the sky was light turquoise.

The sun touched us with warmth. What a beautiful thing is a sailboat with sails full of wind and only the sound of the boat sliding through the water, rustling, and creaking a little. I thought, *We deserve this day. It's like dessert at the end of the meal.* We had intended to sail to Shediac, our final destination for this year. Three miles before buoy X17, the wind was so light that we reluctantly turned on our engines. Just past the buoy, we noticed that our over-the-ground speed had slowed down, the current was turning against us. Jim and I estimated that we wouldn't get to Shediac until after 7:00 p.m., even with engines going and sails up. We held a VHF radio conference and decided to change course for Bouctouche, about ten miles closer. Pete had told *Misty* about a new marina there, which was not on the chart, near Priest Point.

We entered a GPS waypoint for the first buoy in the long series of red and green buoys that would lead us past Dune de Bouctouche and into Baie de Bouctouche. Consulting our charts, we wondered how to get into Buctouche Harbor. Jim and I measured the distance from the last buoy shown on the chart to the harbor entrance—five miles. It would be very difficult to cover that five miles with no buoys to guide us. Then I read the fine print Channel Staked and noted a very skinny channel with depths ranging from five to eight feet.

We took our sails down as we turned into the wind to find the entrance channel. We arrived at our last waypoint buoy about 4:30 p.m. From there on, we needed to find the rest of the buoys and then the stakes. *Misty* was leading, but we were all straining our eyes, looking into the sun with or without binoculars to find each buoy.

There was also a set of range markers on shore, but because we were looking into the setting sun, they were difficult to see. Range markers are frequently used to guide vessels through narrow, curving channels. Two lighted structures are placed in a line, usually on land, one behind the other. The one in front is shorter. As a boat rounds a curve, the markers become visible. The front one appears to the right or left of the back one. When the two markers appear to come together, the boat is on the correct course. I said to Jim, "I've always been confused how to steer toward these markers so that they line up."

Jim thought a minute and came up with this memory device. "Bare bottom, *bear* (steer) toward the *bottom* marker." How easy. Finally, we came to the last green buoy. Where do we go now? Those of us squinting through binoculars could see a skinny stick ahead with a small red triangle on top. *Misty* continued to lead, but for added security, we looked for each marker also. And so we negotiated this last part of the passage, finding more sticks with either small green squares or red triangles. Sometimes it was impossible to identify the shape until we were almost upon it; the sun was shining so brightly behind it. It was highly important to stay on the correct side of each marker, shallow water waited for those who strayed.

Misty, with her shallow draft, arrived at the marina. Jim and I could see the entrance, just past two stakes with green squares. Oops, we strayed, thudded, and stopped. We warned *2nd Wind* behind us to slow down. He touched bottom also but soon got off. We were too far on the green (left) side of the channel.

Again, we needed to use our Florida techniques to get unstuck here. Jim took the six-foot boat pole and climbed down the stern ladder into the dinghy. He circled *Yankee Lady*, thrusting the pole into the water as he went. He found deeper water toward shore. *Misty* sent a Jet Skier out from the marina to see if we needed a tow. We declined; we're used to this. I think Jim was a little insulted by the offer, but it was nice of them to come out. Tugboat Jim nosed the bow of the dinghy against *Yankee Lady's* port bow. The outboard roared at full power against *Yankee Lady*. I applied full diesel engine power and moved the rudder back and forth to dig a channel in the mud. The bow pointed toward shore. Then Jim zoomed around behind *Yankee Lady* and pushed against the stern while I gunned the engine. *Yankee Lady* plowed through several feet of mud, and then she was free. We entered the marina and tied up to the dock, joining the others.

We registered at the small office. We were told that Bouctouche is the birthplace of K. C. Irving, founder of Irving Oil Company. This marina was built by Irving Oil and then sold to a group of people who formed a yacht club. The charge for one night was $23. There were no showers or laundry, and there was one bathroom at the office. However, a security guard was on duty all night. We thought this rather expensive compared to the marinas at Richibucto and Shippagan where the charge was $15 per night and included showers, laundry facilities, and accessible bathrooms. Jim and I noticed a public wharf nearby. If it hadn't been so late, we probably would have moved.

The next morning was quiet, calm, and warm with scarcely a breeze. We left the marina at 9:00 a.m. *Misty* led us back through the narrow, staked channel. At least this time, the sun was higher in the sky, and the glare was not as bad as last evening. Part way out of the channel, Jim asked me if the exhaust water sounded funny. We both agreed that it did; it was barely pumping enough water. We deduced that the raw water filter was full of grass or mud.

How well I remember the first two times this happened to me. Both times, I was alone on *Yankee Lady*. It was the first year I owned her; she was still new. The first instance occurred as I was motoring out of Newport, Rhode Island, harbor. When the exhaust water stopped pumping out, I didn't know what was happening. I turned around and anxiously motored to the Newport Yachting Center docks. I asked for a mechanic, but someone on the dock identified the problem for me and volunteered to fix it while I watched as best I could. The second time, I was on my way from Newport to Old Saybrook, Connecticut. Just past Point Judith, the exhaust water dwindled to a trickle, and black smoke started to blow out of the exhaust pipe. The wind was calm; there was a slight swell in the water. I couldn't sail, and now I couldn't motor. I remember thinking, *Judy, you have to do this. There is no one to help you. You can do it. You have to do it.* I went below to the aft cabin, which was over part of the engine and the shaft. This was where I slept on two adjacent, fitted together, comfortable, blue cushions. I turned on the overhead light because it was dark in the bilge. I lifted the in-board cushion and bent it back to pry it against the top of the cabin out of the way. I loosened and removed the wood cover board (about 3 × 3 feet) that was over the engine shaft. I could see the filter close to the engine block. It was round, about three inches in diameter and six inches high. It had a metal cover, which was tightened against two rods by two wing nuts. The filter was inside a circular glass housing. I would have to loosen the wing nuts, remove the cover, and reach inside the filter basket to clean it.

I half-lay down on the outboard cushion and half-kneeled on the cabin sole. From there, I could extend my arms into the bilge. There was nothing to brace them against; I just had to hold them out there. I needed to shut the raw water intake valve, which allowed water from the ocean into the filter. That part was easy; I had done it before—just take hold of the sea cock lever and move it from vertical to horizontal. Now that no water could come into the boat, I located the two wing nuts and tried to unscrew them. They were really tight; I didn't have the strength to turn them. I needed a wrench, so I had to crawl and back out of the aft cabin. I found my orange Tupperware "toolbox," which was stored on the port shelf of the main cabin. I selected a wrench—not a difficult task because I didn't have very many tools. I returned to my uncomfortable position in the aft cabin. I unscrewed the two nuts, removed the cover, and reached into the filter. It was full of seaweed. I managed to pick it all out (I don't remember where I put it.). I replaced the cover and aligned it with the two rods. I knew I had to get the wing nut screws on tight or the filter would leak. I replaced one nut and tightened it with the wrench. I picked up the other one—and dropped it into the bilge. I knew I *had* to find it. With trembling fingers, I searched underneath the filter and found it. Still not too steady, I managed to place it on the rod, screw it shut, and tighten it with the wrench. Then with trepidation, I opened the sea cock and watched the top of the filter. Victory! Nothing leaked! With great relief, I went back to the cockpit and started the engine. Water gushed out of the exhaust pipe. What a beautiful sight! Relieved and more confident, I continued on my way.

We told the others we would be shutting down the engine to clean the filter when we reached open water. We raised the mainsail, not that it would do much good, but it felt better to have it up when we stopped the engine. Jim went below, opened the filter, and cleaned out a paper plate full of tightly wadded sea grass. How easy it was for him to do this. I restarted the engine; all was normal.

We tried to sail our three boats for a brief time, but the breeze never really strengthened. We dodged lobster boats and pot buoys most of the way to the red and white fairway buoy at the entrance to Shediac Harbor. Here, things got a little confused.

Both Tom Isele and Jim looked through their binoculars trying to locate the next buoy. They saw a red buoy and yellow range lights. Tom was trying to line up these range lights, with Jim following. This was leading us away from the GPS waypoint we had plotted to find buoy XN12. We were about halfway to the wrong buoy when we heard a voice on channel 68 VHF radio. It was Bruce from the Pointe-du-Chêne Marina. He said, "I see three sailboats. They must be the ones we're expecting from Connecticut. Two of them are going the wrong way." *Misty*, meanwhile, continued on the course they had plotted from buoy to buoy.

Yankee Lady and *2nd Wind* regrouped. We found the correct buoys and range lights and, at last, motored into the marina basin through a narrow gap between two breakwaters where we met *Misty*. It was late in the season. This was where we were going to haul out the boats for the winter. If we needed any convincing to stop here, the rapid approach of the remnants of Hurricane Floyd convinced us.

With 150 slips, this is the third largest marina in the maritime provinces of Canada. We felt we were back in "boat civilization." Bruce Thomas, the marina manager, was at each dock to take our lines and welcome us. We were surrounded by other sailboats, a few trawlers and a few "go fast" powerboats. Marina activity was much like any other large marina. Boaters worked or relaxed on their boats, some went day sailing or out for a powerboat ride, and others strolled on the dock, stopping to talk to anyone handy, including us. The main building contained the office, showers, and bathrooms, a laundry room, and a welcoming sitting room, which even had a gas fireplace. A broad porch faced the docks. From its rocking chairs, we could see the wide expanse of Shediac Harbor Island and Bay. No wonder Bruce could watch our approach through the buoys and channels.

The time had come to organize clothes, food, and other items to get ready to leave the boat. I took inventory of our food. We were down to two breakfasts, maybe a lunch and supper. Canned food would not survive the winter; I had five cans—two beets, spaghetti sauce, baked beans, and mushroom soup to contribute to the food bank box. By our last day, Jim and I had one bagel and peanut butter to tide us over to the next restaurant.

Tom Isele had arranged for his daughter to drive his white van to Rosie's sister, Frances, who lives in St. John, New Brunswick, an hour and a half away from Shediac. Malcolm and Frances Barry, together with Rosie's brother, Jimmy, and his wife, Betty, drove the van, plus a car to get home with, to Shediac. We enjoyed visiting with them over lunch.

We planned to take minimum luggage for two reasons. One, six people in the van wouldn't allow for too much space. Two, whatever we took out, we would probably have to bring back. Jim and I ended up with the laptop computer, the printer, a canvas bag of books, the *Yankee Lady* blue duffle bag, a box of clothes, and the good binoculars. Barbara and Tom included her pressure cooker and Tom's tools in their quota.

Bruce Thomas made the logistical arrangements for hauling the boats on September 15. There was a public wharf with a boat-launching ramp on the other side of the harbor. We would motor our boats, one by one, to the section of wharf near the launching ramp. Bruce scheduled a crane to take out the masts and a hydraulic boat trailer from Prince Edward Island to haul the boats out of the water. The trailer would drive each boat to Landry's storage yard, about a mile away. The crane arrived on time, and each mast was unstepped and laid on top of each deck. The first one was *2nd Wind*.

The trailer was late, which meant the tide was lower than originally planned. The driver backed the trailer down the ramp. Tom tried to drive *2nd Wind* over the trailer where four carpet-covered pads would meet the bottom of the boat and then be hydraulically raised to lift the boat. But the ramp was not steep enough and the water not deep enough for *2nd Wind's* five-and-half-foot draft. *Misty*, with shallower draft, was unsuccessfully tried next. After a conference, the decision was made to move the boats to Shediac Harbor, one mile away, where the ramp was steeper. By now, it was 5:00 p.m.

The three boats filed out of Pointe-du-Chêne basin and motored over to Shediac Marina. *Misty* was chosen to be first. *2nd Wind* rafted to a floating dock alongside the boat ramp. *Yankee Lady* rafted to *2nd Wind*. *Misty* motored into position over the trailer, and the pads were raised. After much discussion and repositioning of the pads, the boat was lifted clear of the water. Suddenly, *bang*. *Misty* lurched forward and to port. One of the pad supports had broken, dropping the boat down onto the steel hydraulic arm, creating a one square inch gouge in the fiberglass. Ouch, poor *Misty*. Fortunately, this was reparable. In outward appearance, Barbara and Tom were remarkably calm. I think it was different on the inside. After several more tries to balance the boat on the pads, Jim said, "Enough, you won't do this with *Yankee Lady*." Tom Isele and Tom Frasca instantly agreed. Back, we filed to Pointe-du-Chêne marina and our former docks.

Meanwhile, Hurricane Floyd or its descendant was threatening. Arrangements were made for a large crane from Irving Oil Company to lift the boats at the public wharf on September 16, the next day, and place them on trailers. We drove to Landry's yard to identify trailers that might fit our boats.

We woke to drizzle and rain, which continued off and on all day—so much for leaving dry boats over the winter. Everything was a mess. The crane arrived shortly after 1:00 p.m. We waited patiently while a local boat was lifted to its trailer. Landry's crew drove three pickup trucks and the three trailers we had selected over to the wharf. *Yankee Lady*, being the lightest, was lifted first. She did not fit properly on the designated trailer, so the crew put her on the one assigned to *Misty*. By using extra blocks, the trailer was adjusted to fit her. But the trailer was not very strong; it flexed every time *Yankee Lady* moved. *Yankee Lady* went down the road, rocking as if she were at sea, especially when the trailer bounced over the potholes. We couldn't look. *Misty*, two thousand pounds heavier, would probably not have made it.

Next, *2nd Wind* was placed on a trailer made for a C and C 30, practically a perfect fit. Now, there was one more to go. We waited for half an hour, at $125 an hour, for another trailer to arrive. Finally, *Misty* was loaded, and all three boats arrived at the storage yard. The crane arrived and unloaded the boats one at a time. The yard crew ran out of jack stands, which were supposed to have arrived before we got there, another half-hour wait for us and the crane, putting us into overtime. At last, at 5:00 p.m., we were all grounded. Then we winterized the boats and placed small covers over the hatches to protect them until the boats dried sufficiently to be shrink-wrapped. The cost for removal and placing the boats in storage was $241 apiece. There was no charge for the failed attempts with the hydraulic trailer. We then drove to the motel, rested for a few minutes, and went to dinner. Dinner was well prepared and delicious, but I think anything would have tasted good at this point.

The next day, we rose early enough to eat breakfast and leave around 8:00 a.m. Floyd's remnants were due to travel through New Brunswick and Maine. It was rainy and windy but not enough to keep us from driving. We were somewhat of a puzzle to the customs officer at the Maine border. Jim was driving and so spoke for the group. After asking where we lived, the officer asked, "How long have you been in Canada?"

Jim replied, "Three months."

Looking in the van, the officer asked, "Are any of you related to each other?"

Jim said, "No."

I said, "What do you mean? I'm your wife."

Jim said, "Oh, you mean that way. We're three married couples."

The officer walked around to the back of the van and looked at the luggage compartment. No doubt he was wondering how six people could be in Canada for three months and have so little luggage. He returned to Jim and asked what we had done in Canada for three months. Jim said, "We were cruising on three sailboats, which we left in Shediac." The officer asked how we got the van. Tom Isele replied that it was his and that his wife's sister and brother-in-law had brought it over from St. John.

Finally, the officer mumbled, "I'm not going to touch this one," and waved us through. We arrived in Connecticut ten hours later.

Au revoir, *Yankee Lady*, *2nd Wind*, and *Misty*. See you in the spring.

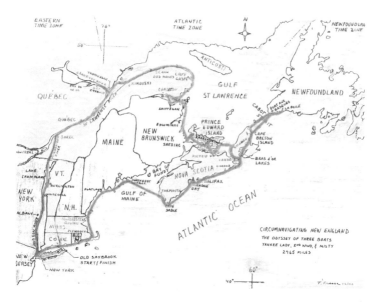

Circumnavigating New England

1950—My first boat, a Penguin sailing dinghy

The crew—l to r: Jim, Judy, Barbara, Tom F., Rosie, Tom I.

Old Saybrook outer lighthouse

Yankee Lady, New York skyline (with World Trade Center in the background)

The little red lighthouse under the George Washington Bridge

Mast down

Canal directions "road sign"

49° 16' 65.9" N   65° 27' 31.4" W. GASPE', QC   8-19-99

Over the top—our highest lattitude Illustration by Barbara Frasca

Yankee Lady in the Saguenay River

The end of a continent, the Gaspé Peninsula

Welcome—Reinhard at L'Anse-á-Brillant

Getting a tow, Mabou, Nova Scotia

St. Peters Lock, entrance to Bras d'Or Lake

A Marble Mountain morning

Yankee Lady at Bras d'Or Lake

2nd Wind in Kelly's Cove, Bras D'Or Lake

Misty at Port aux Basques, Newfoundland

Isle aux Morts, Newfoundland

Rose Blanche lighthouse, Newfoundland

La Poile, Newfoundlancd, an outport

FARTHEST EAST LAT. LONG, TURNAROUND, LA POILE, NEWFOUNDLAND   9-27-2000

N 47°40.7
W 58°58.4

Illustration by Barbara Frasca

MOVING RAFT 2:30 AM INGONISH 8-2-2000

Illustration by Barbara Frasca

Snow crab harvest, Marie Joseph, Nova Scotia

Judy at Taylor Island, Nova Scotia

Lunenburg, Nova Scotia

A Happy Day—Yankee Lady in the background

PART TWO

SECOND YEAR BEGINS: NORTHUMBERLAND STRAIT, PEI, CAPE BRETON, AND BRAS D'OR LAKE

June 16, the day of departure for the second half of our *Yankee Lady* adventure had arrived. We were ready. Jim and I arose at 5:00 a.m. to finish our last minute chores. Tom and Rosie arrived from their house in Old Saybrook about 6:45 a.m. Tom was driving their white Chevy Lumina van. Jim loaded our carefully rationed gear (With six people, there is not room for too much luggage.), and we left at 7:00 a.m. It was to be a long driving day. We drove through Middletown and turned right on the high-speed ramp that connects to I-91 at Rocky Hill, bound for the Frascas' house in Wethersfield. We were pleased to know that Tom Frasca would continue the trip. Traffic was heavy; it was almost rush hour. In a conversational voice, Tom noted that the "check engine" light was on. I didn't think much about it; we've all driven around with that little yellow light on from time to time. Jim and Tom discussed the ins and outs of the use of computers in car engines. Then the van started to slow down. Tom said, "I can't get any power," and kept pressing the accelerator. Oh, no, with Tom's reputation for cranky engines, perhaps he should have paid more attention to the warning light. We were still in the left lane.

From the backseat, I looked over his shoulder at the dashboard and said with some alarm, "The heat indicator is on Hot!"

At that, Tom maneuvered through the busy traffic to the breakdown lane where we stopped. Tom and Jim got out; Tom lifted the hood, and steam poured out. The water pump appeared to be blowing steam, all the water in the radiator was blown away. We weren't going anywhere without a lot of water that we didn't have.

We waited about ten minutes with the hood open, hoping someone would stop. Cars kept whizzing by. Finally, Jim walked ahead a few feet and stuck out his thumb. Within a couple of minutes, someone stopped to pick him up. The driver took him to the Marriott Hotel at the next exit. Jim called AAA and Tom and Barbara.

After another half hour, the tow truck arrived with Jim and the AAA driver; Tom and Barbara arrived in their car. Tom and Rosie transferred to their car; Jim and I crowded into the front seat of the tow truck. The van followed behind the tow truck all the way to Tom and Barbara's house.

Tom and Tom drove to a nearby auto parts store to get a new water pump while Jim took out the old one and refilled the radiator. After the new pump was installed, Tom started the van. Air and water bubbled out of the radiator; water and steam came out the exhaust pipe. Not good. Something was internally wrong. Jim thought it was either a blown head gasket or a cracked block or head. Tom could find no one who could look at the car and analyze the engine immediately. The conclusion? This van was not going anywhere in the near future.

We started thinking about alternatives. Did we know anyone else with a van? Who would drive us? We couldn't think of anyone. Could we rent a van and have Barbara's friend drive it back? She was not available. Could we rent a van and leave it in Moncton, which was a city with an airport twelve miles from Shediac? Barbara called AAA. No vans were available for one-way trips. We sat around, thinking some more. Someone said we looked like we were at a wake. In that case, Jim said, "We should go sit around the Lumina."

Someone suggested we rent two cars and leave them in Moncton. Barbara called AAA again. Yes, that was possible. By now, it was lunchtime. We decided to eat at the Chinese buffet in Wethersfield and think about it. We ate a lot and laughed a lot. Back at the house, Barbara called AAA and reserved the cars to be picked up at Bradley airport. AAA rules required that a member be in each car. Barbara and I were the only AAA members, so we would drive separate cars. Spouses were also allowed to drive as long as there was an AAA member in the car. Tom and Jim came with us to show their licenses to the AAA rental agency and to drive Frasca's car back to Wethersfield. We loaded our luggage into the two cars and left by midafternoon. We arrived in Bangor, Maine, by 10:00 p.m. where we stopped for the night and checked into a Days Inn. Gratefully, we relaxed; it had been a long day.

We left Bangor at 8:30 the next morning. To avoid another day's fees, we needed to turn the cars in at the Moncton airport by three. This put a little speeding pressure on us as we drove over the ninety-mile airline (Route 9) to Calais.

We crossed into Canada at the local Calais bridge, the one just before St. Stephen's. There were no problems although when Barbara, following in the second car, stopped at the custom's window, she said "Ditto."

The custom's lady said, "Wait a minute," and Barbara had to go through the same explanations we did. We stopped at the information building just before the turn off to St. Andrews to pick up a New Brunswick highway map. And then we were off. Because we weren't sure how long the trip would take, Jim, in the lead, drove about eighty miles an hour on the highway. Tom and Barbara followed. Both cars narrowly missed being stopped by a trooper just outside of Moncton. He stopped another car instead.

We arrived in time to drive to Shediac, check into the Four Seas Motel, and unload the cars. When we signed for the cars at Bradley, we had paid for a tank of gas for each car so that we would not have to fill up the tanks at the Moncton end because we figured Canadian gas would be more expensive. Consequently, we wanted to return the cars as empty as possible. It seemed as if Barbara and I drove the cars back to Moncton on fumes. We brought a gas can with us just in case, and we both opened our windows and turned off the air conditioners so as not to use more gas. The little gas pump lights lit up on both our dashboards, and the indicators were on E, but we made it. I think we got our money's worth. We rented a local car for two days, which proved to be invaluable for doing errands.

When we had contacted Jacques Landry previously, he told us there would be a new hydraulic trailer available to launch the boats. When we arrived at the boatyard, Jacques was away teaching a small engine course at a community college. His employees had been instructed to *never* call him at school. They told us he would be back at 4:30 p.m. When Jacques arrived, it seemed everyone wanted to talk to him. Jim waited in line for his turn only to find that Jacques had not talked to the trailer owner yet. I have always said, "There is no such thing as a perfect boatyard" because there always seem to be glitches when it comes to boats, but Jacques's yard was fast moving to the top of my not perfect list. We didn't know when the boats would go in.

The next day, Tom, Tom, and Jim walked to the boatyard to start preparing *Yankee Lady*, *Misty*, and *2nd Wind* for launching. Since Barbara and I were the only ones officially allowed to use the car, we played gofers to get the necessary supplies. Rosie joined us on our trips for groceries, which we loaded into the boats.

By afternoon, we still didn't know when the boats were going in; Jacques was not available. We were getting tired of the motel. We even knew some of the waitresses by name. Finally, Jim obtained the number of the man with the hydraulic trailer and called him. This fancy new trailer had not even been built yet! It was time for us to think of an alternate plan. Jim called Bruce, from Pointe-du-Chêne Marina, who had been our major coordinator last fall when we hauled the boats. It looked like we would need to use the crane and boat trailer method again. It was important for Bruce and Jacques to talk to each other—soon.

Barbara and I made another grocery store and errand run. Somehow, the car turned into the bakery where the delicious bread was made for the motel restaurant. There was a cheesecake on display. Oh well, we bought the whole thing. We put it on ice in the bathroom sink to save for evening. We drove over to the boats and brought back paper plates and silverware from *Misty* and playing cards from *Yankee Lady*.

We had almost memorized the restaurant menu. The vegetables were always the same mixture of broccoli, carrots, cauliflower, and celery. For some reason, Tom Isele seems to get most of the celery. The fish and scallops were delicious, as was the bread. After supper, we moved extra chairs and another table into our room, enjoyed the cheesecake, and played cards.

The next morning, we rushed to complete as many errands as possible before we had to return the car. Bruce arranged for Reggie, a local retired boater, to follow us to the airport and drive us back. Barbara and I checked at the customs office to see if we needed another official piece of paper to finish the cruise. We didn't.

Jacques was still not back during the day. Jim finally talked to him in the late afternoon. Things were still confusing and frustrating.

Another day. Today might be the day for launching. Tom, Barbara, Jim, and I checked out of the motel. The now familiar waitresses and staff wished us a good trip. We carried the remainder of our belongings over to the boats. Tom and Rosie decided to stay another night at the motel. We all continued cleaning and preparing the boats and then walked to the Dairy Queen for lunch. Back at the boats, there was still no crane. We picked out our trailers, and one of the mechanics moved them in front of our boats. We were ready. Where was the crane? By 5:00 p.m., we found out it would not be coming today. Tom, Barbara, Jim, and I settled into our boats for the night. *Yankee Lady* was ready. I plugged in the electricity and made coffee in the electric coffee pot. I warmed some bagels and cooked scrambled eggs for supper. We spent the evening reading and then snuggled into the bunk for a good night's sleep. It started to rain, but that made the bunk seem warmer and drier. It was good to be back.

It was raining when we woke up. I thought that if the crane came while it was raining, it would be a big mess. Oh well, not to worry about that—no crane arrived. First, we heard it would arrive by 9:00 a.m., then noon. We found out that it was still in Moncton working on a big job. We figured that maybe it wouldn't show up today. Then we heard it would be here by 3:30 p.m. It finally arrived at 3:50 p.m., and it had stopped raining. Our energy levels changed from apathetic to lively.

The crane lifted the boats, one at a time, onto their respective trailers. It was a little scary to watch our beloved boats airborne, hanging in a sling, which was attached to a square, which was attached to a cable on the boom of a crane. The two-mile ride to the dock was uneventful. One by one, the crane lifted each boat off its cradle, airborne again and then into the water. First was *2nd Wind*. Tom Isele jumped aboard to check for leaks; Jim was right behind him to help rig the mast. Tom went below and saw a geyser of water shooting up into the bilge. He hollered, "Lift the boat. I've got a hole in it." There's nothing like seeing an unexplained fountain of water inside your boat for causing panic.

Jim looked in and said, "Shut your sea cock." That did it. Tom had forgotten to reconnect a hose. *Misty* was an uneventful second, followed by *Yankee Lady*.

After each boat was in the water, a rope was tied around the mast, and the crane lifted the mast while those below secured the shrouds and stays. Jim was working on the backstay, trying to hurry. *Splash*. There went a U bolt into the water. There is something so final when you watch a metal boat part sink to the bottom. But Jim was creative, born of necessity. He used a piece of string as a temporary replacement.

At last, we were all in the water and tied up to our floating docks. Tom and Rosie had not transferred their clothes from the motel because they had planned to stay another night. They reluctantly left us to our floating homes and went back to the motel.

Our first full day in the water! There was still plenty of work to do including putting on the sails and dodger, checking the engine, cleaning the hull, changing the oil and filter, and more cleaning inside. We were all busy. Tom and Rosie checked out of the motel, walked to the grocery store, and hired a cab to bring them to the marina. Loaded with fresh food, they invited the rest of us to *2nd Wind* for dinner. It was a feast-marinated chicken breasts grilled on the marina's charcoal grill, broccoli, carrots, salad, and rice. There was also fresh bread and more cheesecake from the bakery. I'm sure you have all noticed that we eat well. We continued our card-playing tradition after dinner.

Another busy day with beautiful weather. I took a break and sat for a while in one of the rocking chairs on the broad porch in front of the office building. Looking at the harbor below, I could get an overview of harbor activities while visiting with other porch sitters. On this weekend day, the bay was dotted with sailboats taking advantage of a good breeze and powerboats out for a spin.

The boats were looking a lot more ready, mostly clean, with sails and sail covers on and flags flying. We needed to spend another day on trip planning and navigation.

Today was chart day. We each had forty-three Canadian charts for this part of the trip—twenty-five big picture charts and eighteen harbor charts. Before we left Connecticut, Jim had taken advantage of a large table in our garage to spread out the charts. He had spent hours plotting GPS latitude and longitude points for major buoys along the way. He laid out course lines and headings for potential routes. I then double-checked his figures. It's easy to make mistakes; we always double-checked each other.

The six of us decided to transfer the information from our charts to the charts for the other two boats. This was not an easy task. There were three small tables in the clubhouse that we moved together. This allowed us to spread out the charts sufficiently to work on them although the margins hung over the edges of the tables. Tom Frasca was still working on *Misty*. I read the latitude and longitude numbers and GPS waypoints from our charts; Tom Isele and Barbara had to first locate the latitude and longitude numbers on their charts and then enter the GPS waypoints and course headings. Jim and Rosie kept the charts in numerical order. Before lunch, Tom was taking twice as long as Barbara to record the information because he was writing the GPS waypoints both on the charts and on a separate piece of paper, which he figured would make it easier for him to enter the waypoints onto his GPS. Barbara and I were getting frustrated with the delay. I thought it over during lunch. Since I didn't have to write anything on the charts, I decided I could record the waypoints on the paper. This compromise worked for all of us. However, it still took six long hours for us to transfer the information.

At last, we were ready to start the second half of our voyage around New England. This year, we would cruise through Northumberland Strait to Summerside and Charlottetown on Prince Edward Island and then to Pictou, Nova Scotia. From Pictou, we would go back to the east coast of PEI. Then we planned to cross over to Cape Breton, Nova Scotia, and the Bras d'Or Lake. Heading north, we would cross the Cabot Strait to Newfoundland where we planned to cruise along the south coast although not everyone wanted to do this at first. We would return along the Nova Scotia coast, around Cape Sable to Yarmouth, across the Bay of Fundy to Northeast Harbor, Maine, and then along the New England coast home to Connecticut.

We were about to begin the first leg of this journey, bound for Summerside, Prince Edward Island. We settled our accounts with Bruce and thanked him for all his help, and the ladies gave him hugs. He said he would miss us after all our time spent at the marina. Leaving seemed a little sad knowing that we would not be back. We filed out of the harbor, three sailboats, each flying the Canadian flag and a North Cove Yacht Club burgee from a starboard spreader and each with the American flag waving proudly astern.

It was a calm, sunny day. The water sparkled as we motor-sailed northeast toward Summerside. Jim and I used our autopilot for most of the trip. Barbara and Tom found that *Tilly*, their autopilot, worked reliably for the first time ever (they had taken her to Florida for repairs last fall). I sat below for a while, enjoying the warmth of *Yankee Lady's* cabin, cozy as I watched the sunlight dance off the warm teak cabinets and deep-blue velour cushions. On deck, Jim set up one of our new cockpit cushions, which can be folded at differing angles, from flat to chair. He placed it in front of the mast. It made a perfect perch to get an unobstructed view of the water. We took turns sitting there, watching the ever-changing water as *Yankee Lady* glided along, and listening to the water slide under the hull.

The entrance to the harbor was well buoyed. We called Summerside (Silver Fox) Yacht Club on the radio to request three slips. When we arrived, the dock attendant stood on the dock to guide us. When we registered at the bar in the lounge, someone gave us a tour of this new recreation facility. There is a curling rink, a daytime restaurant, bathroom and showers, and a washing machine and dryer. There is also a comfortable members room (available to yachting guests) full of overstuffed couches and chairs with a view of the marina. The people of Summerside are justifiably proud of this complex.

We woke to a cloudy, off and on foggy day. We didn't care; we weren't going to leave today. We had planned a day of rest and relaxation. I thought I would do the laundry at the marina, sit on the comfortable couch in the laundry room, and type on the computer. All went well as I loaded and started the washing machine. I went back to the boat for the computer and met Rosie who was also heading for the laundry room. I plugged in the computer and typed a paragraph before my wash was finished. I took it out and loaded it in the dryer while Rosie loaded and started the washing machine. The dryer would not accept my quarters. I found someone from the marina who tried the quarters also. No good. After checking with the management, he returned to tell me the dryer was out of order. *Great*, I thought, *now Rosie and I had wet clothes and no dryer.* I could try to dry them on the boat, but there wasn't enough room. Besides, I thought, *I don't even hang clothes out at home. I am strictly a dryer person.* Someone told me there was a Laundromat across the large mall parking lot on the other side of Water Street. That looked like my only choice.

I took the computer back to the boat. Wanting something to do at the Laundromat, I decided to copy the GPS waypoints I had written on a separate piece of paper during our six-hour charting marathon. I put those papers plus extra blank sheets into the outside pocket of my purse. Back at the washing machine, I packed the wet clothes into the laundry bag. Feeling like Santa Claus, I slung the heavy bag over my shoulder and started across the parking lot. Part way across, I stopped at a parked car with two women in it to check on the location of the Laundromat. My ulterior motive was to hope they would offer to drive me there. Yes, they thought the Laundromat was across the street. There was no driving offer. Two-thirds of the way across the lot, I stopped at another car with a couple in it. For sure the Laundromat was across the street; they had been there yesterday. There was no driving offer. Oh well.

I made it across the street. The wind was blowing as I entered the Laundromat. After loading the dryer, I pulled up a chair to the table where you fold the clothes and prepared to start copying. Horrors! I had the blank paper but no GPS waypoints. Those pages must have fallen out of my pocketbook on my way across the street. One minute later, Tom and Rosie appeared, holding some papers. They had found them starting to blow away outside the Laundromat. Saved!

We met in the afternoon to discuss our plans for the next few days. After going to Charlottetown, we would cruise to Pictou, Nova Scotia, on the mainland. From there, we would return to PEI, stopping at Montague upriver from Georgetown, which was on the Northumberland Strait opposite Mabou, Cape Breton. We would then cross the Strait to Mabou. However, we needed to find charts for the Georgetown area.

The commodore from the Summerside Yacht Club stopped by to welcome us. We asked him where to buy charts. He said he didn't think we could find them locally but that Dave, two boats down, might have some. We checked with Dave who said most of his charts were on his computer but that he would look for a paper copy. Meanwhile, Jim and I went out for ice cream. Dave found us at the Cow's Ice Cream store because someone had told him where we were going. I thought to myself, *I love this small town atmosphere. Here we were strangers in town, but people were already keeping track of us.* Dave told us that he had put the chart in our cockpit and we could return it in the morning. I found it and took it to the "office" at the bar in the lounge, another place where local gossip and information were shared. I asked if there was a place to make copies. The bartender said there was a machine at the yacht club, but it was up to the boss. That was easy; the boss was standing right there. I looked at him imploringly and said, "We only need a particular section. Could we get one copy?" I didn't dare ask for three. He took it to his office and came back with a legal-sized copy.

We met for coffee and dessert aboard *Misty* and then adjourned to the comfortable members' sitting room. We reviewed the Charlottetown charts and studied the Georgetown copy.

We had decided on this trip to never pass up a fuel pump as fuel stops may become few and far between. Accordingly, in the morning, we motored to the fuel dock across the channel from our slips before leaving for Charlottetown.

Because of the configuration of *Misty's* keel and rudder, she is difficult to back up. They enlisted us to help. Using fore and aft lines, we walked her back along the dock, about a boat length. Jim took a long bow line to the neighboring slip; Barbara motored forward while Jim pulled the bow toward him. At the last minute, he gave the bow a shove, pushing *Misty* into the small channel. *Misty* had now been backed out and turned to face forward. *2nd Wind* was at the fuel dock. I'm not sure what happened, but by the time *2nd Wind* was out of the way, *Misty* had turned around again and was facing in the opposite direction. That is how she tied up to the fuel dock. We had to help her get turned around again before we left.

We retraced our route to the red and white "safe water" buoy outside the harbor and then turned east toward Charlottetown. The wind was from the west, just enough on our aft quarter to allow us to put out both sails and, at least for a while, to turn off our motors. The mantle of leadership today fell on *Misty*. We had only one good colored chart of each harbor area, so the leader took it. The rest of us had black and white copies, which were not as clear. We all had colored charts of the larger areas.

We passed under the Confederation Bridge, eight miles long and, at the highest point, one hundred eighty feet above the water. It was an impressive sight. The graceful arches and solid piers supporting the two-lane road extended toward distant New Brunswick. This is the only bridge to the island. Before the bridge was completed in 1997, there was only a ferry service to the island. It is also the longest bridge in the world that crosses ice-covered water, not that we wanted to be around for the ice.

Two miles later, we set our GPS for the green buoy at the entrance to Hillsborough Bay outside of Charlottetown. The wind died, and with twenty miles to go, it was time to motor again. We proceeded in lonely splendor, our three boats trudging along, seeing no other boats until we were in the Charlottetown area. The gently sloping shore, green fields, wooded areas, and neat farmhouses attested to the mostly rural nature of Prince Edward Island. Geographically, the island is similar to Cape Cod, low lying and sandy with shallow bays and harbors. The sand, however, is redder than that of the cape because PEI was formed of soft, red sedimentary sandstone. Souvenir shops even sell "dirty" T-shirts dyed with the color from the sand.

We felt we were almost there when we got to the green buoy, but Charlottetown is deep inside the bay. It took another one and one-half hours to get there, which seemed like forever. *Misty* did a skillful job of leading us in, following the buoys and keeping an eye on the range markers.

Before we left Summerside, Tom Isele had called the Charlottetown Yacht Club to inquire about dock space. There were no slips available, but they might have some empty moorings. We tried to call the Yacht Club while underway, with no success. I called the Coast Guard to inquire about anchoring in the harbor and to ask about the Yacht Club's radio. The reply was friendly but governmentally cautious, "There is nothing to prohibit you from anchoring in the harbor, and the holding ground is reported to be good." They also phoned the yacht club for us. Their answer was the same—"Maybe" to moorings and "Yes, we were expecting you." I thanked the Coast Guard for their help, and we continued motoring.

We motored through the narrow passage by Blockhouse Point at the entrance to Charlottetown Harbor, arriving at 6:30 p.m.—a long day. We noticed considerable current here from the Hillsborough River. We finally reached the Yacht Club on the radio. They apologized, but we would have to anchor to the west beyond the yellow fishing boat. *Misty* and *2nd Wind* dropped the mooring floats they had picked up, and we started toward the area. *Yankee Lady* was behind *Misty* when *Misty* suddenly stopped. Aground. What a bummer after leading us in so carefully. Someone from a local boat said the tide was coming in. *Misty* would wait. *Yankee Lady* meanwhile moved on and anchored just past the mooring field. The wind and current were opposite each other, which *Yankee Lady* did not like. Her fin keel was tangled in the anchor line, and she sat sideways to the current. Jim motored the dinghy to the bow and pushed it around one turn, which put the anchor line forward again. Then *2nd Wind* anchored near us and had the same problem. At last, *Misty* appeared and anchored. The tide had risen enough to get her off the mud. Tom and Rosie thought about going ashore to eat but then decided they needed to maintain an anchor guard in this current. The rest of us were too tired to even think about going ashore, and we did not feel secure about leaving our boats either.

Jim and I ate supper in the cockpit and watched the Wednesday evening sailboat race. Bob, from the Bayfield 32 near us, motored over in his dinghy to welcome us to Charlottetown and tell us about various local sights. We spent a pleasant evening watching the harbor traffic and mostly relaxing, watching the drift of the boat as the current changed, and bouncing in a few powerboat waves.

Charlottetown is the economic and political center of the province and one of Canada's oldest cities. It was first surveyed in 1765. Settlement was begun in 1768. Because it is a safe harbor between the York and Hillsborough Rivers, it has provided refuge for ships and boats since the city was founded. The city was named for Queen Charlotte, wife of King George III of England.

In late morning, Jim and I dinghied ashore while Barbara, Rosie, Tom, and Tom took the club launch. Tom Isele spent the better part of the day at Quartermaster Marine getting a plugged macerator line unplugged. Ugh. We walked to the Institute of Culinary Arts for lunch and enjoyed an 8-dollar gourmet affair served cafeteria-style. All the food was cooked by students.

Lunch was delicious. Jim took a picture of the chocolate lighthouse, perched on top of chocolate boulders, just outside the dining room. We spent the afternoon touring the city.

We visited Province House, a national historic site, where the decision was made to unify the western provinces, now Ontario and Quebec, with the Maritime Provinces to form the confederation of Canada. Final confederation was accomplished in 1867 when Queen Victoria gave assent to the British North America Act and issued a royal proclamation, which stated, "We do ordain, declare, and command that on and after the First day of July, One Thousand Eight Hundred and Sixty-seven, the Provinces of Canada, Nova Scotia, and New Brunswick, shall form and be One Dominion, under the name of Canada." July 1 is now celebrated as Dominion or Canada Day.

Due to the construction at the yacht club, the ladder leading to the dinghy float was in use elsewhere. This led to a couple of small adventures. Barbara was going for her usual early morning run. In order to do this, she had to take the dinghy into the under construction yacht club. When she arrived there, she couldn't find a place to dock the dinghy. So she motored around and went to the new floating docks where there were a few boats. She figured there must be a way off at this dock. Wrong. The docks were not attached to the wall, and there was no ladder. However, it was 7:00 a.m., and the workmen had just arrived. Small and slight, Barbara asked a workman for help. He said, "Give me your hands and put out your foot." He grabbed her hands. Her "put out" foot kept her off the wall—up she went. Thus, she arrived. Departing was equally interesting. She startled a tall, blond, crew-cut young workman who was standing on the floating dock when she asked him for help. She put out her hands, but instead of taking her hands as she expected, he grabbed her by the waist and plunked her on the dock. A little ruffled, she said thank you and proceeded to the dinghy trying to look dignified. She thought, *I better not blow this departure.* She wrapped the dinghy painter around one end of the cleat on the dock and held it with her foot while she started the engine (which had no neutral). The painter slipped off the cleat as planned, and she headed out into the harbor, laughing all the way and looking like a pro.

When Jim and I returned from shopping, it was low tide, too far to jump. A club member led us across the docks to the club launch. The driver gave us a very short ride around the corner to *Yankee Lady's* dinghy. Tom and Barbara took the launch back to town later; it was a lot easier. Tom Isele appeared at suppertime. He told us *2nd Wind* had been assigned to a nearby mooring.

During the course of our stay here, the yacht club launch stopped by regularly to see if we needed anything. They were continually apologetic about their lack of dock space and moorings.

Aboard *Yankee Lady*, Jim and I celebrated our fourth anniversary with the others—strawberry shortcake, coffee, and cards. Ever thoughtful Rosie bought us a jam jar with hand-painted lupines on it.

We left Charlottetown the next morning at 8:00. The weather forecast was for light winds and scattered rain showers. Our spirits were high even though it was a cool, gray day. We motored across Northumberland Strait on our way to Pictou, Nova Scotia. After a small shower, we saw fog near the Nova Scotia coast. Jim took the radar out of its "cooler" home, plugged it in, and turned it on. The fog dissipated, but it was good practice to get used to the radar again. It's very likely we will need it when we reach the Atlantic coast. We followed our various GPS waypoints to the head of the harbor at Pictou, motored through the "narrows," and called the Hector Heritage Quay. Yes, they had three slips, at least for one night.

After we settled in, Jim and I guided the others three blocks to the Old Stone Pub, a restaurant we had found while exploring with our camper last fall. It is the former Custom House; the stone walls were about three feet thick. We found a table for six in the small, unoccupied room next to the main dining room. The food was delicious.

We walked through the small town on the way back to the marina. Recently, the waterfront has been restored as the main tourist attraction of the town. Beside the marina, there is a gift shop, an artist's studio, and a carpentry shop. The former train station nearby houses a museum. But the centerpiece of the restoration is probably the replica of the tall ship *Hector*. Pictou became the Birthplace of New Scotland in 1763 when Scottish emigrants arrived aboard the Dutch ship *Hector*. The *Hector* was followed by other ships. Many of the houses in town were built from the stone ballast carried in the holds of these ships.

When you're cruising, the basic things in life take on new importance. This marina had one of the largest shower areas I've ever encountered. There was a sliding door that opened into a spacious room with a large bench. The shower stall was normal size, but this was a "stand you against the wall" water pressure shower. Everything was clean and neat. There was also a working washing machine and dryer where we all did our laundry. Way to go, Pictou!

The next day was Canada Day, July 1, and there were a series of festivities planned. At 10:00 a.m., Jim and I walked a short block to the Hector museum at the old railroad station. A young girl played the bagpipes while a red-coated Royal Canadian Mountie raised the Canadian flag. A soloist sang *O Canada*, the national anthem. Then the Nova Scotian flag was raised, followed by the unveiling of the new Pictou flag. The new flag was designed by a local craftsman and contains the heraldic seal of the municipality. Listening to *O Canada* always reminds me of my Canadian roots through my grandmother who was born in Thorold, Ontario. I have always felt a special affinity for this country.

Most of the events took place near the marina. At 11:30 a.m., there was a Strut Your Mutt contest. The prize for the cutest dog went to a Skipper look-alike puppy, white, bouncy, and fuzzy.

The prize for the dog-owner look-alike contest went to a woman with long auburn hair and her long-eared Doberman. Barbara, a former Doberman owner, gravitated to her while I held the fuzzy puppy.

Lunch was a barbecue at the marina—grilled hot dogs and pieces of cake that had been frosted to resemble the Canadian flag. A small jazz band played to add to the celebration.

During the afternoon, we visited the Hector museum whose exhibits depicted the voyage of those first Scottish settlers.

Some referred to the *Hector* as a miserable wreck. She was already fifty years old when she made this voyage. During bad weather, the passengers were crowded together in the eighty-five-foot-long hold, dark and damp, with little ventilation. The ship was so rotten that passengers in the hold could pick the wood out of her sides with their fingers. They met with a severe storm off the coast of Newfoundland and were driven back so far that it took fourteen days to regain their original position. Food and water became scarce. Disease took its toll, mostly on the children. The pilgrims kept up their spirits as best they could, often by playing the bagpipes.

After twelve weeks, the *Hector* entered the calm waters of the Pictou River. The emigrants lined the sides of the ship, relieved yet anxious to see their new home. It is recorded that the young men arrayed themselves in their kilts. As the *Hector* dropped anchor, the piper blew his pipes, the thrilling sounds startling the echoes among the solitude of the forests.

As we cruise along in our sturdy boats, it is well to remember that the "romance" of the sea can have its darker side. We are grateful for our inboard engines, ready food supplies, and the opportunity to stay in sheltered harbors during stormy weather—hats off to all those pioneers who crossed the ocean on sailing ships.

Eight sailboats arrived from Charlottetown to participate in a race from Pictou to Charlottetown that will take place the next day. The pace of life on the dock picked up. The feeling was definitely one of a holiday. During the fading hours of daylight and well into the evening, there were clusters of people here and there, talking and laughing.

We left promptly at 8:00 a.m. bound for Montague on the eastern side of Prince Edward Island. After motoring out of the harbor, we turned to port and passed rural Pictou Island. We motored across a smooth sea under an almost cloudless sky, feeling at peace with the world. This is one of those instances I wish I could save in a can to be opened during one of life's darker moments.

We passed by Cape Bear, leaving it on our port side, and noted a square lighthouse perched high on the red sandstone cliff. It marks the southeast tip of Prince Edward Island and was the first land station to receive the distress call from the sinking *Titanic*. During World War II, it was useful in spotting German U-boats that neared the coast. But the submarines were hard to track. They disappeared from view when they reached the deep trench that lies between the Magdalen Islands in the Gulf of St. Lawrence and Prince Edward Island. I don't think most people realized how close the Germans were to our shores during this war.

We had not originally planned to go to Montague, which is five miles up the Montague River from Georgetown, but everyone we talked to about Georgetown recommended Montague instead. Tom Isele agreed to lead, so we gave him the one copied chart we had obtained at Summerside. We followed him into the harbor, past Georgetown, and up the Montague River.

The sides of the river were lined with mussel beds, an aquaculture industry of the area. When I first saw them from a distance, the buoys marking the tops of the columns of mussels looked like a flock of birds all sitting in the water and facing the same direction.

We motor-sailed up the curving river, following the marked channel and enjoying the rural scenery. It was almost dead low tide when we arrived at the town, unsettling for us in this unknown territory. Long floating docks lined both sides of the river. There were spaces for boats to tie up on either side of each dock. The marina dock was on the right, and the government dock, crowded with lobster boats, was on the left. *2nd Wind* pulled into the first available space at the marina. The dock boy appeared and directed us to a space further up the harbor. I started to motor *Yankee Lady* forward, but Jim and I were confused about where to go. I shifted into reverse and backed up to *2nd Wind*. After more discussion, the dock boy told us we could motor to the inside of the dock and tie up across from *2nd Wind*. *Misty* was already there. We motored in, still apprehensive about the depth, and docked in front of *Misty*. Then someone said *Misty* would have to move. This was beginning to feel like musical chairs (boats). *Misty* went back to the outside of the dock; the rest of us untied the boats in front of *2nd Wind* and walked them forward on the dock to make a space for *Misty*. We had arrived in Montague.

Montague is the service center of eastern Prince Edward Island. There are banks, grocery stores, a hardware store, gas stations, a museum, gift shops, and restaurants. Still, it is a quiet and peaceful small town.

After seeing all those mussel beds on the way in, Jim figured he could find some to eat. He asked at the marina office. The captain of the tour boat, *Manada*, happened to have some leftover from his last cruise to watch the seals. He was just leaving his office next door. Voila, Jim, Tom, and Tom bought seven pounds. Jim steamed them with onion and garlic powder in our big pot over the propane grill. They were delicious. I became a convert. When we were through with the appetizer, Barbara cooked spaghetti, I heated sauce, and Rosie brought a salad. Those who wanted to added leftover mussels to their spaghetti. Jim will make chowder the next day with the rest.

I found more information on harvesting mussels at the tour boat office. Mussels are grown in two stages. First, seed mussels are collected. Mussels spawn from the middle of June to the middle of July when the water reaches fifty-six degrees. The females release eggs, the males fertilize them, and little mussels happen. The larvae swim freely for two weeks when they become adults and form a hard shell. They become heavier than water and sink. In order to continue to grow, they have to find something to attach to.

The farmer puts out lines of buoys with weighted vertical ropes attached, about nine feet long. When the little mussels come in contact with the ropes, they attach themselves. At first, they are extremely small; they look like little specks of pepper, but they are fully formed adult mussels. They stay on the ropes until October, growing to about three-fourths of an inch. The farmer takes the rope out of the water and strips off the mussels.

At the start of the second stage, the farmer fills up a nine-foot-long netted sock (sort of like giant panty hose) with about 2,500 seed mussels. The socks are tied back on the line below the buoys. The little mussels do not stay inside the sock. Within twenty-four hours, they begin to move out through the mesh and then cling to the outside. They move out with the help of little hairs, which stick out of their shells. They are dependent on passing food provided by the flow of the tide. They stay there for two years until they are ready for harvest. It's a labor intensive, time-consuming process, but Prince Edward Island mussels are famous for their high quality. They are shipped all across North America.

Today was explore Montague day (It's not very big.). There was fuel at the next set of docks, but we were not sure of the water depth. Anyway, it was easier to put all of the jerry cans into *Yankee Lady's* dinghy than it was to untie the boats and redock. Jim dinghied over and filled up the diesel jugs. The large gas storage tank was empty, so Tom I. left his containers at the gas dock while we went for lunch. We gathered together at the Window on the Water restaurant, just above the marina. It was a nice view, and they had good food. We watched the Irving truck drive to the marina to pump gasoline into the storage tank. Well, we thought, some of that is meant for *2nd Wind*. What a service. Jim and I walked across the bridge over the Montague River to check out the hardware store. Among other things, Jim bought an oyster knife, made especially to open oysters. We have heard that the Bras d'Or Lake is full of mussels and oysters.

Jim and I went under the bridge and upriver in the dinghy to see what we could see. As we looked at the narrowing river, its steep banks crowded with dark green firs and lighter green hardwoods, Jim said, "It's a good thing we remembered the camera," which was, in fact, still on *Yankee Lady*. We followed an S curve, motored under an old bridge, and continued another five hundred feet. It was beginning to look shallow; we were at high tide. If the water receded too fast, we could be walking in mud. We stopped for a few minutes to listen to the wind in the trees and the birds singing before motoring out.

The young man in the marina office had loaned us a Cruise Cape Breton book, which contained really helpful information about the Bras d'Or Lake. There was too much in it to digest all at once or even to copy quickly. Remembering the gentleman in Tadoussac who lent us his St. Lawrence cruising guides, I asked today's dock lady if she could find out if the owner would let us borrow the book and return it this winter. He happened to be standing three feet away. It was probably a redundant question because he had obviously heard our conversation, but she asked him anyway, and he said yes. Gratefully, I said, "Thank you."

At the moment, Barbara and Jim are the champion soup makers—Barbara for her lentil, bean, and barley soup and Jim for the mussel chowder he made for supper today. Tom, Barbara, Jim, and I feasted on both soups together with the fresh bread and broccoli contributed by Barbara. Rosie hasn't been converted to liking mussels, so they ate on *2nd Wind* and came over for cookies and cards later.

We woke early to listen to the weather at 7:00 a.m. and then conferred with the others by radio. Our next destination is Mabou on Cape Breton. We have to cross Northumberland Strait—over thirty miles of open water. We agreed that today would not be good. The wind was forecast to be twenty-five knots with fog and a few showers. Cabot Strait, at the tip of Cape Breton, had gale warnings.

Since there were now spaces available, we moved the boats to the upriver end of the marina near the bridge at the head of the harbor to take advantage of closer drinking water and nearby electricity. Each of our boats carried a water hose and an electrical cord.

I don't particularly like hoses. I always seem to have a hard time screwing the hose fitting into the water spigot so it doesn't leak. Somewhere early in my boating career, I had learned that "right is tight and left is loose." This piece of information has been invaluable to me over the years. At least I know which way to turn the hose fittings even if I don't get the threads lined up or I don't get the hose screwed on tight enough.

The long yellow electrical cord is also a challenge. It is about one-half inch in diameter and fifteen feet long. To me, it is heavy, bulky, and difficult to move around. When I try to pick it up from the outside storage compartment, it usually gets stuck on something on the way out. After I plug it into the cockpit fitting (more turning and screwing), I have to lead it behind the wheel, then between two stanchions, and over the side onto the dock, then get off the boat and plug the cord into the electrical outlet. Then I need to make sure it lies flat along the dock or is coiled near the outlet so that no one will trip over it when walking by.

But these luxuries were worth it. Water at the dock makes it easy to fill up *Yankee Lady's* water tank and also to give her a good washing. Electricity is wonderful on a cold night when we could plug in the heater and stay cozy warm. We could also use the electric coffee pot and the toaster. The hot water heater is "ambidextrous"; we could get hot water either when we were plugged into the dock or when the engine was running.

The wind roared, rain poured, lightning struck (not near us), and thunder boomed all night. We were glad to be safely tied to the dock. It was obvious we were not leaving in the morning.

At various times, we engaged in more shopping, more walking, and more grocery store and bakery trips. Jim and Tom F. deleted old and entered new GPS waypoints. Tom I. fixed a leaking window and put a new polypropylene painter on his dinghy. Jim replaced our lower lifeline with polypropylene.

Another day, and the wind was still blowing hard. We'll stay put—more shopping and more eating out. Tom and Rosie suggested that we go to the local community hall to play Bingo in the evening. The six of us walked over, purchased our cards and markers, and found a table in the smoking section. After the first game, we moved to the nonsmoking room. We noticed a lot of serious people playing this game. None of us won anything, and several of us agreed that this was about as much fun as watching the grass grow or watching paint dry. I hadn't played in probably forty years, and I can wait another forty to play again.

At last, there was a weather window to cross the forty miles of Northumberland Strait bound for Mabou Harbor. Several people had cautioned us about the entrance to this harbor. They said that it shoals in, stay to the left, enter at half tide or above, and it's very difficult. As I have mentioned before, we listen to everyone and then draw our own conclusions. Nevertheless, we spent a good bit of time discussing the entrance before we left. We weren't sure if we could get to the entrance at half-tide—low tide was 9:40 p.m. We left at 8:00 a.m. This should get us there no later than 6:00 p.m.

We retraced our watery path out of the river and the harbor. We passed one of the larger Canadian buoys, which had a flat platform attached to it and noticed a seal resting comfortably on this ideal haul out surface. The harbor widened; we passed the red and white "safe water" buoy and were on our way. It was cool and cloudy at the start; we were thankful for the protection of our dodgers. It warmed up a little when the sun came out. The wind had been predicted to come from the southwest, but it was from the east instead. Since we were heading almost east, it was too much in front of us for good sailing. We put our mainsails up to provide some stability and motored. We gained about two-tenths of a knot in speed with our sail power. We tried using our jibs some, but they didn't really hold the wind. The waves varied between one and three feet, not big enough to be uncomfortable. We put on our autopilots and settled in for the day's crossing.

The time passed quite quickly. First, Jim and I took turns taking naps. Next, lunch preparation and eating took an hour. Finally, we just looked around and thought our own thoughts. We checked our progress against our GPS heading to the buoy just off the Mabou Harbor entrance. The distant blue-gray cliffs of Cape Breton gradually became larger; we could see green meadows and white houses. The indentation that was Mabou Harbor became clearer. Then we saw the red entrance buoy ahead; it was almost camouflaged against the red-brown sandy cliff behind it. We arrived at 5:00 p.m., which meant it was half-tide approaching low.

Jim analyzed the chart and the location of the sandbars. *Yankee Lady* was in the lead. Looking through the binoculars as we approached the entrance, we could see a series of small red and green buoys. We could also see waves breaking on nearby shoals to our right. The current was rushing out, moving at about four knots. With full power, we honored the buoys. We really had no problems following the buoys two miles to the head of the harbor. Water depth was not a problem either. Our lowest depth read 6.7 feet; then, it was back up to 7, then 8, and soon we were in 15 feet or better. So much for the "dire warnings" from boaters who have "been there." We found out later that the buoys were put in every spring with adjustments for changing shoals. Why did the so-called experts not even mention the buoy system?

Yankee Lady motored toward the head of the harbor. We stopped and turned around in the narrow channel when the depth dropped from fifteen to seven feet. We were about one-half mile from town. The others were not far behind. On our way in, we had noticed an attractive little cove with a sailboat moored inside. Tom Frasca suggested we try the cove, figuring that if a sailboat was already moored, there should be enough water for us. We agreed. It was so peaceful inside, we decided to raft together. Barbara circled *Misty* around her anchoring spot to determine that there would be enough water all around, no matter which way the boats turned; then she dropped anchor. *Yankee Lady* tied up on one side of her, and *2nd Wind* tied up on the other. Jim used our dinghy to put out a second anchor.

What a beautiful spot. We were surrounded by gently rolling hills and were protected from wind and waves from every direction except southwest. Even if it blew from that direction, the water would not be really rough. The sailboat we had seen from the channel was moored inside the cove's entrance behind a sandy point of land. It floated gracefully in a deep pool of calm water, completely protected from every direction. We noticed a small white overturned dinghy pulled up on the sand above the high watermark.

Part of the sandy point was used as a beach. Three people were swimming. Jim, not to be outdone by the swimmers on the beach, went below, put on his Speedo, and *splash*, he was in the water. He reported that there was warm water at the top three feet—below that was much cooler.

A rural two-lane road crossed a small bridge at the head of the cove. The bridge became a handy spot for some of the local people to view three strange boats anchored in their cove. We could view yellow, white, and purple wild flowers that decorated the banks on either side of the bridge. The surrounding hills were a patchwork of green fields, farmhouses and stands of fir trees.

After supper, we gathered for our now usual dessert and game of cards. Tonight was my turn to be hostess. Rosie brought fresh strawberries while I supplied angel food cake and Cool Whip. When Tom and Rosie walked back across *Misty* to *2nd Wind*, they found a mysterious box of fresh strawberries in their cockpit. Who brought the strawberries? What a welcoming surprise!

The mystery was solved in the morning. A man in the white dinghy rowed out while we were all sitting in our cockpits shortly after breakfast. I called out, "Are you the strawberry man?" He was. His name is Earl Frank, and he owns the moored sailboat. He has a farm and a sawmill up the road a couple of miles. He appeared to be of retirement age, a lean man with a ruddy face, a glint of humor in his eyes, and a smiling mouth. He had dreamed of cruising to far off places, but sadly, he said his wife didn't like to go offshore. He had even sold his cows to get some money ahead and to lessen his land-based responsibilities. He listened a little wistfully to our tales of adventures and offered to drive us to get supplies. We thanked him and said we were all set. We invited him to bring his wife out for a visit. Each boat crew gave him an address card before he rowed ashore.

It was time to visit the town. We dinghied past the sandy point and then turned left heading toward the main road. Jim and I skimmed over the water at the top speed of our 5 hp outboard, quickly covering the mile and one-half to the newly built town dock, which was at the base of the main road bridge. The town was a block up the hill to the left.

While waiting for the others, we noticed that Tom and Barbara, with their 3.5 hp motor, were towing Tom and Rosie. Uh-oh, what happened? When they arrived, Tom I. said his motor wasn't pumping water. Jim took a look. Perhaps the cooling water overflow was plugged. They needed something long and skinny to poke into the rubber tube. Nothing was available until we could look in town.

We walked up the dirt pathway to the main road. We arrived at MacMillan's Store, which was located on the main road near the bridge. A large painting on the side of the building read, Welcome to Mabou. Passing by at walking speed, we probably appreciated the welcome more than someone in a car who might have missed the message if they had blinked while driving by.

It was Rosie who noticed the bakery sign first. Since we knew she was naturally attracted to bakeries, this did not seem unusual. As we followed the smell of baking bread, we saw that it was also a restaurant, which served home-cooked food. Later.

We continued up the slight hill to a one-room local museum. Here we observed pictures, articles and memorabilia from the early days of Mabou as well as documentation of present day activities. As in Pictou, the displays highlighted the traditions and culture of the early Scots settlers. One student had interviewed old timers about the use of the Gaelic language still spoken in many homes. We learned that courses in Gaelic were taught at the high school. These were accepted for credit as a second language, part of the language requirement for graduation. The museum also displayed articles written in Gaelic by a few of the high school students.

We next stopped at the Red Shoe Pub, which had a large collection of many styles of red shoes, including sneakers, in the window. Various kinds of musicians, mostly fiddlers, play here several times a week.

Musical traditions brought over from Scotland by the original settlers have been preserved and enhanced by succeeding generations.

We crossed the street to Cathy's Consignment Shop where I bought a red and white shirt for a dollar. We next stopped at an art gallery/gift shop and chatted with the owner. We told her we were living on boats, and she replied, "Oh you're the three boats in the cove." The little road at the end of "our" cove goes to the point of land at the harbor entrance where the fishing boats are tied up. She lives on that road and had seen us when she crossed the bridge.

We walked a little farther and came to The Mull Restaurant. To the side of this building was Suzanne Craig's gallery where she sold bioprints, pressed images of assorted flowers, reproduced in a special way on her color copy machine. The six of us trooped into her small establishment. We hadn't said more than a few sentences when she said, "You must be the folks on the three boats from Connecticut." How I love small towns! You can't get away with anything. How did she know? She confessed that she was a friend of Earl's and had spoken with him that morning.

At this point, we had reached the end of town. We walked back down the hill, checked out the Red Shoe's menu, and decided to go to the Shining Waters Bakery & Eatery. This was a busy place. Both locals and tourists were eating here. We walked in, put our coats at an empty table, and then stood in line waiting to order. All the bread was homemade as were the chili and the chicken curry soup. Rosie bought an apple pie for later.

On the way back to the dinghies, we stopped at Macmillan's grocery store. It had a little bit of everything, but there were more groceries than anything else. It was one of the focal points of the community. The young lady at the cash register told us people leave things all the time for someone else to pick up. She told us that yesterday when she came to work, there were two cats in cages waiting for the vet to pick them up on his way to his office in Inverness. We needed something skinny for Tom Isele's outboard. Tom and Jim asked her for a paper clip. She didn't have one, but she did have packets of bobby pins for sale. She opened one, took out a couple, and gave them to Tom, saying, "Nobody in Cape Breton will ever miss them" as she handed them over.

Barbara decided to walk back to the cove (about a mile). Tom could pick her up at the little beach on the point. The rest of us walked back to the dinghies. The bobby pin worked, and Tom I.'s outboard was restored. Shortly, we were back at our boats.

By universal consent, I made strawberry jam with Earl's strawberries—one for each of us and one for Earl. We relaxed, read, and puttered until supper on our respective boats. It rained some. We gathered on *2nd Wind* for apple pie, cards, and a discussion of our next port, which we agreed should be Port Hawkesbury past the Canso Locks. We also listened to the marine weather. A front was coming through. Tomorrow didn't look good for leaving.

Morning dawned cloudy and windy. It rained off and on. Tom, Barbara, Tom, and Rosie left during a dry time to walk to the bakery for breakfast and then to go to church. Forty-five minutes after they left, the skies opened up, but they were safe and dry in the bakery. By noon when they returned, the skies had cleared, and the sun was out.

Tom, Rosie, Jim, and I took advantage of our 5 hp outboards to speed two miles to the beach at the harbor entrance. Jim and I detoured to look at a couple of deserted coves, too shallow for *Yankee Lady*. Then we joined Tom and Rosie at the beach.

The beach was made of coarse sand. We walked by the remains of an old wharf and breakwater, victims of the pounding sea. Sand dunes, covered with tufts of grass, framed the back of the beach. Little air holes dotted the waterline, indicating clams hiding below. They were too deep for us to dig up by hand. We knew that because Jim tried. We walked to a small freshwater (Tom tasted it) brook and climbed the dune to see what was on the other side. We saw a pond surrounded by trees near the base of a small hill. There were no houses near it. Across the brook, a small group of people sauntered on the beach, and one person was swimming. Someone was flying a kite. It struck me as a typical summer beach scene. It could have been the subject for one of Barbara's watercolors. Rosie was barefoot, but the rest of us didn't want to take off our shoes to cross the brook, so we turned around and went back to the dinghies. We motored across the entrance channel to the small fishing wharf, where nine boats were tied up. We explored another cove. We looked up and saw an eagle.

Toward evening, we listened to the weather. A gale was forecast for late tomorrow with wind gusts from fifty to sixty-five knots predicted for the Cape Breton highlands twenty miles north of here. I hoped the wind would know the difference between the highlands and where we were. We went to bed in the calm, wondering what tomorrow would bring.

We planned to go to breakfast at the bakery, but first, we listened to the weather again. The gale was still coming. We did not want to be rafted together in high winds, so we decided to split the raft before breakfast (that's asking a lot before coffee). We moved *Yankee Lady* to about fifty feet from the shore, still in twenty feet of water. Each of us put out two anchors.

Tom, Rosie, Jim, and I walked to the bakery (We thought the waves could become wet and messy if we took the dinghies.). It was around 10:00 a.m. By then, we were really hungry—a good thing because the breakfast was really huge.

We walked to Macmillan's store and then to the post office/office supply store. We found we could get copies of our borrowed Cape Breton book for 10 cents a page. We left them for the post office lady to copy. Jim and I walked back to the dinghy; Tom and Rosie did some more shopping and then picked up the copies. Jim and I got back before the rain arrived. It started to rain before Tom and Rosie returned; someone gave them a ride part way.

The gale came; we hardly knew it. We sat snug and secure in this little cove. The boats moved gently back and forth on their anchor lines. There was hardly a ripple in the water. We could see the trees on the hill blowing in the wind. Darkness came. Jim lit a candle and put it under the grate of our alcohol heater. We sat there in the ambience of our cozy fireplace until we went to bed.

We woke at 7:00 a.m. and listened to the weather. We all agreed it sounded okay. By the time we were organized, it was 9:30 a.m. Earl rowed out just before we left to offer to take us to his house for showers and to do laundry. We told him that we were getting ready to leave, thanked him again, and gave him the strawberry jam. We were all reluctant to say good-bye.

We motored through the shallow mouth of the river with no problems. The wind was blustery, and the sky was gray until after we passed Port Hood; then the wind diminished, and the waves flattened. We continued motoring for the rest of the day. When we entered St. George's Bay, just before the Strait of Canso, we said good-bye to Northumberland Strait, our watery home since we passed through Escouminac last year.

The Strait of Canso is a narrow body of water that separates mainland Nova Scotia from Cape Breton. A causeway and a swing bridge were built in the 1950s to allow traffic to drive across the strait. Prior to that, vehicles had to use a ferry. A lock system was also built to allow vessels to pass through the causeway. Boats, including large freighters, are now locked through. We called the lockmaster on the radio to arrange to enter the lock chamber. By now, we felt like pros at locks. This one was easy. When we had risen less than three feet, the lockmaster called the swing bridge that opened for us. We passed through, and now we were on the Atlantic side of our passage.

I called the Strait of Canso Yacht Club two miles away in Port Hawksbury and arranged for three slips at their floating docks. *Yankee Lady* led through the buoys straight into the harbor. We all turned left and docked at three slips next to one another.

Port Hawkesbury has been nicknamed Cape Breton's Front Porch. It is still a large commercial port, second only to Vancouver, British Columbia, in tonnage shipped. We, however, did not encounter large vessel traffic during our transit of the strait.

Our next destination, St. Peters, was at the southern end of Bras d'Or Lake. At 8:00 in the morning, we moved our boats to three finger piers by the fuel pumps—easy in, easy out. Fueling done, we walked to the clubhouse to pay our bills. While we waited for everyone to check out, fog rolled in, accompanied by a rainbow across the harbor. It was scenic, but we wondered if we should leave. We decided to wait an hour to see what would happen. Fortunately, the fog lifted, and we were off.

We quickly passed the industrial area of the strait including a storage terminal where a three-hundred-foot tanker was unloading fuel. We turned left at our first GPS waypoint and entered the Lennox Passage with *Misty* leading.

Lennox Passage twisted through twenty miles of tree-clad shores between Cape Breton and Isle Madame. The ride was a smooth one thanks to Isle Madame, which protected us from the surge of the Atlantic.

Midway through the passage, we arrived at a bascule bridge, which opened on demand. As far as we were concerned, this structure was a bit ornery. When *Misty* called for the opening, the bridge tender said he would open when we arrived at the last green buoy. Fine. We arrived—and waited. The bridge went up about a quarter of the way and hung there. We wondered if it was broken. After a few minutes, it went up a little more and then a little more until finally it was all the way up in the air. We think the bridge tender was waiting to see if we could fit through the partial opening. *With our masts? No way.*

We entered St. Peters Bay, which was open to the Atlantic. It was a calm day; we encountered no rough water. However, a few of the buoys that we actually passed by were not indicated on our charts. This was a bit disconcerting, so Jim and Tom Frasca quickly plotted some GPS waypoints. Then we could accurately check our positions as we traversed the bay.

The St. Peters Lock and Canal system connects the southern portion of Bras d'Or Lake with St. Peters Bay. It is operated and maintained by Parks Canada. When we arrived at the entrance to the lock, *Misty* radioed the lock tender. There was no answer. Another boater heard Barbara on the radio and told her to tie up at the entrance and wait for the green light. We, of course, were listening to the conversation. Once inside the lock, we spoke to a ranger/lock tender who instructed us to wait for the amber light before leaving. I noticed that the land on both sides of the lock was well-kept and neat. A cement walkway ran along the top of the lock walls; green, mowed grass extended about twenty-five feet toward the wooded hillside. I don't remember whether we were lifted up or let down on this lock trip because of the unique nature of this lock. In most locks the high side is always at the same end of the lock, but because of the variation in the timing of the tides between the Atlantic Ocean and the Bras d'Or Lake, the high side could be at either end. It depended on the tide cycle for that day. At any rate, once the 4.5-foot tidal difference was equalized, we locked through. The lock tenders operated both the lock and the swing bridge at the end of the canal. Once we were out of the lock, they drove their vehicle to the end of the canal and opened the bridge. We proceeded through the narrow canal, cut deep into the rock; no houses were visible along the entire half-mile passage, just wooded shores, tree-clad granite hills, and the road to the bridge. We passed through the now open bridge and, with anticipation, entered the Bras d'Or Lake. Another one of our major destinations accomplished! This lake had seemed so far away when, at home in Connecticut, I had read other peoples' stories in cruising magazines. Now we were really here, and I could tell my own story.

We had left the ocean again and entered a lake—a salty one. The Bras d'Or Lake is actually an inland sea extending deep into Cape Breton Island. It is considered to be one of the great cruising grounds of the northeast. An irregular shaped lake, its many indentations and coves provide sheltered anchorages and fog-free cruising. The larger basin is the southern one, which is connected to the northern basin through the narrow Barra Strait. The lake is connected to the Cabot Strait in the north by two natural channels: Great Bras d'Or Channel and Little Bras d'Or Channel— more about these later. Suffice it to say here that Great Bras d'Or Channel was memorable.

The narrow portion of the lake spread before us, sparkling water and forested islands. We turned left and motored a quarter of a mile to the St. Peters/Lions Club. Yes, they had slips for three boats. We glided into the docks and tied up. Actually, we obtained the last three spaces. There was, however, plenty of room to anchor just off the docks. Three boats were anchored, and several more arrived later—most flying the American flag.

We gathered in the marina's large room, which contained two washing machines, two dryers, two long tables, and several chairs. A picture window afforded a view of the harbor. We took turns doing laundry. I asked another cruiser about her favorite places in the lake and wrote down some of them. Some other experienced boaters who have cruised to Newfoundland told us that the best time for crossing the Cabot Strait was between July 15 and August 15. Hopefully, we would find that weather window.

In the morning, there were small craft warnings, but the wind was predicted to diminish later in the day. We planned to sail as far as Marble Mountain, twenty-three miles from St. Peter. We walked the short distance to town in the morning for groceries and other odds and ends. The grocery store clerk practically begged us to accept a ride back to the dock, so we did.

We left the marina after lunch; the wind was still howling. *Misty* and *Yankee Lady* reefed their mainsails; *2nd Wind* motored and then put out their jib. We set out to negotiate the winding, well-buoyed passage into the Great Bras d'Or Lake.

Jim and I circled in *Yankee Lady* while waiting for the others. I guess I wasn't used to sailing; it had been awhile. I accidentally jibed—the sail and the boom flew across the cockpit—*whomp.* The boom was too high to hit anyone's head, but the pulley system of the main sheet hit Jim in the arm. For most of the rest of the day, his arm hurt, and I felt guilty.

It was a typical north wind day. One minute the wind roared, the next minute, nothing. *Yankee Lady* and *Misty* put out their jibs. One minute, the rail was almost in the water, the next, we were upright. Nevertheless, Jim and I turned off the engine (bliss) and were able to sail the passage. Wouldn't you know we met a tug and barge at one of the narrow points. Jim contacted the captain on the radio and arranged to pass port to port. There was no problem.

When we entered the open lake, the wind was blowing a sustained twenty knots with gusts to twenty-five—so much for diminishing winds. The wind was too much on the nose to sail, so we furled the jib, left the reefed mainsail up, and motored. The main gave us a little extra push. We bounced through the short, steep chop until we were about three miles from the entrance to Marble Mountain Cove. We had set a GPS waypoint for the middle of the passage between the two islands that formed the entrance. It led us perfectly between the red and green buoys. We closed in on the shore, making a gradual turn to starboard until we spotted the sandspit that jutted out to form a small cove. There was one other boat at anchor. We nosed past the anchored boat and motored slowly to the limit of the deep water. The anchor dragged the first time we set it. When we pulled it up, it was loaded with grass. However, the water was so clear we could see the bottom. Jim saw a grass-free spot and dropped the anchor again. *Success.* The others rafted up to us. I thought we were three boats in a perfect setting—well maybe a little too much civilization; there were a few houses and a road.

Jim and I beached the dinghy on the sandspit. We were barefoot, and I don't "do" pebbly beaches, so I stayed in the dinghy and followed him along the beach while he looked for oysters and mussels. *No luck.* He got back in the dinghy, and we sped across the water to a small bridge. We saw lots of grass but no shellfish. We motored a short distance, then stopped at a small motor boat to ask the fisherman where to find mussels. He told us it was to the left of the bridge. Back we went. They were there for the picking, both mussels and oysters. Jim was in heaven. He gathered a small bucketful. It was suppertime when we returned.

Jim put one oyster on the grill with the pork chops. He will cook the rest tomorrow. The oyster opened easily, and Jim said it was delicious. I may have to learn to like oysters.

We woke to a beautiful Marble Mountain morning. The trees were mirrored in the still water, crows conversed in the woods, and songbirds chattered. On one side of the cove, a green ridge of trees framed a few summer cottages nestled near the water. A white farmhouse stood at the head of the cove flanked by a green shed with lobster pots stacked next to it. There was an old blue fishing boat tied up to a rundown dock in front of the farmhouse, and a blue skiff was pulled up on shore. Another small boat covered with a blue tarp lay in front of the shed. On the third side of the anchorage, a low wooded peninsula ended at the treeless sandspit. Our raft of three sat gently in eight feet of clear water; we could see our anchor lines snaking across the mostly grassy bottom. The morning rays of the sun warmed us as Jim and I ate breakfast at the table Jim had made for *Yankee Lady's* cockpit. We heard the quiet sounds of activity on the other boats, a muted good morning, and a fly buzzing by. This morning was one of the rewards for putting up with too much wind or not enough wind or bouncing about in large waves. I will always remember the peace of this Marble Mountain morning.

Jim and I went messing about in the dinghy. He found a patch of oyster beds, but they were too deep to reach in and grab. The oysters lay on the bottom mixed in with grass and sand. He said, "My brain is going a mile a minute. I've got to think of a way to get them—maybe a forked stick." We figured other coves would also be loaded, but we never did get any more oysters.

On the way back to the raft, we noticed that the anchor lines were twisted under water. Jim tied the dinghy to a *Yankee Lady* cleat and pulled the boats around in a circle to untangle the lines. How many times in his boating career has he done this? But this time, he could see what he was unraveling. The others ventured forth in their dinghies for various reasons. Everyone picked some oysters. Tom and Rosie toured the harbor. Barbara rowed to a nearby Styrofoam mooring float, tied up to it, and sketched a picture of the white farmhouse scene.

Midmorning, we left for Maskells Harbor in calm winds and calm water. After lunch, I went below to take a nap lulled by the sound of water passing by the hull. I woke to rocking and rolling. Was that a powerboat? No, the wind had freshened. It doesn't take much to stir up the water on this lake. There was a fairly strong current running when we reached the narrow Barra Strait. The current flows through the strait at midflood and at midebb with a speed of up to three knots. We must have arrived during that timeframe because we entered the bridge channel slightly sideways, just like some days at the Connecticut River breakwater. The bridge opened; we passed through. Now, there were no more waves; we were in the lee of the land. With jibs out, we sailed four miles to the entrance to Maskells Harbor.

Maskells Harbor was flanked by steep, wooded hills. A sandbar jutted out from land and extended part way across the opening. Behind it, the anchorage was completely protected. One house and two boathouses were the only evidences of civilization. We anchored separately. The guidebook noted that this was a popular harbor because of its proximity to Baddeck. By nightfall, there were thirteen boats anchored. This didn't thrill us; we were looking for solitude.

Jim and I made oyster/mussel chowder from an old Portuguese recipe. We invited any and all for supper—Tom and Barbara accepted. The chowder was good, but to my way of thinking, the flavor of the oysters did not equal the flavor of mussels or clams. Our Richibucto chowder was the best.

The next morning, we left Maskells Harbor in sunshine and followed the coastline a short distance to Baddeck Harbor, arriving around noon. The harbor lay between two peninsulas and was sheltered behind Kidston Island.

Baddeck has been the headquarters for boating in the Bras d'Or Lake since the early 1800s. Baddeck Marine was next to the large government wharf, which was lined with charter boats, fishing boats, and cruising boats. Tourists and boaters strolled along the wharf to see the boats and to view the harbor.

2nd Wind secured a slip at Baddeck Marine. There was some confusion about slips for *Yankee Lady* and *Misty*. The girl in the office said they were moving boats around to make room for us, "Could we stay on a mooring for a few minutes?" We picked up two moorings between the government wharf and Baddeck Marine. We found out that slips were ninety cents a foot; moorings were $15. Jim and I decided to stay on the mooring. When we dinghied over to the dock, the girl told us we were not on a Baddeck Marine mooring; it belonged to the small boat rental business next door. We dinghied over there and found we could stay on that mooring for $8 per day. Tom and Barbara arrived after finding they were on the wrong mooring also. They decided to stay on the 8-dollar mooring as well. Thus, we bumbled upon a good deal.

The one main street was a block uphill from the waterfront. You could walk the length of it in about fifteen minutes, but there were a variety of shops and restaurants in that short distance.

We talked to a taciturn charter captain on the public dock, a seaman who had sailed around the world in the merchant marine and retired from the Canadian Coast Guard. We asked about crossing the Cabot Strait. He was not forthcoming with information until we told him of our many years experience and our trip around the Gaspé. We immediately won his respect. He said, "You sailed in the Bay of Chaleur? That's a lot more challenging than the strait. If you can sail there, you can sail anywhere. If you watch the weather, you should have no trouble. Don't go in an east wind. The prevailing wind is southwest—it's easier going across, but it could be an upwind beat coming back." We were also meeting more boaters who had been to Newfoundland and heard about their favorite harbors.

We watched the end of a sailboat race from our mooring. The finish line was just off the government dock. The first two boats crossed close hauled, sails trimmed tight, and boats heeled over. The staccato shot from the yacht club's gun signaled the arrival of each boat as it crossed the finish line. The wind in the harbor died before the last three boats could finish. One red boat, sails flopping, took about forty-five minutes to cover the last few yards. They tried tacking; they put the spinnaker up and took it down, and they waited. They all wore blue shirts, the uniform of a maritime academy. At last, the gun signaled their finish. An exuberant cheer arose from the boat. They motored to the government dock, laughing and congratulating each other. A short time later one, then another, and another, crew member jumped fully clothed into the water. When they climbed back to the dock, they noticed that the captain was still dry. *Not for long.* Four of them overcame his resistance, and in he went.

Jim and I ate supper in the cockpit, enjoying the view of the harbor and watching the tour boats leave and return. The calm early evening followed a beautiful sunny day. It's hard to believe messy weather will be arriving tomorrow.

We woke to fog. I called over to the charter schooner captain. "I thought it didn't get foggy in the Bras d'Or Lake."

He replied, "It'll be gone by noon," and it was. We decided to walk to the Alexander Graham Bell Museum after lunch. The sun came out.

First, we stopped at the former stone post office building. It housed a display about the ecology of Bras d'Or Lake. It was formed during the last Ice Age and remains pretty much the same today. As with the Saguenay River, cold water flows in from the ocean underneath the warmer water from the lake, which flows out. Arctic organisms live in some of the deep, cold trenches. Because of the freshwater rivers, which drain the surrounding hills, the lakes are about 10 percent less salty than the ocean. Certain ocean fish, such as cod, have adapted to this change and have become a slightly different species, living only in this environment. A large picture, taken by satellite, gave us an excellent overview of where we are and where we are going.

We walked on to Alexander Graham Bell's house. So often, genius in a person is accompanied by lesser human qualities such as greed and self-centeredness, not so with Alexander Graham Bell. His story is an inspiration to me. He considered himself first as a teacher of the deaf, and he was a successful one. His wife, Mabel, was deaf, a former student. Theirs was a lifetime love story. They died within five months of each other. They had two sons and two daughters; the sons died at birth. He discovered the telephone as a relatively young man and gave Mabel 90 percent of the shares in the company. She managed their finances and their household, freeing him to concentrate on a ceaseless flow of ideas. He maintained an enthusiasm for new ideas throughout his life and could often be found pacing the floor in the middle of the night, thinking of a new concept. He moved his family to Cape Breton because it reminded him of his native hills in Scotland and because he wanted a place to raise his daughters where they had the freedom to wear trousers to play in.

East wind, clouds, rain—another no-go day. We decided to meet in the large room at the yacht club to regroup and review our plans. Jim asked the big question, "Should we go to Newfoundland?" To get there we would need to consider the following:

- Head north about twenty miles to one of two coves to wait for a favorable tide and current to go out the Great Bras d'Or Channel
- Leave the Great Bras d'Or Channel and go to Ingonish, about twenty-five miles
- Leave Ingonish and go to Dingwall, about twenty miles

- Wait in Dingwall for a weather window to cross the seventy miles of the Cabot Strait

Given the weather patterns to date, we didn't know how long we would have to wait.

We had heard conflicting reports from cruisers and locals who have been there. Among them were the following: "There may be or there may not be enough water in the channel to get into Dingwall" or "It's impossible to predict the current at the north end of the Lake," or "Call the Coast Guard, and they will tell you" or "There is a formula you can use" or "Climb the hill from the cove, and look to see which way the current is going" or "Don't call the Coast Guard. They don't know" or "Don't be afraid of it, if you've been through the Bay of Chaleur, you've been through worse than that."

Weather was the biggest problem. To cross the Cabot Strait, we agreed to wait for winds from the south or southwest at no more than ten to twenty knots, with a prediction of diminishing (not increasing) wind.

Time was the next biggest problem. How long should we wait? What are our options? Tom Frasca said that so far we have averaged fifty-seven miles per week. It was generally agreed that with the present weather patterns, we wouldn't be able to get back to Connecticut even if we started now. Tom Isele didn't really want to go to Newfoundland. He perceived it as too remote. The rest of us, with varying degrees of enthusiasm, wanted to go. Jim said, "We've come this far. It would be frustrating not to go."

I said, "I really want to go."

We discussed many options. There were two towns that we knew of on the south coast of Newfoundland that had travel lifts. If we went, we could haul the boats at one of these travel lifts if we ran out of time and good weather. We could go to Dingwall and wait—but for how long? How long was not decided. If we went over and returned, we could haul the boats in Baddeck. But maybe we could get farther down the coast or we could forget Newfoundland for this year, haul in Baddeck, and come back next year. Jim also suggested to *2nd Wind* that maybe they could wait for us in the Bras d'Or Lake and spend the time cruising there, perhaps with some of their family. We didn't want anyone to go where they didn't want to. Tom said he'd think about it.

We walked to *2nd Wind* (at the dock) to call Sydney Coast Guard for advice about the current out of the Great Bras d'Or Channel. The Canadian tide and current book that we had didn't give us this information. The CG officer referred to another current chart from the Canadian government. He gave us times of slack water. He also told us that ebb current flowed into the channel (219 degrees) and flood current flowed out of the channel (40 degrees). Later, we consulted Reeds Almanac, which had information about tide and currents for the entire Atlantic coast. This almanac said the channel floods at 219 degrees and ebbs at 40 degrees; the exact opposite of what the Coast Guard said. Now who do you believe? We were inclined to believe Reeds; it seemed more logical for current to ebb out into the ocean and for flood to enter the lakes, but we will see.

Enough of that for now. We ate supper on our own boats. Tom and Barbara rowed over to *Yankee Lady* for dessert. It was raining, so Tom and Rosie decided to stay at the dock rather than get wet in the dinghy.

The weather was still iffy. The morning was gray, misty, and foggy. Jim and I decided to look for a secluded anchorage in Baddeck Bay, which extended approximately two miles to the northeast and contained a number of anchorages under the rolling hills of Beinn Bhreagh (Beautiful Mountain). But first, we had chores to do. We spent the morning getting fuel and water, doing laundry, going to the grocery store, and talking to Tom and Rosie at the dock. We were pleased to hear that they had decided to go with us to Newfoundland.

The sun came out; it was even hot in town. Jim and I ate lunch at the Chinese/Canadian restaurant, retrieved our laundry from the slow-drying dryer, and dinghied back to *Yankee Lady*. We told the others we would monitor channel 78, dropped the mooring, and motored into Baddeck Bay.

We passed the harbor anchorage, which was a basin inside a long bar, and continued to Herring Cove at the end of the bay. As we turned toward the southwest, the fathometer read 50, 60, 45, etcetera. But I thought, *Sometimes the dots between 5 and 0 (5.0) etcetera don't show up clearly, so I'm not really sure how deep the water is.* We slowed as we approached a small cove, and Jim dropped the anchor. It immediately sank fifty feet. Oops, I guess the readings were right. Jim raised the anchor, and we continued closer to shore where the depth read sixteen feet, and Jim dropped the anchor again.

I stood on the deck, looking around; there was something under the water to the right. We both looked. We had read about Captain Irving Johnson's former ninety-foot schooner, *Yankee*, which had sunk somewhere in this cove in the 1950s (Johnson, by now was sailing his brigantine, *Yankee*, around the world). There was the schooner. The water was still and clear; we could see the skeleton of the entire vessel. We slowly motored over it in the dinghy feeling, for some reason, the need to be as quiet as possible. The main deck and bulwarks were a few feet from the surface. We could have touched them with the bottom of an oar. We passed over a huge manually powered anchor windlass with a metal ladder tied to it. Proceeding around the hull, we observed an open hatch, about four square feet. Fifteen feet after that, we observed another open hatch. Farther aft, we came to a raised companionway, which was where the crew would have entered the living spaces. It was an eerie feeling, something like walking in a cemetery late at night after listening to ghost stories. It was not rational, but it gave us both the shivers. Imagine what it would have been like to find the *Titanic*. This was not a good place to stay; we were too close to the sunken boat, and it was a little too spooky.

We weighed anchor and motored back around the corner to the harbor. We eased our way in past the bar and continued to the next small cove where the water was fifteen feet deep. *Perfect.* Jim dropped the anchor and let out 110 feet of anchor rode. There were two small boats moored in this cove and a couple of empty moorings. No houses were visible on this side although we could see houses and the road on the other side of Baddeck Bay. "Our" bar was covered with low shrubs and wild roses. The land surrounding the cove and the nearby hills were wooded. We were pooped. We sat and then took naps in the cockpit, enjoying our privacy. We ate a light supper outside and went below when the mosquitoes came out. Another sailboat picked up an empty mooring just before dark.

We woke late to fog and mist. We called *Misty* and *2nd Wind.* They asked us to listen to the weather. The prediction for today was for clearing and for southwest winds twenty to twenty-five knots with gusts to thirty-five in the channels of the Bras d'Or Lake, right where we were going. We didn't think they would want to go, but the trip would be downwind, and they were up for it. So were we. First, we toured the harbor in the dinghy, observing lots of forest and a couple of houses at the end.

At 12:30 p.m., we raised the anchor, motored out of Baddeck Bay, and met the others just outside of Baddeck at 1:00 p.m. We could still change our minds, but in effect, we had committed ourselves to the journey to Newfoundland. With partially furled jibs, we motor-sailed toward Otter Island, which was just before the high bridge of the Trans-Canada highway.

There were some heavy-duty gusts but nothing to bother any of us with so little sail up. The channel narrowed as we approached Otter Island; it seemed more like a river. At one point, we passed a light rock cliff with some statues carved into the pillar-like formations. There were houses here and there and a few cleared fields, but mostly, we saw trees. We arrived at Otter Creek at 3:30 p.m. It seemed too soon to stop. We decided to continue to Kelly's Cove, which would be the last anchorage before Great Bras d'Or Channel and the approach to Cabot Strait. The narrowest part of the channel with the most current was just over the hill from Kelly's Cove.

As we passed under the gracefully arched, one hundred plus feet high bridge, we noticed our speed over the ground picking up. The red buoy near the bridge was leaning slightly toward the ocean, and the ripples going by it indicated the current was going out. Jim had figured, incorrectly, that it would be coming in. By some dumb luck, we had the current with us. We arrived at Kelly's Cove an hour later. After all the confusion about how to calculate the direction and timing of the current at Great Bras d'Or Channel, we now knew for a fact that it was ebbing at 4:30 this afternoon because we were in it. After we anchored, we observed several other indicators that the current was ebbing. Jim noticed that our knot meter read about one knot of current—going out. He observed a green lobster boat across the channel heading up current, also indicating the water was flowing out. It was now 5:00 p.m. Therefore, we figured that the current would be going out thirteen hours from now, in the morning. We should be able to leave around 6:00 a.m. According to our calculations, Barbara would not have to climb the hill to take a look.

There was a small L shaped dock at Kelly's Point. After Jim and I anchored, we dinghied over to talk to someone on the dock about staying at the dock instead of anchoring. They said it would be okay to raft to the lobster boat on the inside or to tie up at the end of the dock. We decided to stay anchored as did *2nd Wind*. We were dug in, but *Misty* wasn't. They went to the dock.

The harbor was rural and picturesque with a few small houses, a beach at the end, and hills in the background. *Yankee Lady* and *2nd Wind* did a graceful dance back and forth as the wind, now light, and the current pushed us gently around. Before the sun set over the western hill, its slanting rays shone on the small fishing village across the channel. In our harbor, the dock, fishing boats, sailboats, and nearby trees and hills were also illuminated—peaceful and beautiful.

NEWFOUNDLAND

We woke at 5:00 a.m. to listen to the weather—west winds were predicted to be twenty to twenty-five knots with gusts to thirty knots diminishing to west, ten to fifteen knots. We figured that since the west winds would be blowing from the land, we wouldn't get huge waves. It's a go for the trip to Dingwall. Jim and I ate a hasty breakfast, although it seemed like it took forever for the coffee to perk. We left with the others at 6:00 a.m.

The Great Bras d'Or Channel is one of two channels that open to the Cabot Strait. It is a narrow, quarter-of-a-mile funnel between the ocean and the lake. There are shoals and an eleven-foot bar at the entrance, and the current could exceed six knots. At times, it could be a boiling cauldron of frothy water, sharp, steep waves, and racing current. *Well*, I thought, *this might be the description of the Race on Long Island Sound or Hell Gate at the entrance to the East River near Manhattan. We've been through both, but there, we could depend on the accuracy of the current and tide charts.*

After all the worry, the channel out was simple. We had the current running with us, but that was not due to a lot of pre-planning on our part. I noticed a few eddies and ripples, nothing serious. Watching the water move past the buoys, Jim and I estimated that the current was running at about three knots in the narrowest part of the channel. So far, so good, but we were planning to return through this channel on our way back from Newfoundland. I wondered what it would be like then, but that's another story.

What scenery! The highlands of Cape Breton came into focus to port, and the wide Atlantic appeared to starboard. Shortly, the Bird Islands appeared to starboard. Jim nosed *Yankee Lady* closer, about fifty feet from the island; *2nd Wind* followed us. We were rewarded. There were gulls, cormorants, guillemots, and, best of all, puffins. Jim and I figured they must be tough little birds because they appeared to have the most sheltered spots in the nooks and crannies of the cliffs. We saw four perched on their own little porch (ledge) looking over their world. They were compact little birds with their puffy white breasts, short legs, eyes framed with black feather trim, and orange around their beaks. Some singletons were perched in front of little cave-like holes (a roof over their heads) in the cliff. Some flew by and landed in the water.

Halfway down the second island, underneath the lighthouse, a bald eagle sat on his ledge, white-feathered head majestically looking out upon the ocean. Although we saw no other boats, these islands are a major tourist attraction. There were several tour boat companies that sailed here regularly. But for me, it was a privilege to see these islands from the privacy of my own boat.

We continued along the bold coast of Cape Breton. We tried sailing after we left the islands, but there was not enough wind. I thought it would probably come up later. It did. At 10:30 a.m., the wind arrived and gradually increased. We estimate it increased to twenty or twenty-five knots with thirty-knot gusts. We continued to use the motor for maximum speed. The waves were moderate, rocking us somewhat, but not so that we had to hold on all the time. The wind chill made it cool enough to wear sweatshirts and long pants.

We passed the entrance to Ingonish Harbor. Perhaps we'll stop here on the way back. However, this day we were committed to Dingwall; turning around would have faced us into the wind and waves and would have been very uncomfortable.

We marveled at the wooded slopes, steep cliffs, and tiny settlements nestled at the base of the Cape Breton highlands. After we rounded Cape Egmont, we had five miles to motor through

Aspy Bay to reach the harbor entrance flanked by two sets of breakwaters.

This bay was ringed with mountains. As with the Saguenay River, everything looked tiny set against the grandeur of the hills. It made judging distance difficult. Jim and I searched frequently with the binoculars for the harbor opening. We saw a red tour boat (whale watching) and a fishing boat, which we thought might be close to shore. A little later, we saw a schooner leave the harbor, and then we were able to locate the breakwaters. When we were one-fourth mile from the entrance, we looked back. The tour boat looked tiny; it was much farther offshore than we thought.

As usual, we had received all kinds of advice about entering a strange harbor. As well, the chart noted that the buoys approaching Dingwall were frequently moved because of shifting shoals. We read that no one should go in there without local knowledge. Well, we were committed. We remained in deep water until just before the breakwaters. I was steering as *Yankee Lady* approached them. I noted what looked like dark fingers extending shoreward from each breakwater. I said, "I hope that's not shallow water."

Jim said, "Just stay in the middle." We couldn't even slow down because we needed almost full power to keep steerage into the whistling wind. Eyes glued to the fathometer and the channel, we passed between the breakwaters in nine feet of water. *Phew.* The buoys into the harbor were spaced close together so that we followed them with no problem.

We needed to find either dock space or an anchorage. There was a public dock on the right, but we noted on the chart that the general store was on the left. We decided to continue into the harbor. We approached a fish plant on the left, which had a long face dock. Jim and I pulled close and asked a couple of fishermen where three boats could tie up. They said, "Right here." So we did, followed by *2nd Wind* and *Misty*. Lobster season ended five days ago, and crabbing season wouldn't start until Saturday. This was an open time at the dock; no fishing boats would be docking to load ice or to unload fish. *Wow*, I thought, *timing is everything*. I marveled at the way solutions have been found on this journey. The fishermen were very friendly and interested in our trip. They said that other cruisers had stopped here from time to time and that they even met someone heading for Greenland. I thought, *Newfoundland is far enough for us, but there would always be another destination just over the horizon.* We told them about the conflicting reports we received about entering this harbor. One fisherman said there was six feet at low tide. He told us that in the old days, when the gypsum plant was open, large boats were able to enter. He noted that the harbor was dredged every so often now but probably would not be deep enough for really large boats

We had more than enough room at the dock, about 150 feet. The adjacent building, built on the dock, was one hundred feet long. The inside was clean and almost empty, waiting for the next round of activity. The middle of the building contained an ice room, about forty square feet. We knew that fishing boats needed to take ice to preserve their catches while on the water, but the process of making it was new to us. Above the room, a large machine made shaved ice by the ton (from saltwater). The ice dropped into this storage room. From the storage room, it was piped through the floor into an auger, which pushed it into a blower. Then the ice was blown into a pipe, which delivered it into the boats. When we looked in, the room was partially full, a cool summertime snowscape.

We walked a short distance up the road to the small general store—a combination sandwich/pizza/groceries place. Even though it was only 4:00 p.m., Tom and Barbara and Jim and I bought steamed mussels and pizzas. Tom and Rosie ate ice cream cones, and we all talked about plans for tomorrow. We needed to check the weather again, but it looked positive for leaving. We thought we should leave at 4:00 a.m. to allow twelve to fourteen hours for the trip. We definitely wanted to arrive in Port aux

Basques in the daylight. We conferred once more before going to bed. We were still planning to leave.

At 3:45 in the morning, there was a knock on the hull. It was Barbara whispering that we better listen to the weather again. She went to wake up *2nd Wind*. Things had changed overnight, and the weather was predicted to be unsettled. At 4:15 a.m., Tom, Rosie, Tom, and Barbara stood on the dock next to *Yankee Lady*. I looked out the companionway to talk to them. Jim was still in bed. We all, including reclining Jim, agreed this was a no-go day. It was disappointing because we were all psyched to go, but the last thing we wanted to do was cross seventy miles of open water in iffy weather. We concluded that Dingwall was a beautiful spot, well worth taking a day to enjoy.

Jim and I spent the morning rearranging our clothes, books, canned food, and pots and pans. *Yankee Lady* felt a lot trimmer. The others went for a walk. At noon, Jim and I started to walk up to the lodge to see if we could get lunch. By the time we left the dock, it was 1:30 p.m. This was because there was always somebody to talk to, and we were caught up in exchanging stories. Later, it took Jim twenty minutes to walk twenty-five feet to *Misty* because a man and his seven-year-old son started asking him questions.

We walked up the country road a half mile to the Markland Resort. Wild flowers, including my favorite blue-lavender chicory, decorated both sides of the road.

We found that the lodge did not serve lunch, so we walked back to the boat and made sandwiches. Jim plugged in the power cord so we could have hot water, and I took a delicious shower. We could do this in ports where we could get more water. We also needed ice. The fish plant manager gave us two buckets full of shaved ice, which we poured into the ice chest. That ice was remarkable. It seemed to last forever. I found out later that saltwater ice lasts a lot longer than fresh.

In the evening, the six of us listened to the weather and decided it was a go again. Up again tomorrow at 3:45 a.m.

Actually, we got up again at 4:00 a.m. (but what difference does fifteen minutes make at that hour?). Barbara, the early morning person, listened to the weather at 3:30 a.m. and found the report to be confusing. The two-day synopsis mentioned winds of twenty plus knots for the Cabot Strait, but the specific forecast for today called for light winds. We decided to radio Sydney Coast Guard for clarification. An officer told us that the twenty plus knots winds were predicted for the next day. We're leaving.

We left the dock at 4:30 a.m. and at 5:30 a.m. and at 6:30 a.m. The first time, as soon as we were a few feet from the dock, Tom Frasca noticed that *Misty* wasn't pumping water. He went back to the dock while we circled. Then I dropped Jim at the dock and continued circling. Tom, with a little bit of help from Jim, checked the water pump impeller. It was fine. They packed it with Bag Balm, which helped to prime it. Off again. This time, we made it through the breakwaters and into Aspy Bay. It was not good; there was still not enough water pumping out of *Misty's* exhaust. *Misty* and *2nd Wind* went back to the dock. Jim and I thought that was the end of this try to cross the Cabot Strait. We decided to put up the mainsail in the light wind and drift around in the bay for a while. Maybe we would see a whale. Then, at 6:30 a.m., we heard *Misty* call us on the radio. "We think we've found the problem, and we're ready to go again. Should we go?" Yes, we all agreed. It was time to get excited again.

For the first time ever, we filed a float plan with the Coast Guard. They asked us to describe our boats, how many persons aboard, what type of safety equipment, and what was the estimated time of arrival. We estimated it would take us twelve hours to cross. They emphasized that we must close the float plan with Port aux Basques Coast Guard when we arrived in Newfoundland. Otherwise, after a two-hour grace period, they would begin searching.

It was a beautiful day. The soft morning light made the mountains look like green velvet. The seas were calm with gentle Atlantic Ocean swells, not uncomfortable. St. Paul Island appeared bluish, twenty miles away. Newfoundland was out of sight, sixty-seven miles away.

The sun gradually warmed us. As the day progressed, Jim's three layers of clothing became two layers, then one layer, then less than one layer. Within a few miles of land, one layer went back on. Around the bend into the harbor and wind, another layer went on. When we stood on the dock talking to local residents and other cruisers, the third layer was on.

Several times, we saw schools of porpoises around our boats, a nautical reminder that we were not alone. St. Paul Island became more distinct as the Cape Breton Highlands receded to a blue line on the horizon. We passed St. Paul, leaving it four miles to port. We saw a little fog in the distance; Jim got out the radar just in case. We were actually never quite out of sight of land, at least when looking through the binoculars. About halfway across, I looked through them and saw a thin blue line on the horizon—Newfoundland. As we progressed, we watched the outline become more distinct; hills and cliffs appeared and then the cluster of buildings that was Port aux Basques.

I decided to cook beef stew while en route so we would have something warm to eat when we arrived. Over the radio, I invited the others to a potluck supper aboard *Yankee Lady*. I started simmering the meat when the GPS said we were two hours (about twelve miles) away from the entrance buoy. I put the potatoes and onions in when we were six miles from the buoy. The carrots went in two miles from the buoy. Just before docking, I turned the stove off.

Port aux Basques is the ferry terminal for ferries from Sydney, Nova Scotia. Since the entrance channel was not that wide, the chart and the guidebook indicated we should call Port aux Basques traffic control on channel 14 when we were two miles out. We did and were informed there was no big traffic at this time. The ferries were still on the Sydney side. We entered the harbor, a straightforward approach. The guidebook noted that there were floating docks, as well as three large public wharves. It cautioned against using the north-facing floating dock because there was a large rock in the way. However, the directions weren't really clear to us. Jim and I approached one of the wharves and asked two men standing there about the floating docks. Again, we heard, "There's plenty of water over there." We decided to try. A boy ran over to guide us in. Close to the head of the dock, he pointed and said, "There's a rock right there. Go around it by that wharf and then you can pull in." Jim was on the bow; I inched in. I called out, "The fathometer says 4.2." *Crunch.* We can verify that there is a rock there. We backed out and went to one of the public wharves. Using our St. Lawrence River experience, we pulled up to a ladder and tied up. The others followed us in. Jim called Port aux Basques Coast Guard and closed our float plan. I climbed the ladder and stepped onto Newfoundland.

It seemed like our arrival was big news, almost as big as the ferry arrival. Small groups of people sauntered by and left to be replaced by others. Many questioned us about where we were from, where we came from today, etcetera. One grandmother said, "I saw you from my window coming across Cabot Strait. It looked very pretty to see three boats with their sails up." She came to see us with her ten-year-old granddaughter. The granddaughter was curious about the boat, so we invited her aboard although I felt a little hesitation about having a child climb down the ladder to the boat. But as she descended, she said, "I'm good at ladders." And she was.

Jim invited a little boy to see the boat, but he politely said, "New, thank you." We were finding that there was a definite Newfoundland dialect.

The potluck supper hit the spot for all of us. Rosie brought salad and cookies, and Barbara brought steamed cabbage.

Everything fit in nicely with the beef stew. After the long day, we enjoyed the warm meal in *Yankee Lady's* cozy cabin.

The ferries arrived after supper while we stood on the dock. The ferry terminal complex was across the harbor from us. Whenever a ferry landed, we could hear announcements over the loudspeaker at the terminal—"Attention please," …. I thought this was probably an indication of the importance of the ferry operation to this town.

Seeing the size of the first one, we understood why this port needed traffic control; we would not want to have been in the same channel with one of them. As we were talking to some other cruisers from Maine, the second ferry, a fast catamaran, arrived. Jim looked over at *Yankee Lady*. She was rocking badly at the dock from the wake of the ferry. He feared for the radar that he had mounted on a two-inch aluminum pipe (designed by him) on the starboard side of the boat, the side we were tied up to. It could be damaged if it hit the dock on a rolling swing. It was dark and damp out. We were tired, but we climbed down the ladder, turned on the engine, untied all the lines, and moved to the other side of the dock where we could tie up on the port side. We slept well.

The wharves were in good condition, and the town had added electric hook ups if you could get the right adapter from the harbor manager. This was Sunday. We were told he was away fixing up his cabin to get ready for moose hunting, which would begin next month. Nobody else, that we could find, had the key to the office, so we couldn't plug in. This didn't really matter; we were all self-sufficient. The Harbor Authority building containing bathrooms and laundry facilities was also locked. But Jim, never one to take the first no for an answer, walked across the street to try the door. He found that by putting a little pressure on the handle, the door opened. Thus, those of us who wanted to could take showers and do laundry.

Port aux Basques, with a population of six thousand, retains its image as a historic fishing community. It is one of the oldest fishing settlements in Newfoundland partly because it is a deep and ice-free port. It was named by Basques fishermen in the1500s.The first ferry crossing between Port aux Basques and North Sydney, Nova Scotia, took place in the 1890s. The town is still the gateway for the majority of people, goods, and services entering Newfoundland.

Situated on two peninsulas, which form the harbor, it seemed to me that this is a town that faces the sea with fortitude. Most of the buildings are old and weather-beaten; strong storm windows provide protection from the harsh weather. The houses are clustered together in a ramshackle sort of way as if to take comfort in neighborliness. Turquoise is a popular color, which offered a bright contrast and cheery note to the otherwise gray and white buildings. The hills and plateaus behind the town were barren. No trees of any consequence could grow because of the constant wind. Here, perhaps more than some other places, weather could define one's mood.

Newfoundland had been explored and settled by Europeans for centuries; the remains of a Viking settlement have been discovered at L'Anse aux Meadows at the northern tip of the island. Before 1497 when John Cabot landed there, the waters off Newfoundland were known and frequented by fishermen from Portugal, Spain, and France. The English established a settlement in St. John's Harbor by 1583. Most of these settlers and fishermen were from the English West Country. Irish immigrants formed a second major population group, particularly in the later 1700s and early 1800s. The language and dialects heard today reflect the influence of both these groups.

Fishing has formed the culture of the people and has been a major industry in Newfoundland for five hundred years. For most of these years, fishermen used long lines, with hooks spaced intermittently along the lines. They would row out from the mother ship in dories and row back when their dories were full. But the introduction of huge draggers and factory ships, mostly from foreign countries, has intruded on this way of life. These ships anchor offshore, catch and process huge amounts of fish, and deliver the processed fish to Canada and to other countries. Local people are harmed because there has been a drastic decline in cod, so much so that the ground fish population cannot sustain itself. In 1994, the Canadian government forbade fishing for cod anywhere in Newfoundland, but the factory boats stayed far enough offshore to avoid this restriction. Now, I understand, the government has allowed Newfoundlanders to fish periodically throughout the year, two weeks at a time. Unfortunately, the majority of the population is unemployed.

I have read conflicting reports about the size of Newfoundland. It is either the tenth or the seventeenth largest island in the world. Anyway, it is rather large—we would have to travel approximately 3,200 miles to cruise around it. This was slightly more than the distance of our entire journey. It would take us two more summers to circumnavigate Newfoundland—more time than we could spend.

Cape Spear, east of St. John's, is the eastern most point of land in North America. Since they are so far east, Newfoundlanders have created their own time zone—one-half hour ahead of Atlantic time. We found this a little hard to get used to. It's hard enough to remember the one hour difference between Eastern and Atlantic time. If it's 4:00 p.m. in Connecticut, it's 5:00 p.m. in Nova Scotia, but in Newfoundland, it would be 5:30 p.m.

The south coast of Newfoundland, where we plan to cruise, has steep cliffs with fjord—like arms cutting through the cliffs and extending inland for many miles into the tundra-covered wilderness. We read about streams cascading into the sea where you could take a shower, an intriguing thought should it ever warm up. A large portion of this coast is still connected to civilization by ferry/mail boat; there are no roads. This is what we came to see.

Jim and I went out to breakfast at the one restaurant in town, halfway to the ferry terminal. We sat at a table between two tables of local men, so we joined their conversations.

Wherever we go, we find common threads of life to talk about with the people we meet. This morning, we all talked about the ups and downs of human nature, especially in a marriage. One man said his wife wanted everything done just so in the kitchen. The only thing he was allowed to do was barbecue. So he didn't have to do dishes, and he stayed out of the kitchen. He wasn't unhappy about that. Jim and I talked about early marriage challenges and how we had adjusted as co-captains (the one behind the wheel is the captain). When they left, another couple sat at the table. The man grew up in East Providence, Rhode Island, not too far from where Jim grew up. He was a commercial fisherman who fished out of Point Judith, Rhode Island. He has fished as far south as North Carolina in his seventy-six-foot boat. We talked almost nonstop with them for the next hour. I think we were in the restaurant for over two hours.

Then we met the others when they came back from church and joined them for lunch at the restaurant. Even though it was crowded, the waitress was cheerful. She greeted us with a friendly, "What can I get for you m'love?" Sometimes, we found it hard to understand the Newfoundland dialect. I have particularly noticed that many people add an *H* before words that begin with a vowel, *hother* for *other* or omit the *H* where it was usually pronounced, *ouse* for *house*. They also used different personal pronouns after verbs, "Never mind they" instead of "Never mind them." We frequently asked people to talk slower so we could understand them better.

After lunch, we stopped at a couple of stores and then visited the local museum. Most of the stores were closed on Sunday. The streets were very quiet, only a few cars and a few pedestrians. The museum has an original astrolabe, dated 1628, found by a diver off the town of Isle aux Morts—one of four left in the world; it was of Portuguese origin. The astrolabe was a forerunner of the sextant. With it, sailors could determine longitude, but not latitude. It was better than any other instrument of the time, but ships would frequently be as much as four hundred miles off course.

Jim and I returned to *Yankee Lady* after stopping at a Newfoundland crafts shop and buying an ice cream cone at the convenience store. It started to rain. We lit the alcohol heater and stayed aboard for the rest of the night.

In the morning, we started looking more seriously at our Newfoundland charts and the cruising guide. While we were not in uncharted country, we were in an area where there were fewer detailed charts. The cruising guide was not complete either. One of our charts was reproduced from a British Admiralty chart, last surveyed in 1890. Its ancestry goes back to original surveys by Captain Cook in the 1700s. The first Canadian edition was issued in 1955, reprinted in 1980. There were no latitude or longitude references on the perimeters of the chart, so it would be impossible to plot a GPS course or to know where we were except by reference to landmarks and use of the compass. There was, however, a scale of latitude and longitude, so we could figure the distance of a nautical mile. Coordinates were also given for the Rose Blanche lighthouse at the very bottom corner of the chart. Jim studied our other charts of the larger area of the coast. He was able to transpose one latitude line and one longitude line onto the admiralty chart. Then he could use the mileage scale to find other positions. I was impressed again with his creative problem-solving ability.

The other charts also cautioned that mathematical adjustments would need to be made to make them more accurate. Our calculations, and therefore our GPS entries, could be off by as much as three tenths of a mile.

We spent the rest of the morning grocery shopping, getting fuel, and getting somewhat organized. Jim and Tom Frasca spent time looking at the charts; Tom had plotted the GPS waypoints for the next segment of the trip, and Jim copied them. Right after lunch, we decided to leave for Isle aux Morts ten miles down the coast. We did not have time to double-check the waypoints, and I did not have time to look at the chart.

Just after Jim untied *Yankee Lady's* lines and I had called traffic control to get permission to depart, the fog started to roll in. Tom Frasca pointed it out and asked if we should stay. We were attached to the dock by one line, ready to let it go. Jim said, "We're going." We had one hour before the high-speed ferry arrived. While it was a short distance out of the harbor, we didn't want to linger.

We started out. I called traffic control to say we were leaving. The fog became thicker, and the waves increased. We held a radio conference. Tom Isele asked, "How are we going to get down the coast of Nova Scotia to go home if we're afraid of going in the fog?" He and Rosie voted to go. Jim voted to go. Tom and Barbara didn't want to go. I didn't feel ready. I had not had a chance to look at the chart or plot a course. I didn't know what buoys to look for. We were bouncing in the waves and *Yankee Lady* did not have the GPS waypoints entered or the radar set up. We also had our dock lines all over the place. I voted to go back. That made it three to three. We turned around; I called traffic control. Then Tom Frasca, with a deciding vote, changed his mind. We turned around again. I called traffic control again, which was embarrassing. The operator was very polite, but I wonder what she was thinking.

We headed out as the fog thickened. *2nd Wind* was in front, *Misty* was next, and *Yankee Lady* was last. We pretty much stayed in single file, keeping within sight of each other. There were three-foot swells, so we rolled a lot, but Jim managed to get the lines put away while I steered. By the time we got to the first way point, QW1, we had our GPS in order, the radar on, and the lines put away and had notified traffic control that we were clear of the control area. Tom Isele did an excellent job of leading us to Western Passage. Once we were in this passage, with land on both sides, the fog lifted. First, we saw the dark shape, almost a shadow of land, with a white line of waves hitting the shore. The radar said land was a mile away. As we motored closer to land, a few gray wisps lingered, and then there was bright sunlight, a rocky shore and green tundra.

We continued through a now not scary narrow passage (we could see) toward Isle aux Morts. Just past Fox Goose Island, a tiny passage appeared on our starboard side. It led to a small, almost landlocked cove called Squid Hole. It would have been a great, unspoiled, protected anchorage. *Another time.* We wanted to see Isle aux Morts and check out the travel lift reported to be there.

We continued straight to a public dock, with railings painted yellow, and nosed around to the inside. There was a large fishing trawler tied up, and there was not really room for the three of us. *Misty* called to remind us that the chart showed another public dock on the other side of this small peninsula. They led the way. The entrance was narrow; there were islands scattered about on the starboard side. A small, red nun buoy marked the entrance on this side. These islands afforded the harbor protection from winds off the ocean. On the port side, rocks were visible between the green buoy and shore. Rocks also lurked at the head of the harbor, just past the wharf. *Misty* went in, followed by *2nd Wind*. We waited for them to tie up before motoring in also. I was really glad that *Yankee Lady* had such a short turning radius. It didn't look like a lot of room between the dock and the other patch of rocks. We had all arrived safely. It was a hectic departure, but all's well that ends well.

This is another picturesque spot. Fishing dories and old fishing shacks line the shore. Houses cover the hill that the town is built on. Again, turquoise houses added bright color to the scene. And again, we were a major attraction. People walked or drove over to stroll on the dock and look at us. We talked to lots of them; almost all of them said they wouldn't live anywhere else. This, even though the fish plant has closed and there is no other industry here. *Yankee Lady* and *2nd Wind* invited some of the children aboard. One little boy asked if we were part of the tall ships. They were visiting Halifax and had been in the news.

Another lady asked us if we knew what bakeapples were. She and her family had been out on one of the islands looking for them; they were just now turning ripe. She showed me one that wasn't quite ripe; it looked like a yellow raspberry. When they are ripe, they taste something like apples. The low plant grows mostly in bogs or other marshy areas and grows abundantly in Newfoundland. I thought, *It's too bad they weren't ripe yet. I would have tried to make jam.* In my book, anything that resembles a raspberry has got to be good.

Jim and I walked around the town, as did the others. We stopped at the grocery store, which also sells outboard motors. The view from the top of the small hill was spectacular. We could see the Western Passage we had come through as well as clumps of islands and rocks scattered throughout the harbor. We looked down into a dried out cove and saw four large wooden fishing boats, high and dry. Their paint was chipped and fading, and they were starting to rot away—another sad reminder of the state of the fishing industry here.

Jim walked to the marine service center to inquire about the travel lift. There are two of them; one was able to lift one hundred tons. The fee was $85 (American) out and $85 in, $2 a day for storage. Given prices in Connecticut, I thought that was quite a bargain, except, of course, that we were really far away from home.

Community spirit was high in this small town. Several people told us they were getting ready for Come Home week and for a Christmas in July celebration. Come Home week is a tradition in many of these small communities. Friends and family who grew up in town and had left the island return for a giant homecoming, more than doubling the regular population of nine hundred. Many houses appeared freshly painted and were neat and clean. The three picnic tables at the waterfront park were so newly painted bright red that the paint cans were still there. Strings of small multicolored triangular flags were strung across streets, and many houses had Christmas lights strung outside.

We continued to find Canadian hospitality exceptional. Perhaps the Newfoundlanders raised it to new heights. We were invited to stay for the homecoming celebration, but we didn't have time. Another cruising couple had told us they were invited to a wedding held at an outport to the east. They went, together with the whole town.

Isle aux Morts (Island of the Dead) was so named because of the many shipwrecks off its rocky coast. We plan on avoiding these rocks. In the early 1800s, George Harvey, his daughter, Ann, and their Newfoundland dog, Hairy Man, twice saved shipwrecked sailors. In one instance, Harvey rowed his small punt, with Ann and Hairy Man, over a mile to the wrecked boat. He could not get close enough without going on the rocks himself. The story goes that he told Hairy Man to swim over. Newfoundland dogs have oil in their coats to protect them from cold and large, webbed feet for swimming. The dog brought back a rope in his mouth. The rope was used to set up a breeches buoy to get the victims to shore, and all were saved. The two Toms, Rosie, and Barbara walked part of the Harvey trail, which memorializes this event.

The sign at the waterfront park indicated that the astrolabe we saw at the museum in Port aux Basques was found near here. The ship it was on was wrecked a little over a mile offshore. That's not very far away. We could pass right by it and not know the ship was there. Minus the houses, we were looking at the same coastline the sixteenth century English, Portuguese, and Basques sailors saw.

After a supper of grilled fresh salmon bought in Port aux Basques, we met on *Misty* for strawberries and cookies and to discuss our next few ports. We picked out four or five we would like to see before heading back to Nova Scotia. We were limited to about two weeks. I wished we could stay the whole summer.

Our next destination would be Little Garia Bay, twenty-five miles from Isle aux Morts. Jim spent two hours trying to figure out adaptations for our GPS headings, given the errors on the charts. I tried to double-check everything. We were both getting headaches from all this mental effort. When we finished, we took the charts over to *Misty* and went over everything with Tom and Tom.

A little fog threatened way offshore, but there was none near us. We left around 10:30 a.m. and followed the buoys out of the Eastern Passage. We probably looked at the rocks where the shipwrecks were. Our GPS heading to the first red and white buoy was off by about a half mile, so we thought it looked like we were no further ahead than before all our calculations.

We continued eastward along the coast to Rose Blanche, noting the reconstructed lighthouse. It was difficult to see because the native granite stonework blended in with the rocky cliff. It was no longer active; the beacon had been replaced by a smaller mechanical structure and light on the next point. Using our revised figures, we were again at least half a mile off the next red and white buoy. We decided to use the figures obtained from the chart, rather than trying to make corrections.

We rounded the next peninsula and motored into Little Garia Bay. We saw one other boat ahead of our little group. We kept Pigeon Island to port and crossed the relatively deep west side of the entrance bar into the inner harbor. There was a small red cabin to the right and two other cabins at the head of the harbor on the left. A large waterfall flowed into the bay at the head of the harbor on the right. Jim and I circled and tried to anchor in two different places before the anchor finally held on the third try near *Misty* and *2nd Wind*. *Tarka*, a boat from Maine, was anchored nearby also. We had met the couple who sail it at the wharf in Port aux Basques.

We were surrounded by hills covered mostly with small bushes and moss. A few stands of fir trees grew in sheltered spots out of the wind. Jim and I took the dinghy and tried to find the path that led to the top of the hill by the waterfall. Nothing seemed to open up. We dinghied around the head of the harbor, thinking there might be another outlet to the waterfall.

A couple from one of the cabins waved at us, and we motored over to talk to them. They told us that the path was by the white spot (a bleached out tree trunk) to the right of the waterfall. The couple, Cecil and Dorothy Parsons, were from Rose Blanche, which we had passed, seven miles ago. He was a fisherman; she was his crew. During the fishing season, they fished on a large ocean-going trawler. Here, they come and go in a twenty-foot, extremely rugged, sea-going open boat, powered by two huge outboard motors. There are no roads; the only way to get here is by boat. They lease the land their cabin is on for $5 a year from the provincial government. His brother owns the camp next to him, and his son owns the red one across the harbor. Cecil told us that his brother's cabin is for sale for $15,000. We knew it wasn't practical, but we daydreamed for a few minutes about what it would be like to own it. They used the cabins summer and winter for hunting and relaxing. Caribou and moose roam the hills. The tundra vegetation is perfect for these animals, and there is plenty of water in the freshwater lakes high in the hills. We thanked them for the directions.

We saw Cecil and Dorothy leave before we found the path to climb the mountain. I had a moment's hesitation before we started because coming down is harder on my knees than climbing up. But then, Jim found a natural walking stick, which I adapted. We climbed almost to the top ridge. The first part was narrow and steep, damp and slippery in spots. We saw fresh caribou tracks in the mud but no animals. We scraped through bushes, slid a little, and balanced ourselves by holding onto some small, beautiful, sweet-smelling balsam trees. The mountain leveled off a bit as we entered meadows of spongy moss, blueberry bushes, and wild flowers. We were rewarded with a spectacular view. Looking toward the harbor, our sailboats looked like toys. Gently rolling hills, covered with tundra-like vegetation, extended inland as far as we could see. Slightly below us to the right were three lakes, one flowing into the other. The lowest one flowed into the waterfall. There was a small, naturally dammed area that formed a large pool, probably suitable for swimming. The noises we heard were not man-made. There were bugs buzzing around, but they didn't seem to bother us. Jim heard an owl. It was primitive and beautiful.

It was getting late, about 6:00 p.m. Regretfully, we started climbing down. The walking stick was wonderful. I placed it in front of me and leaned on it with each downward step. I arrived at the bottom totally together.

We stopped to tell *Misty* and *2nd Wind* about the view. *Misty* hadn't seen us start out. They said they had looked up at the ridge, saw something moving, and thought it might be a bear or a caribou. They looked again and said, "It's Jim and Judy." I think they were a little surprised since I didn't join in their long walks. It's all a matter of motivation.

We returned to *Yankee Lady*. Jim put the nozzle of the sun shower through the hatch over the head (bathroom) so I could take a shower in privacy. The water was warm and wonderful. He put on his bathing suit and dove into the water, which was warm on top but cold below, his brand of shower. While he was swimming, Cecil and Dorothy returned and motored over to us. Cecil asked us if we wanted some fresh caught fish. We think that when we saw them leave earlier, they were planning on giving us some fish. We accepted with enthusiasm. Cecil filleted and skinned them and gave us enough for more than the six of us. I asked, "How much do we owe you?" Their reply was nothing. It's impossible to convey the total feeling of hospitality we felt from meeting people like this. They were so genuinely happy to see us and interested in where we had been. They did not feel as if we were intruding on their privacy. We told them that what they had here couldn't be measured in money. Jim and I cooked some of the fish for supper and saved the rest for a potluck supper with the others the next night.

Rosie and Tom climbed the mountain in the morning while we watched their progress from the boat. I thought that it was a lot easier to watch someone else do it. We all met on *Yankee Lady* to review the guidebook and plan the day. We decided to continue on to La Poile later in the day. It would be a short trip, only ten miles. This would be our first outport. The only access to this town is by boat!

We took some strawberry jam to Cecil and Dorothy. They met us at their sturdy dock and invited us in for coffee. We climbed the steep ladder from their dock and walked across the little yard to the cabin, passing a small garden where they were growing strawberries for their granddaughter. Between the two cabins, there was a freshwater stream cascading down the mountain. They had channeled it through a pipe and used it for their water supply including drinking water. What a testimony to the remote and unpolluted nature of this tundra wilderness. The kitchen was the large main room. Cabinets and a propane stove lined one wall, a day bed covered with a blanket and a propane refrigerator were set against another, and the table and chairs sat in front of the window, which looked out over the harbor. Two small bedrooms and a bathroom with a Porta Potty completed the rest of the cabin.

While we drank coffee, they talked about this country. They frequently see caribou and moose. They told us that last year, a bear had broken into their son's cabin and caused a lot of damage. Like any self-respecting bear, it had found the sugar bowl which it left halfway up the hill. The bear had also broken into their cabin but didn't cause much damage. Cecil had devised a "bear repulsion" plan. He hammered nails, sharp points up, into a piece of plywood. Now, when they leave, they place it in front of the door. It seems to work. He also obtained a bear hunting permit, but I don't think he has shot one yet. They were so pleased to meet us representing, to their eyes, a more sophisticated way of life. We were so pleased to meet them representing to our eyes a simple, wholesome way of life. We gave them our "boat card" with our names and address and invited them to stop to see us in Connecticut if they ever traveled that way. We couldn't stay long because we had to get back to the others and leave.

It was threatening fog. Jim and I discovered that our radar wasn't working. This equipment failure had important implications for all of us. Until we could get it fixed or get a new one, we would have to rely on the other two boats when we were in dense fog. This would not be easy for self-reliant Jim. It was unlikely we could get it fixed until we arrived in Halifax, which seemed to us like a long time to be without such an important instrument. After we told the others, we all agreed to put *Yankee Lady* in the middle, between *Misty* and *2nd Wind*, a *Yankee Lady* sandwich. However, this day, the fog never developed.

We retraced our path to the Cabot Strait and continued east. We turned to port a little before Naked Man Rock and entered La Poile Bay. During our approach, we passed the eastern most point of our voyage—58 58' 4" longitude. I wished we could go farther. There were so many places to explore and so little time to do it in. We turned to port before the large headland that formed Little Bay. We motored toward the town noticing the colorful houses perched together on the side of the hill. The tall, stationery public wharf and the floating docks next to it constituted the downtown section of La Poile. Several fishing boats were attached to the floating docks; there was no room for us.

We tied up on the far side of the public wharf, hoping this was not where the ferry landed. *2nd Wind* went in first, and *Yankee Lady* followed. *Misty* rafted to *Yankee Lady*. We adjusted all our lines, climbed onto the wharf, and walked the short distance to the store and the post office. There, someone told us that the ferry unloaded at the face end of the dock, but then, since this was Thursday, it would be tying up for the night where we were. After the ferry arrived to unload, I walked over and politely asked the captain if he could stay where he was for this one night. He said he couldn't because he and his crew would need the outlets for the power and telephone lines.

We had to move. The dock was shaped like a backward L. We walked across it to see if there was room enough for the three of us on the shoreside. It looked like a tight fit; the channel was narrow, and a ledge extended out from shore, but we thought we could do it. We really had no choice. *Yankee Lady* went in bow first, as far as possible. *Misty* rafted to us, also bow first. Then, using long bow and stern lines, we helped *2nd Wind* back in through the narrow opening. All went well, which was comforting since we had an audience of local people watching our maneuvers.

As we walked up the path to the post office, we passed the sign that read, Welcome to La Poile, Population 150. The town is set on the north side of Little Bay, which turns shallow from here and continues past the town. It is one of the few remaining outports in Newfoundland, towns that can only be reached by water. There are no roads to this town, and consequently, there are no roads in town, only footpaths. Walking sets the pace of life. There are no noisy car motors, no honking horns, no exhaust fumes, no street lights. The only things motorized are two four wheelers which pull little trailers which are used to meet the (little red) ferry and carry the heavy loads. Electricity has recently been brought in from the east through underground cables. This has eliminated the noisy, local generating plant and made the supply more reliable. The ferry runs six days a week; *everything* comes by boat. This is a fishing community; the wharf is the focal point of the town. Old fishing shacks, dories, and fishing boats cluster together at the wharf and on a few floating docks. Even though fishing has been severely curtailed by the government, the fishermen still work on their boats and gather around the docks.

The houses are set randomly on the hill; a footpath leads to each house. Blue is a popular color, along with white; some houses are white trimmed with pink. The crest of the hill seemed like a protective presence, shielding the settlement from the wilderness. By land, the nearest road through this wilderness is one hundred miles to the north. Small shrubs, moss, and Christmas tree–sized fir trees cover the hill and the land in between houses. Most houses have small neatly kept yards; some had painted wooden figures, animals, and people for decoration. There were a lot of welcome signs. There are two small stores, one at each end of town. We visited each. The school has sixteen students, K–8, and three teachers. The high school students attend school in Port aux Basques, boarding with local families and coming home on weekends. Everyone knows one another, and most are related. As Jim and I passed by a black, barking dog, a local man said he only barks at strangers. We were obviously strangers.

There was a path that continued out of town past the dump and into the tundra. Several young men and women were being paid by the government to extend the path to the headland that extended into the bay. They used shovels and spades to dig into the spongy tundra and a wheelbarrow to carry dirt for filling swampy places. *No machines here.* They had placed white painted benches at three lookouts. We sat on one to enjoy the panoramic view of the bay. They were a cheerful group, obviously enjoying what they were doing. Jim called them the "road crew." Some of them attended college in Port aux Basques or Nova Scotia; some remained in town.

During the evening, we sat in our cockpits and talked to the fishermen on the dock. Tom Isele joined some local folks fishing off the other side of the dock. He caught a small mackerel, walked over to show it to us, and then threw it back. That represented the sum total of fish caught by us this trip, not that we were really trying.

The weather forecast was favorable; everyone else thought we needed to start heading back toward Port aux Basques in the morning. I didn't. I was angry. I had come a long way to find this remote place, and I wanted to stay and savor it. The other couples, seeing my dark mood, left Jim and me alone. Jim was quietly patient with my outbursts. We were able to take time to explore the town a little more. Jim and I walked to both grocery stores, bought two rolls of paper towels, and mailed some postcards. The post office was on the other side of one of the stores. It had its own entrance. We walked out the path the kids were making, talked to some of them, and sat on the farthest bench to enjoy the view. My rational self returned.

We left at lunchtime, motoring out of the bay in hazy visibility. We passed the now familiar entrance to Little Garia Bay and saw the tower of the restored Rose Blanche lighthouse silhouetted against the sky. The lighthouse grew clearer as we approached the red and white whistle buoy marking the entrance to Rose Blanche Harbor (the locals call the buoy The Groaner).

Once we entered the harbor, it was confusing finding the right cove. First, we followed the red and green buoys into the large cove by the fish plant. There were rocks sticking out of the water on either side of this buoyed channel. This was where the little red ferry docked; the town was too far away. *Not inviting.* We turned around, passed the red and green buoys again, and turned to port, staying close to the far shore where the chart showed deep water. There was a small red buoy just before a floating dock and a fishing wharf. Keeping the buoy to starboard, Jim and I docked *Yankee Lady* at the floating dock.

I stepped off and walked to the nearest person I could find. Yes, it was okay to dock here. *2nd Wind* docked by a ladder at the fishing wharf, *Misty* tied up to the inside of the floating dock. A pickup truck drove to the end of the wharf. The front license read Coast Guard Auxiliary. I thought, *Oh, no they're going to tell us to move.* Wrong. They just came to say hello. Later, a fisherman told us that if it was crowded, some of the fishermen would move their fishing boats to make room. Here, as in the other small ports, there were no officials to tell you what to do. The fishermen welcomed us!

This was a small cove tucked in at the end of the larger harbor. Fishing boats were tied up on both sides of it inshore from our boats. A large red ocean-going fishing boat lay diagonally across from us. We found out later that it belonged to our Little Garia Bay friends, Cecil and his partner. There was a large white building on the wharf near *2nd Wind* where the fishermen prepared their fishing gear.

As usual, this town is built on hills, but these hills seemed steeper. The road from Port aux Basques ends here; the roads through town are steep, narrow, and winding. White, blue, and turquoise houses cover the hillsides. There is a small grocery store and a hardware store just around the corner from the wharf. The lighthouse is set on the point across the harbor from our dock.

A little blonde girl, whose name is Michelle, her brother, and another boy came to meet us. Her mother works as a guide at the lighthouse. They had lots of questions. Jim and I gave them a tour of *Yankee Lady*, as did *2nd Wind*. A fisherman, Wayne, spied the name *Yankee Lady*. He said, "You must be Jim." *How did he know?* It's a small town and word travels; he was a good friend of Cecil Parsons. He joined the six of us for coffee aboard *2nd Wind*.

The next day, we explored the town. A short dinghy ride or a longer walk would take us to a bed-and-breakfast/restaurant and gift shop at the entrance to the lighthouse park. We decided to walk, stop at the restaurant for lunch, and then tour the lighthouse. A "short cut" footpath led us practically through peoples' yards and then to the road by the next small cove. Instead of walking around the hill on the paved road, we could take another footpath at the head of this cove. It went under the cliff and over a small wooden bridge to a parking lot. We noticed a sign that said, Danger, Falling Rocks. We asked a teenager if the footpath was useable. He confirmed the sign, saying, "Don't use the path. There are falling rocks under the cliff." We walked a few feet farther and asked a man with gray hair the same question. He said, "Yes, there are falling rocks, but nothing has fallen in my lifetime." We took the path.

The restaurant was a "loving hands at home" experience. It had been open for two months. The local ladies that ran it prided themselves on cooking everything to order. This must have meant boiling the potatoes for Barbara's mashed potatoes after she ordered it. We all ordered Fisherman's Platters. At least three of the ladies checked to see what we had ordered. It took about one hour to get our food. We were running out of conversation. When the food came, there wasn't that much, which was okay because it wasn't that good. We lied to the ladies, though, because they were so anxious to please.

Michelle's mother, Shawndra, was our guide on the path to the lighthouse. The granite for the original and the restored light-house was quarried on site. The lighthouse began operation in 1873 and continued until the early 1940s. The fixed white light shone out from an elevation of ninety-five feet and could be seen for thirteen miles on a clear day. Nevertheless, several ships were lost in the vicinity of this lighthouse.

Inside, the thick stone walls muffled the sounds of the wind and sea. They must also have provided some insulation from the heat and cold but not from the dampness. The living quarters consisted of a living room and office on the first floor and three bedrooms on the second floor. I wondered what it would have been like lying in one of those beds listening to the wind howl-ing on a bitter winter night. The lighthouse keeper would probably have been in the tower tending the light while his family lay sleeping below.

Someone had told us that the Barachois waterfall, which we had seen from the ocean as a silver sliver high on a hill, was about a twenty-minute walk from the "gas bar" at the end of the village. Shawndra heard us talking about walking to it. She said, "It's a longer walk than that. Here are the keys. Why don't you use my car? I'm through here at nine, just be back by then." She handed the keys to Jim. How could we not accept? It was at least eight miles from town, one way. I didn't think even runner Barbara would have made the round-trip.

We parked just off the road and walked about half a mile on the boardwalk to arrive at the base of the falls. The boardwalk was laid over spongy peat moss, which would have been very difficult to walk through. The water cascaded over a steep cliff, falling between tundra-covered hills. The resulting brook, near our feet, rippled between stones and boulders to a small lake. We thought it was worth the car ride to see it.

We returned to the boats. Jim dropped the five of us at the dock and drove back to the lighthouse to return the car. Tom Isele volunteered to meet him with his dinghy, but I said, "No, I like 'messing around' in small boats." I skimmed across the harbor to the gift shop dock. After I picked up Jim, we explored the small bay by the lighthouse, edging over to a narrow cut that led out to sea, so calm inside, so lumpy outside. The lighthouse looked really tall from the perspective of a rubber dinghy.

In the morning, we decided to leave for Port aux Basques, eighteen miles away. First, we walked down the wharf to say good-bye to Wayne and the others and to ask him to say good-bye to Michelle and her friends for us. We were told that the government had opened the cod fishing season for a two-week period. Six men and a woman were in the white fishing shed cheerfully preparing their lines to go fishing on Monday. They used the old-fashioned long line method. For the past two days, several of them had taken their dory-type boats out early in the morning to catch mackerel, which they used for bait. Today, they cut the mackerel (now frozen) into chunks and baited the hooks. There were three hundred hooks on a line. These were spiraled into a tub, ten tubs per boat. That's a lot of hooks and bait. To fish, they weight the line and let it out of the tub as they motor forward. At the end of the day, they would return to haul in their catch. Every fishing day, they immediately bleed and gut the fish they catch and then throw them into a compartment containing crushed ice. This produces good quality fish, which brings in more money. At the end of the day, they would unload the fish and rebait the lines, all three thousand hooks. They work about eighteen to twenty hours a day, and they wouldn't earn a living any other way. You could tell that it felt good to them to be working again.

We decided to make a run for Port aux Basques today because the weather forecast for the next few days didn't sound good. This will put us in a good position for recrossing the Cabot Strait. The wind was on our aft quarter starting out at ten knots and building to fifteen to twenty. The seas were rough, five to six feet. It was a bouncy trip. *Yankee Lady's* autopilot worked well, as did *2nd Wind's* autopilot. However, *Tilly*, aboard *Misty*, wasn't up to it. Barbara had to steer the whole way, which was not easy in a following sea. The red and green channel buoy at the entrance to Port aux Basques was a welcome sight, as were the empty wharves. We pulled in and tied up to ladders. We heard that a ship carrying an entire winter's road supply of salt would be arriving the next day. It would pull into the other side of the wharf where we were.

In the morning, we were about to eat a leisurely breakfast when Barbara called down from the wharf, "Jim and Judy, have you seen the salt ship? It's going to be dirty. Do you want to move?" Before coffee, decision making was difficult. We ate a hurried breakfast and then prepared to cope with the day. I looked out the companionway to see a very large (four hundred feet) ship slowly approaching the dock. We didn't understand the process, but before the ship reached the dock, the crew let out a port side anchor to slow them down. The chain creaked and groaned as the ship inched forward to the dock and the crew secured the dock lines.

Tom Isele talked to the captain who said *2nd Wind* would be okay at their far end of the wharf. *Yankee Lady*, however, was right next to one of the clam shell shovels; we could see that salt dust would sift all over us. *Misty* had already moved one wharf over. We decided to join them. The wind was howling, and rollers (somewhat diminished) and white caps covered the harbor. Jim untied the lines, and I backed *Yankee Lady* out past the end of the wharf. It took two tries to ease into the space in front of *Misty*.

Trucks rolled onto our former wharf, and the ship's crew began unloading salt immediately. Two clam shells suspended from two cranes dug into the ship's hold, scooped up salt, and dropped it into the waiting trucks. Yes, there was salt dust. We still got a little, but it wasn't horrible.

We met the others for lunch at the restaurant and then walked to the ferry terminal. The catamaran ferry was canceled for the day due to high winds and high seas. We watched the other ferry, the six-hundred-foot Caribou, dock, unload, and load. Everything was touristy and official.

At 6:30 p.m., we noted that the wind had died down, at least for the moment. Jim and I were sitting in *Yankee Lady's* cockpit, enjoying the evening sunlight. The tide was rising; we could gradually see the top of the wharf and the salt ship still unloading buckets into the waiting trucks. We could hear the trucks rumbling into place, the sound of the crane, and the whoosh of salt falling into the trucks. When the trucks hit the speed bump in the road, there was a loud boom. With each rattle, a little salt dropped onto the road; it was beginning to turn white.

Diagonally across the road, at the little bandstand, a group of Salvation Army faithful were singing gospel hymns—very off tune. Jim said, "It's a good thing you can get into heaven without carrying a tune." The Salvation Army flag was waving in the breeze. Next to us, Barbara and Tom were talking at the dock to the grandparents of the boy who was singing off key. They said the great grandmother was playing the drum accompaniment.

Tom Isele decided to move *2nd Wind*, now a little more salty, because the ship would be unloading salt until 11:30 tonight and would start again early tomorrow morning. He motored to the end of the last wharf, which was across from us. We met him there and used his bow and stern lines to turn him around. He tied up at the far side of the dock with the help of the Salvation Army singing "Praise God" several times.

We were sitting in the cockpit just before dark when a man came to the edge of the dock to ask about our crossing. We told him we had crossed last week. He said he was the cook on the salt ship. Yesterday (gale warnings) had been really rough, but it didn't bother him. He was from Havre Boucher, Nova Scotia, and had been sailing on this ship for twenty-four years. He has been to within one hundred miles of the North Pole where the ship carried supplies to a Canadian outpost. He told us that all daily living activities at this outpost took place inside, partly because of the cold and partly because of the polar bears. There was even an indoor golf course. The ship has traveled throughout the Great Lakes, to Maine, and south to New Orleans. He said that he was home about four months a year, and that his house and his truck were all paid for. The ship had a crew of twenty-one; he had two women working for him, and the third mate was a woman. Since he was the cook, he could say with authority that they all ate well. Sunday was usually roast beef or roast turkey (with all the trimmings) day. He made all the bread. I said that everyone must be nice to him. He said, "Oh yes, nobody bites the hand that feeds him." It sounded like a pretty interesting life.

The wind changed direction. *Yankee Lady's* bow started hitting the dock with a jerk. Jim and I took turns getting up in the middle of the night and early morning to adjust our fenders. Finally, while it was still dark, he tied another bow line to the other shore, and we were settled again.

We were still waiting for a weather window to cross the Cabot Strait, maybe tomorrow. This was a catch-up day for me. I needed to straighten up the inside of *Yankee Lady*, wash my hair, and go to the grocery store. We ran the engine to charge the battery. This made enough hot water so I could take a shower on the boat instead of coping with feeding quarters to the shower timer at the Harbor Authority building. Things were looking up.

After dessert aboard *Misty*, we walked over to the bandstand to hear another concert—country music. There was quite a crowd, the music had a good beat, and the children were "dancing" to the music, wherever they happened to be standing. One baby was bouncing on his father's lap. The music was loud; we moved across the street to save our ears. We walked back to the dock just as the freighter, now sitting high in the water, was getting ready to leave.

It was a tight fit for the freighter between wharves. On its approach, about one boat length out, the crew had lowered a very large anchor with very large chain, presumably to keep the wind from blowing the ship against the dock. Now, as the freighter backed away from the wharf, the crew proceeded to pull the anchor up. Something got stuck, and the anchor would not come up, leaving the ship swinging in the wind toward other docks, which were occupied by fishing boats and pleasure craft (Not us, we were gratefully on the upwind side of all this.). It drifted closer and closer and came within five feet of some rock ledges. After several back and forth maneuvers, the captain finally got the bow facing out. The anchor still did not come up. Rosie, standing next to us, said, "Should I get (anchor man) Tom to give him some advice?" The captain finally used full power to drive the ship and dragging anchor out of the harbor, leaving swirling whirlpools and eddies of green water behind from his prop wash. We heard him one-half hour later, talking to Port aux Basques traffic control. He was a mile and a half from the channel marker trying to resolve his anchor problem. Finally, he did. It was a "hold our breath" sight to see this whale of a ship very close to being out of control.

The Cabot Strait smiled again. We filed a sail plan with Port aux Basques Coast Guard and departed at 5:30 a.m. We had light northwest winds with sea swells running about five feet. These swells were off our aft quarter; it was sort of like backing up and down a hill, not unpleasant. It was an uneventful thirteen-hour trip. We saw a few freighters entering or leaving the strait, not very close to us. A couple of porpoises cavorted around. While Jim was lying down, I saw what I thought was a very small whale breach out of the water close to our starboard side and fall back into the water with a smacking sound. I called Jim, but I never saw it again.

A few miles from Cape Breton, Tom Frasca called Jim. He said the rpms on *Misty's* engine were increasing and decreasing. *What did Jim think it was?* Jim replied that it was probably a clogged fuel filter. Tom agreed. The Atlantic Ocean was not the place to change a fuel filter; there was nothing to do but keep going. This made for some anxious moments aboard *Misty*. We watched the Cape Breton highlands turn from blue to green and finally arrived at the K4 red buoy, which marked the entrance to South Bay Ingonish. After two more miles, we arrived at the red and white buoy, KM, just before the narrow entrance into Ingonish Harbor. Jim cautioned Tom that *Misty's* engine might stall at low rpm. He said we would go through the entrance first to see if it could be done at full throttle.

The entrance was well buoyed. The channel flowed between a man-made point of land and a sandy, shoaling spit of land. The waves from the ocean surge rose up and broke on the shoal, approximately forty feet from us—too close for any mistakes. *Yankee Lady* powered through in no less than twenty feet of water. *No problem.* We let *Misty* know we were through. *Misty* and *2nd Wind* powered through also.

Ingonish Harbor was deep, forty to fifty feet almost to its shores. We motored to starboard and circled in front of a dilapidated wharf. A cruising boat was tied to it; there were no ladders, and there was not really enough room for the three of us to tie up. The cruisers told us there was also a new pier at the head of the harbor, but it had no planking on top. *Yankee Lady* continued past the wharf and saw a sailboat anchored. The passage was narrow; some people would consider this a perfect gunkhole, but we decided to check out the small indentation behind the breakwater to get a better view of the harbor. We motored back across the entrance and turned to port. The chart indicated a small strip of water eight feet deep, followed by a large area with a six-foot depth. We circled the area and found forty feet of water almost to shore. We were tired and hungry. It was flat calm, and we decided that with enough scope out, this would do. We suggested rafting. *2nd Wind* anchored first, putting out 140 feet of line. *Yankee Lady* and *Misty* pulled up on either side of *2nd Wind*. Jim used the dinghy to put our anchor out with 130 feet of line. It was a beautiful spot. The harbor was surrounded by forested mountains, which dropped to the shore. A few houses were visible through the trees. Within two hours, we were all in bed.

At 2:00 a.m., the wind picked up. *Yankee Lady's* main halyard started beating the mast. *Twang, bang.* I struggled out of my warm bed to fix it. Since I was up, I checked the anchor line. The whole three-boat raft was pulling on our line. I was worried about the short scope. I let some more line out and waited, shivering in the cold. Jim got up. We decided to adjust *2nd Wind's* line to even the load. We tried to go back to sleep. Jim was now nervous about the anchors, so he lay down on the couch in the main cabin. About an hour later, he called, "Judy, come out here."

I pulled on my sweatshirt and struggled to put my jeans on. They were half inside out, but I wasn't going into the cold without them. Jeans on, I climbed out to the cockpit barefoot. Then Jim said, "Everybody, wake up. We're dragging!" We were in seventeen feet of water and about twenty feet from shore. Tom Isele pushed the starter button on *2nd Wind*.

He said, "Oh no, my engine won't start" as the engine cranked over, and nothing else happened. *Yankee Lady's* and *Misty's* engines were running. There was nothing else we could do but stay together. We became a trimaran or a ship with two propellers. Jim said we needed to get the anchors up and then find shallower water to anchor in.

It was a beautiful, starry night, but we didn't have time to think about that. It was also dark. Our first task was to get away from shore without tangling our keels or rudders in the anchor lines. There was an old ferry dock with a few boats tied to or moored near it. It had a bright light on it, which helped illumine the anchor lines. It also gave us a safe direction to head toward while the men pulled in the anchors. This was not so easy. The anchor lines were twisted around each other. Tom Isele pulled his anchor line in, picked up his heavy anchor, reached out, and, holding the anchor, passed it over *Yankee Lady's* line. Then Jim was able to haul *Yankee Lady's* anchor in. Meanwhile, Barbara and I were steering the boats away from shore.

In a crucial situation like this, someone needed to take charge; there was no time for discussion. Once before, one morning in the 1980s, *Yankee Lady* (Judy aboard), *Albatross* (Jim and Carol aboard), and *Wings* (Allen Brown aboard) had dragged, rafted together, toward a sandbar in Point Judith (Rhode Island) Pond. We had successfully powered our raft back into deep water. Drawing on this "vast" experience, Jim and I took charge. While the men went forward to tend to the anchor lines, Barbara and I took charge of steering. *Misty* was the starboard hull; *Yankee Lady* was the port hull. I told Barbara to increase her throttle to help us turn to port (toward the light). She did. Then she throttled back, and I increased throttle to turn to starboard toward the center of the harbor.

We started heading into the middle of the harbor. The water was black; the sky was dark. We couldn't see much. Jim found *Yankee Lady's* spotlight and plugged it in. It didn't reveal much over the open water. We could see lights on shore, but judging their distance was difficult in the dark. They were much too far away for the spotlight to find. Tom Isele kept trying to start his engine with no luck. Jim, Tom Frasca, and I checked our charts. Jim and I had Tom Isele's because in the confusion, we couldn't find ours (remember all he had to do was hand it over). The chart showed that almost the entire harbor had depths of forty to fifty-eight feet. There was a twenty plus section close to shore. *But how close?* Toward the head of the harbor (the opposite end from us), the chart indicated depths of twenty-eight feet, then dropping off to sixteen and nine feet. Jim said, "When we get to twenty plus feet, we'll drop the anchors." Jim took *Yankee Lady's* helm while I went below to stop shivering and to put on shoes and a coat. I found our chart (the original, not a copy) and noted that a point of land stuck out on the left side of the harbor. I climbed back to the cockpit and suggested to Jim that maybe we should head to the right side. He went below and double-checked while I steered. I noticed that we were roughly lined up with the red blinking buoy at the entrance to the harbor. Aha! I switched with Jim, went below, and plotted a course from the buoy to the head of the harbor—295 degrees (we were heading 308). Back out, I suggested the change, and we made it. Following this course, we should have no obstructions in our way. It made us feel a little better; we weren't just heading totally blindly into inky black water.

Barbara and I continued steering. Our engine speeds were pretty well matched because we tracked a straight line without making many adjustments to our throttles. I was able to make small adjustments with *Yankee Lady's* wheel to keep us on course.

It was sort of like flying on instruments, nothing to see, just watch the speed, the compass, and the depth. There was a piece of tape wrapped around *Yankee Lady's* wheel that, when centered on the top, indicated that the rudder was straight, not turning. It was so dark I had to keep feeling for this tape to judge the position of the wheel. Jim stayed on the bow, every now and then shining the searchlight. Tom and Tom stared ahead or watched their fathometers. Nobody panicked. For my part, I was determined that we could do what we needed to do.

We kept our speed between one and two knots. It felt as if we were crawling across the harbor. It seemed like the fathometer stayed stuck above forty. We watched someone launch a boat from a ramp on shore. They headed across the harbor behind us, presumably knowing where they were going. We must have been a strange sight—three ghostly boats with red and green running lights on at least one of them and a white steaming light part way up the mast. To starboard, we saw a light next to the water and a shadowy shape next to it. As we got closer, Jim shined the spotlight on a moored small fishing boat. We passed by with enough room. We saw a few yellow lights well ahead of us and thought that must be the land at the head of the harbor. Finally, the fathometer started to drop into the thirties. When I called out thirty-one feet, Jim said, "Put the engines in neutral" and then to Tom Isele who was waiting on the bow, "Drop the anchor." The wind pushed the raft sideways while the anchor line paid out. Jim let out our anchor also.

I prayed, "Please hold, anchors." They held, but the boats didn't swing into the wind like they were supposed to. We sat broadside to the wind, which put more strain on the anchors. Tom's anchor line had caught in *Misty's* rudder.

By now, it was getting light. Jim pulled on our anchor line to try to take the pressure off Tom's. Tom let his out all the way— two hundred feet or better. Nothing happened. Jim took our entire three hundred feet of anchor line out of the well, crossed

2nd Wind's and *Misty's* bows keeping the anchor line outside of everything, and put it on the winch in *Misty's* cockpit. Tom Frasca winched it in until it took some of the pressure off *2nd Wind's* anchor line. Then Tom took all of *2nd Wind's* line and carried it to the back of *Misty*. At last, it floated free of the rudder. At this point, we were hanging backward on *Yankee Lady's* line, which was on the back of *Misty*. Jim took *2nd Wind's* anchor line, put it on *Misty's* bow, and cleated it tight. Then he released our anchor line on *Misty's* stern and carried it up forward and back over to *Yankee Lady*. He pulled it in and cleated it, and at last, we were facing properly into the wind with pressure on both anchors straight ahead, almost.

After the anchor lines were dropped, I went below to take a break. I could see our American flag on its flag staff in the stern. It was waving briskly, pointing sideways on the boat. This meant we were still broadside to the wind. *Please move*, I thought. Every now and then I looked up—still sideways. After what seemed like a very long time, I saw the flag shift and start blowing aft. I stood up to look out; we were facing in the right direction. Wow, we did it, and we were all safe. *Misty's* rudder will have to be checked later.

We were finally straightened out. Should we stay up and eat breakfast? I think all of us elected to go back to bed. Jim and I got up a couple of hours later. Coffee and food helped perk us up. It was a beautiful morning and a beautiful spot. As we looked around, we saw we were a comfortable distance from shore. The water was calm, the sun was out, and the mountains rose up from the land. We observed the winding trails of a ski resort. Ironically, we saw the new wharf a short distance away, over in the direction of the ski lift.

Tom Frasca found water and dirt in his Racor fuel filter. He changed it. Jim decided that since we bought fuel at the same places, he better look at *Yankee Lady's* also. There was dirt and water in it also, so he changed it. Tom Isele found a broken wire on the fuel pump. He fixed the wire, but the engine still wouldn't start. Jim went over. Together, they tested the fuel pump; it was getting plenty of fuel. They checked the spark plugs and found them wet and shorting out. They changed the spark plugs. Tom turned on the engine; it coughed and sputtered and then purred contentedly.

One hears the strangest conversations when boating. Tom Frasca asked Barbara if she was going to take the broom to fix the knot meter. *Broom?* Yes, she got in the dinghy with the broom and pushed it under the boat to try to spin the little paddle wheel that turns to indicate speed.

We had originally planned to leave at 10:00 a.m. to pick up a favorable tide to the entrance of the Great Bras d'Or Channel. We weren't sure about the current in the channel itself. The Coast Guard had told us that slack was at 8:25 a.m. *Slack what—high or low?* We really had no choice; we had to leave when we were ready. It was twenty miles from Ingonish to the channel; we would have to take our chances.

We negotiated the entrance to Ingonish Harbor successfully, leaving the red buoys to port and hugging the green ones to starboard. We motored a safe distance from the high cliffs of Cape Smoky, which stood boldly out to sea. We rounded the point and continued along the cliff-lined coast, heading slowly away from it on an almost direct course to the channel entrance. The cliffs looked like they were covered with green tree frosting, with here and there a bare spot, and with dollops reaching over the cliffs toward the water. The cliffs themselves were a bare reddish-brown.

We made excellent time, getting a push from the current as Jim had figured. We passed the Bird Islands on the Atlantic side where the rocks sloped gradually into the water and saw a couple of puffins swimming around. A seal surfaced and inspected us.

We arrived at buoy Q1 and approached the channel. At first, it looked as if the current was with us. The GPS read five knots over the ground. But it was not to be. As the passage narrowed, the water started to eddy and boil. Birds sat facing into the wind on the flat edge of a buoy. They looked like they were surfing through the rushing water flowing by. I watched the GPS read two, then one, and then zero. We were just inching by the buoys, swaying in the current. We held *Yankee Lady's* engine at 3,000 rpms. *Misty*, with the same engine but a different propeller, had to put the rpms at "red line" max—3,400 rpm. We all had moments of hanging on with white knuckles. At times, the current was running out at five to six knots. Our boats could only go a little over six knots, maybe seven when pushed. *Yankee Lady* was in the lead.

We called the other boats to see what they wanted to do next. *Misty* wanted to head right into Kelly's Cove to regroup and wait for the current to change. Someone said the current would change at 9:00 p.m., which was too late for us. We and *2nd Wind* wanted to continue six miles to Otter Cove where Jim had seen moorings on the way out. We would be out of the current and the wind there. *Misty* agreed to go along.

We were not through the worst of it yet. The highway bridge crossed another narrow part of the channel. We could see white water flowing under the bridge. *Oh great,* I thought, *back up to 3000 RPM's.* We inched along under the high span. Then the channel widened again and the knot meter read three knots. Finally, we reached Otter Island and turned to starboard to enter the sheltered water of Otter Cove.

There was a small dot of an island in the center of the cove which had a small lighted beacon on it. Moorings were inshore from it. I motored to a mooring with an orange ball; Jim picked up the mooring line with the boat hook. We had stopped. I turned off the motor, sat down, and felt the stress drain away. There was a twenty-three-foot powerboat tied to a dock near us. Jim dinghied over to ask about moorings for the other two boats. The captain said that the four moorings with white markers were his. He had put them out for anyone to use. We directed *2nd Wind* and *Misty* to those moorings. The one we were on belonged to a fisherman who hardly ever used it. I was sure we were not the first to take advantage of these moorings provided by thoughtful local boaters.

Peace again! It had been quite a day.

The next day, *Misty* and *2nd Wind* decided to leave for Baddeck, but first, Jim volunteered to dive under *Misty* to check for rudder damage. Tom dropped his mooring and rafted *Misty* up to *Yankee Lady*. Jim dove in and wiggled the rudder while Tom held the tiller. Jim came up for air (It always seemed to me that he could hold his breath longer than anyone else I knew.) and reported that there were no breaks in it. Then he took a batten to use as a straight edge, dove again, and placed the batten vertically and then horizontally against the rudder. He surfaced and reported that there were no bends or curves. Tom and Barbara left for Baddeck much relieved. Tom and Rosie followed them.

We stayed in the harbor, rejoicing in the quiet stillness of it. To me, it gave vibrant meaning to the verse from Psalms, "He leadeth me beside the still waters. He restoreth my soul" (Psalms 23:2–3, KJV). There were three other boats: the powerboat tied to the dock, a small runabout on the next mooring with no one in it, and the blue ketch from Ontario that we met yesterday.

The owner of the docked powerboat had been coming here for over twenty years. He told us that rum running schooners used to anchor here during the days of prohibition. The captains would sail here from the French Islands of St. Pierre and Miquelon, which were just off the southeast coast of Newfoundland (We didn't have time to go that far.). Shore boats could be rowed through a shallow, narrow channel into a small lagoon where the smugglers could deliver the liquor. Now the lagoon was a source of freshwater for cruisers. Springwater cascaded down the mountain where a rusty pipe channeled it the last few feet to the beach. Before they left, Tom and Barbara rowed in and returned with four gallons of water. Later, we dinghied through that watery path and found the place. I decided that if Tom and Barbara didn't worry about the rusty pipe, we wouldn't either.

Since we were not bouncing around and we had plenty of time, I made pea soup. While it was simmering, we washed *Yankee Lady* with a scrub brush, cleaning detergent, and buckets of harbor water. She sparkled after we scrubbed her clean of Port aux Basques salt and dirt. The pea soup was a just reward for our efforts.

We napped in the cockpit and then explored in the dinghy—rest and relaxation surrounded by silence. Jim went after mussels. He cooked spaghetti, which we ate with canned sauce. He put the cooked mussels in his spaghetti. We sat around for a while; the kerosene lamp glowed and warmed the cabin.

We woke to a slightly cool, gray morning. There was a whisper of a breeze, and the tops of the hills across the channel were smothered in fog. We sat in the cockpit eating breakfast and listened to two gulls create quite a commotion. One was perched on the green day marker, the other floated nearby. Their calls echoed around the harbor. One said squawk; the other said coo. Jim's translation—"Please" and "No" repeated frequently.

Many times we never knew what would be around the next bend. After breakfast, we dinghied back to the lagoon to fill our five-gallon jug with water. We took it back to the boat, and Jim poured it into *Yankee Lady's* water tank. Then we motored around Harbor Point to explore Barge Cove. A majestic eagle flew over us—white head, brown wings, and white tail feathers clearly visible. He landed in a tree. We approached slowly, camera ready. I think I got a pretty good shot of him. We rounded another point before heading into another small cove. We could see the former sand and gravel quarry and the remains of a bulkhead where the barges probably landed. A dirt road touched the beach. Other than that, it was the birds, the water, the forest, and us. We doubled back to Barge Cove, saw another eagle, and dinghied to the head of the cove. There were the three sunken barges the guidebook had talked about. We did not think anchoring in here would have been feasible. We went back for more water and then prepared to leave Otter Cove.

We motored toward Baddeck into a light southwest breeze. The water was slightly choppy, just enough to give us a rocking chair effect. Just before Big Harbor, I sniffed suspiciously and said to Jim, "I think I smell diesel fuel." I went below to look in the bilge. "Yes, I see something. You better come check." It's great to travel with someone mechanical, but he can't smell. I come in handy for that. Jim looked and checked the filters. The secondary filter had a small leak. I shut down the engine while he put on a new washer. I restarted the engine, and we were on our way again.

We heard *Misty* and *2nd Wind* on the radio. Baddeck was crowded. *Misty* was on a mooring near the dock, but they said they might have to leave. There was one empty mooring close to the gray building, but it was not for rent. *2nd Wind* was at the other boatyard. There were no slips at Baddeck Marine because there was something like a powerboat convention arriving. We would have to decide what to do when we got there.

We pulled into Baddeck Marine to get fuel, outboard gas, replacement fuel filters, and stove alcohol. On a hunch, I decided to walk over to the lady in the gray building. We had rented from her when we were here before. Her father had told her not to rent the empty mooring because there was a large houseboat coming in for water, and it might be too crowded. I said we were only twenty-eight feet and would only be here for one night. She said she'd call her father. He agreed to rent it as long as we could get the boat out of the way if the houseboat needed more room. We agreed. We had a mooring.

We almost didn't get it. Just as were getting ready to leave Baddeck Marine, a large sailboat headed right for the mooring. A crew member was standing on the bow with a boat hook. I called over to him, "We just rented that mooring." After a little confusion and a few more comments, they left it. Hurriedly, I backed

Yankee Lady away from the dock and over to it. Jim picked up the mooring line. I hoped that now we were on it, "possession was nine-tenths of the law."

Jim went to the hardware store to get a bilge pump switch and then joined me at the bakery and the grocery store. I picked up a gooey dessert for Barbara who was hostess for the evening. There were also fresh raspberries at the grocery store. I quickly bought a quart to renew my raspberry jam supply. Back at the boat, Jim started to put the switch in the bilge. It was a longer job than he had figured; suppertime was approaching. I managed to keep out of the way until he was done and then made a coordinated effort to get the jam made and supper done by 7:00 p.m. We dinghied over to *Misty* with the dessert and two jars of jam, one for *Misty* and one for *2nd Wind*. We sat in their cockpit and watched a crowd of power boaters assemble for their big day tomorrow.

This was Poker Run day for the powerboaters. They planned to speed around Bras d'Or Lake, stopping at four different ports and returning to Baddeck, altogether a distance of 130 miles. At each stop, the captain of each boat was given a playing card. Whoever had the best poker hand at the end of the day was the winner. The participants were in a festive mood. Many wore blue-gray shirts, which read Baddeck, 10th Annual Poker Run. We saw the captains meet on the public wharf, and shortly after, we watched them leave the docks and assemble at the starting line. *Vroom*, they were off, heading north.

We left an hour later, put up our sails, and sometimes sailed, sometimes motor-sailed to the narrows at Barra Strait. Barbara called the bridge tender to ask for an opening. The bridge tender asked her if we knew about the powerboat race. She replied, "Yes, we were aware and would proceed carefully, but they were much faster than we were." As we approached the drawbridge— *vroom, vroom, vroom*—one after another the powerboaters sped by us heading for their next destination at Iona, just after the drawbridge. As *Misty* and *2nd Wind* were proceeding through the bridge channel, one powerboat came roaring by, sped in front of *Misty*, and tried to pass *2nd Wind*. Somehow, *2nd Wind* eased over to the right a little. There was not enough room for the powerboat to pass, so he had to slow down. A big wake in this confined area could have caused serious damage to a sailboat.

After the bridge, we changed course slightly and were able to sail, no motors, most of the way across the Greater Bras d'Or Lake. Close hauled, full jib out, heeling over nicely, it was a perfect day for *Yankee Lady*. We arrived at the St. Peters/Lions Club Marina around 3:00 p.m., ahead of the powerboaters who had been due in at 2:30 p.m. Thankfully, we were securely tied to our slips at the floating dock when they started to arrive.

It was quite a sight. Powerboats rafted everywhere possible— to the gas dock and in two columns, ten deep at the end of the long, floating face dock. There was constant jockeying for position at the gas dock. The dock girl wore out the path between the office and the gas dock. It seemed most people paid with credit cards. The manager told us later that the marina had sold 3,400 liters (898 gallons) of gasoline in the hour and a half that the powerboaters were here. One of the last boats arrived with flair. The crew had dressed up as "singing" nuns. Their chorus was led by an Elvis look-alike, guitar and all. For the time they were here, the marina was something like pandemonium. We visited with some of the crews—nice people having a good time.

I watched the "nuns" arrive as I sat on the bow of a fifty-four-foot trawler from Fire Island Pines, Long Island, New York. The couple had lived aboard for eleven years, traveling around the United States and the Caribbean. Their little black dog, who loved to swim, was named SCUBA, soaking canine until brought aboard. Jim joined us on the deck. We compared cruising notes and lent them our Cape Breton cruising book that we had copied in Mabou.

And then, with roaring engines, the Poker Runners left. How quiet the marina became. The six of us walked the short distance to town. We ate an early supper at the MacBouche Pub—good and inexpensive food. The others went to church. We went back to the boat to make coffee to bring to *2nd Wind* later where we planned the beginning of our trip down the Nova Scotia coast.

NOVA SCOTIA'S EASTERN SHORE: WILDERNESS, SNOW CRABS, AND LUXURY

Before getting ready to leave for St. Peters lock, I sat in the cockpit for a brief moment while I finished my breakfast coffee. The breeze skimmed lightly over the water, and a blue heron fished from a partially covered sandbar. The pointed fir trees covered the dome of Hadley's Island and directed my gaze to the pale blue sky and white clouds. It was quiet on the docks. Here and there, I heard muted voices saying, "Good morning" and "How are you?" What an inspirational way to begin the day.

We motored to the lock and tied up to wait for an opening. I called the lockmaster on the radio—no response. I walked toward the swinging bridge and saw a telephone with a sign saying To Call the Lockmaster. I picked it up and dialed zero—nothing. I started walking toward the lock where I saw a sailboat locking through and coming our way. That meant the lockmaster would have to drive over to open the swinging bridge. We could get his attention then. Meanwhile, Jim called to me, "There's a telephone here." Right, I saw it. The only difference—the lockmaster answered it when Jim dialed. *Hmph.*

After we locked through, we used our GPS waypoints to pass through St. Peters Bay, across the entrance to the Strait of Canso, and into the town of Canso. There were many rock ledges to avoid. However, we found the passages to be well buoyed.

On this segment of the voyage, we would be cruising along the Eastern Shore of Nova Scotia to Halifax. This part of the shore is considered to be more rugged than the southwest coast after Halifax. We encountered small fishing villages, wilderness anchorages, and one elegant lodge.

As we motored across the calm water of St. Peters Bay, two humpback whales made a brief appearance and then disappeared. Several seals also monitored our progress. We passed along the eastern coast of Isle Madame, which forms the western boundary of St. Peters Bay. Our course took us between a small, barren, rocky island and the town of Arichat on Isle Madame. I noted a lighthouse and outbuildings that sat boldly on top of the island awaiting the storms that were sure to come. Arichat has a small harbor and government wharf. Its weathered houses face bravely toward the Atlantic Ocean.

Jim and I passed by the red and white buoy at the entrance to Canso Harbor and followed the range lights and buoys to a red buoy just before an island. The harbor was visible to starboard. Momentarily we were uncertain which way to turn. The chart showed two small islands that needed to be kept to starboard. These were in front of us. After a few more feet, we saw the channel to follow. If we had turned before the islands, we would most probably have found an unwelcoming rock. After the islands, we turned to starboard and saw a green building with Marina painted on it situated behind two breakwaters. We called the marina, but there was no answer. Regardless, *Misty* and *2nd Wind* motored in and found slips at the floating docks. Jim and I toured the harbor we had seen from the first red buoy. We saw several commercial wharfs, fishing boats, and a fish plant. Then, we joined *Misty* and *2nd Wind* at the marina. We were the only sailboats there. Several small runabouts were docked a few slips away at the shallow end of the lagoon. Happily, we were at the quiet end of town. The marina was not fancy, but there were clean bathrooms, showers, a washing machine, and a dryer. The dock had water and electricity.

The owner was out of town, but a friend of his collected the dock fees, and we enjoyed the luxuries of civilization.

Canso is the oldest continuously inhabited town in Nova Scotia, officially dating from 1601. It is the closest unfrozen corner of the North American mainland to Europe.

After settling in, we toured the historic settlement on Grassy Hill Island, the site of the first government of Nova Scotia, and then walked to town to shop at the grocery store. I picked a few raspberries along the way.

Back at the boat, I enjoyed raspberries and cream. When the supply was not plentiful, Jim would defer to my love of raspberries and eat another snack. For supper, I saved the chicken meat from the roasted chicken I bought at the store and used the bones to make chicken noodle vegetable soup. We'll eat the chicken the next day. We met on *Misty* for dessert and cards. The weather didn't sound favorable for the next day. We planned to stay another day.

We had blueberry pancakes for breakfast. Jim spent most of the morning charting and plotting courses, with consultation from me. We were thinking of taking the gunkhole route through some of the narrow passages. Around 11:00 a.m., all six of us sat at a picnic table to plan our courses for the next few days. It took a couple of hours to do it. Jim and I finished the chicken soup for lunch.

Tom Isele took his dinghy to the fishing docks to see if he could get some crushed ice for *Yankee Lady* and *2nd Wind*. Since Barbara was primarily a vegetarian and was lactose intolerant, she didn't need to keep food cold, so *Misty* traveled without ice. It was about half-tide when Tom arrived at the dock, which was high above him. He called up to a fisherman who said he could get the ice. Tom climbed onto a very black, old rubber tire, used as a fender for fishing boats, reached up as high as he could, and gave our plastic bags and his canvas bag to the fisherman who then returned them with ice. How different from driving to the corner store or supermarket.

Tuna season is starting this month and will last into October. Don Millen, the marina's owner, told me that over a hundred tuna boats would be arriving in this harbor within the next two weeks. We thought this marina was quiet and out of the way. Not always. Again, our timing had been perfect. The tuna boats will fill the entire marina. The captains pay one thousand dollars per season to stay here. Other boats will raft to one another off the public docks. Canso will be a busy place. Tuna is big business. The Japanese will pay thirty thousand dollars to fifty thousand dollars for a prize fish. When the tuna are landed, they are prepared for shipping. The heads and tails are cut off, and they are gutted. They are kept on ice for twenty-four hours to cool them down to the appropriate temperature. Then they are trucked to Halifax, placed on a plane, and flown directly to Tokyo.

We spent the late afternoon relaxing and preparing to leave the next day. I took a long, luxurious, hot shower at the marina; Jim put in GPS waypoints and filled the water tank. We met on *2nd Wind* for dessert. Rosie made a lemon pie with Shirriff lemon pudding mix and a prepared cookie crust topped with Cool Whip. We have become addicted to Shirriff lemon pie.

Morning dawned relatively clear and calm. The weather forecast was for southwest winds, ten to fifteen knots, becoming south, thirty knots, near the coast after midnight. Fog banks and occasional showers were predicted for Thursday. We planned to cruise to Isaacs Harbor, thirty-five miles away. Don Millen stopped by *Yankee Lady* to talk about navigating this area. He gave us some helpful hints about going through Andrews, Little Dover Run, and Dover Passages, noting that if the weather turned bad, we could anchor just past Dover Passage at Port Howe. How prophetic that was. We departed at 8:30 a.m. as planned.

We left the cliffs of Grassy Island behind, carefully following the charted buoys that led through Andrews Passage: red buoys on the left, green buoys on the right. We turned almost ninety degrees to the right at buoy PM9. Our course curved behind Andrews Island. Some of the buoys were small and hard to see; they would probably not show up on radar, so we kept our binoculars handy. The passage was beautiful yet threatening. On either side of us, the rocky coast bordered the northern woods. Some of the rocks and ledges extended ominously toward the channel. On a lighter note, we saw one small island on our starboard with a cabin and a sign which read Gilligan's Island.

At the end of the passage, we needed to make a sharp right and then a sharp left turn, honoring two very small buoys, one green and one red. Jim and I were leading. We found them with the binoculars. We also saw the waves breaking on the ledges *just* outside of these buoys. Shortly after this, we needed to choose between Little Dover Run Passage or the outside (seaward) passage. Barbara called on the radio and told us to look toward the ocean. We saw thin, gray wisps of moisture tickling the outer islands. We looked further and saw more gray—*fog*. Unanimously, we decided to take the outer route, which had no obstructions. The fog moved in quickly. Someone was watching over us while we had negotiated Andrews Passage!

The waves increased rapidly as we headed into open water. Soon we estimated we were climbing up and down ocean rollers at least ten feet high. The three-foot choppy waves, which mixed in with the rollers, made steering even more difficult. All we could see was water, water, and more water. We could barely see each other. Now, all that time spent planning and charting this section of the trip was about to pay off. Jim and Tom Frasca had calculated all the inner and outer GPS waypoints. We had written them on the chart and entered the buoyed ones into our GPS. Tom Isele had most of them; we read the rest of the coordinates to him over the radio. We set course for bell buoy PP1. *Misty*, with radar, took the lead; *Yankee Lady*, without radar, was in the middle; and *2nd Wind* was last. The GPS led us right to the buoy. We heard it before we saw it. We rounded its shadowy green presence and turned slightly to starboard heading for red whistle buoy P20.

Now the waves were at their worst. *Misty* was having trouble making headway. Barbara reported that she was also having trouble reading the compass and that her GPS was not working properly. *2nd Wind's* autopilot was not working, so Tom Isele had to steer manually. He could not see the radar that was in the cabin. *Yankee Lady* had no radar, but her GPS was working fine although the road tended to bounce left and right a little in the waves. Jim was at the helm while I looked at the chart, not easy in the bouncing and rocking boat.

Somewhere around buoy PP1, Barbara asked whether we should consider an alternate harbor such as Port Howe or Whitehead Harbor. *2nd Wind* wanted to keep going. Jim thought the waves might straighten out farther offshore. We decided to continue toward buoy P20 and make a decision en route.

Things got worse. Tom Isele radioed that he could not leave the wheel because it was too rough for Rosie to handle the boat. *Misty* could not hold her course in the waves. Jim was concerned that there was no margin of safety if an engine stopped or a rudder broke. No one could help anyone in these conditions. None of us had sails up in case an engine failed. The rocky coast offered no room for drifting. I looked at the chart and saw that we already had GPS waypoints calculated for two spots, Port Island and Whale Shoal, although they were not entered into the GPS because there were no buoys there. But these spots could guide us into Port Howe. Jim and I were confident in the numbers because we had both calculated them in the shelter of a safe harbor. Port Howe was close by and would get us out of the waves. *Misty* concurred with this analysis, and we all decided to change course for Port Howe after we passed buoy P20.

Just as we arrived at P20, I heard a call on channel 16 over our handheld radio, "Vessel in the vicinity of buoy P20, this is Blue

Bell." We were bouncing around; I needed to enter the new numbers for Whale Shoal, the first spot needed to enter Port Howe, into the GPS and/or plot a course on the chart to get a heading. The others were monitoring channel 78. I responded to Blue Bell who requested we switch to channel 68. I should have requested that we go to channel 78 so the others could hear, but in the confusion of the moment, I didn't think of it. I told him we were three sailboats. The captain told me he saw us on radar. He stated his heading and said that Blue Bell was a fifty-three-foot sailboat. I couldn't give him our intended heading after P20 right away because I was in the process of calculating it. I called the others to have them switch channels to 68. He said he was going to pass on the inside of the buoy. I told him we were already inside the buoy. He said, "Okay, I'll go outside and pass behind you." Shortly after that, Tom Isele, who was behind us, told us he saw them on radar, and soon we had passed safely. *Misty* never saw them on radar, and we never saw them visually. I was embarrassed because I had sounded like I didn't know where I was going. At last, I entered the new waypoints.

We changed course for the GPS spot we had entered outside of Whale Shoal. Whale Shoal was thirty feet below the surface, not really a shoaling problem for boats with five-foot drafts or less. Since this was simply an imaginary spot and there was no buoy there, I double-checked the coordinates with *Misty*. We agreed. The waves were now on our beam. *Misty* was having a difficult time. She would climb almost to the crest of a wave, stop her forward progress, and then slide sideways down the slope, veering away from her course. Briefly, Barbara couldn't use the GPS because Tom was entering the last waypoints. *Yankee Lady* was trying to follow close because of the fog, but it became difficult because we had to dodge *Misty*. At one point, we were within feet of her. Finally, I called to Barbara, "We can't follow you. It's too dangerous." Passing Whale Shoal and with a mile to go to the spot at Port Island, we decided it was safer to get in front of

Misty, even if we didn't have radar. I radioed to Barbara that we were going ahead.

There were many reasons for making this decision. This was a time when Jim and I were grateful for our past experiences. We were confident in ourselves; we knew we could rely on each other. We were confident in *Yankee Lady*; she had proven herself many times in wind and waves. The GPS was working well, and we were lined up correctly from our last waypoint; the "road" should lead us between obstacles. After a short passage between two ledges, the chart indicated deep water right up to shore. If we overshot our mark, we would see the land, even at ten feet, before we hit it. We were very alert as we continued shoreward.

We asked the others to tell us if they saw anything in front of us on radar. By now, in the lee of islands, Tom Isele was able to leave the wheel long enough to look at his radar. The tenths of miles went by quickly. We knew we were getting close to land but still could see nothing but gray. Then, at the same time that *2nd Wind* said, "You have land on your starboard side," we saw rollers breaking on our right, rising up, and crashing on Snorting Rocks Ledge. They were close, but safely away from us. Then the dark shape of Port Island appeared in front of us. It was comforting to find the land where it was supposed to be. We continued to within two-tenths of a mile from our final waypoint, which was another spot slightly to the northeast of Port Island. Again, *2nd Wind* said, "You better turn. There's land in front of you," just as we saw it. Following the charted deep water, we headed three hundred degrees into Port Howe Cove. We could then see the shadowy shapes of the island to our left and make out the land that defined the cove.

We all arrived safely. We circled in fairly close to shore where the depth was thirty feet. We decided to anchor here, individually, leaving lots of scope on our anchor lines. The current, wind, and tide change did weird things to our anchored positions. *Misty* had to anchor twice to get away from *Yankee Lady*. We thought the three boats were settled when suddenly, without any help from anyone, *2nd Wind* silently drifted by *Misty* and *Yankee Lady*. Tom Isele said quietly as he passed within three feet of us, "I always knew *2nd Wind* was a fast boat." Then his anchor line tightened, and he went back where he came from. We each decided to put out two anchors so that we could hold our positions better. This worked.

We were around the corner from the opening out to sea. At times, the fog lifted slightly, revealing the entire harbor, Port Island and Dover Passage beyond it. We could see the breakers foaming onto the rocks at the harbor entrance. We rolled gently in the swell, which worked its way in from the breakers. This was truly a harbor of refuge for us. It looked like we would be here for a day or two until things calmed down "out there."

Jim and I ate lunch and then settled down for a relaxing afternoon. I took two naps; Jim dozed on and off. The fog lifted a little and then clouded back in. We felt secure as we listened to the waves hitting the rocks. Every now and then, we heard the clang of a far-off bell buoy or a whistle buoy's mournful warning. We could see one small summer cottage on the nearest point of land, surrounded by a forest of pine trees. *Yankee Lady* had enough water and food to last for a few days. We were content.

I decided to try a new culinary endeavor. I wondered if our propane grill could be used as an oven. I had bran muffin mix, an egg, water, and a six-muffin pan. On faith, I invited everyone over for dessert after supper. Jim lit the grill and covered the grate with aluminum foil. I mixed the muffins, put them in the pan, and placed them in the grill. Twelve minutes later, we had fragrant, hot bran muffins. I kept them warm while I cooked the second batch. Everyone arrived. We ate fresh, warm bran muffins topped with home-made strawberry or raspberry jam or honey. *Tomorrow, I will try bread.*

The fog persisted. It was damp and cool, a good morning for sleeping late. We didn't wake up until 9:00 a.m. I looked out the hatch after breakfast and thought we were getting closer to the rocks. Jim reasoned that we had too much scope out which put us uncomfortably close to the rocks behind us. There wasn't much wind; we weren't pulling hard on either anchor line. He went to the bow and shortened our primary anchor line, then climbed in the dinghy and, still attached, pulled the boat backward toward the rocks. I cleated the line before he got too close to them. Then he backed the dinghy again while I tested the anchor line. It didn't budge. *Good.*

Given the success of the propane grill, my creativity went into high gear. Maybe I could find a way to use the alcohol stove inside the boat. My twelve-inch stainless steel Revere Ware frying pan with its domed lid was stored in a compartment under the V-berth. I also had a small, square wire rack that I had found at a tag sale and brought along just because. I mixed the bread, put it in a loaf pan, and placed it on the wire rack inside the frying pan. I lit the stove and monitored the heat by intuition and the smell of the bread. Everything worked and out came a real loaf of bread. I count this as one of my major cooking discoveries on this trip, and from then on, we had an "oven" on *Yankee Lady.*

Jim and I left the bread to cool and went for a dinghy ride around the harbor. We took the hand compass in case the fog returned and an umbrella in case it rained. We found a small cove (Casey's) at the head of the harbor. There was a rope stretching from tree to tree across the tip of the cove. We thought that locals perhaps pulled in here and tied up to the rope. To the right was a small, ramshackle dock with a sturdy ladder built onto it. A winding path led to a cabin on top of the hill. No one appeared to be there. We continued around the cove, passing by a small islet covered with trees. We crossed over to the next small peninsula where there was a small dock and a shack. We saw no one around any of these buildings. It seemed we three couples were alone in our protected "wilderness" cove. We rounded the peninsula and motored up the narrow Northeast Arm. Almost at the end, we shut off the motor to listen to nature noises. We could hear the brook rushing over the stones and boulders at the end of this small bay. Jim got this "aha" look on his face, reached into the dinghy, and pulled out our "golf" umbrella. He opened it and held it open in front of him, and we sailed downwind with our red, yellow, blue, and green dinghy spinnaker invention. We "docked" at a rock. I waited while Jim explored further upstream by foot. We motored back to the boat through some choppy waves, leftover swells coming in from the ocean. Once we reached our side of the harbor, it was relatively calm. We decided it was the best anchorage around.

Meanwhile, aboard *Misty*, Barbara spent time programming their GPS. Usually, Tom did this, but after yesterday, she decided they both should be able to do it. Then, they initiated their new propane grill by cooking peppers, onions, and sweet potatoes. While these were cooking, Tom sat in the cockpit near the dinghy which was tied amidships. He stood up to check the food. He heard a loud splash! He jumped, as did the seal, which had been about to board the dinghy. They could see the footprint left behind where the seal dove under the water. We met on *Misty* after supper. We, especially *2nd Wind*, hoped we could leave tomorrow. There were too much woods for Rosie and no dock.

It was clear enough to leave. We motored past the other side of Port Island and rejoined our original route to the GPS waypoint near Whale Shoal. As we looked at the narrow passages, the rocks, ledges, and breaking rollers nearby, we marveled at our safe voyage through them in the fog.

The seas were lumpy with five- and six-foot rollers, but it was nothing we couldn't handle. The primary challenge was to avoid staying below long enough to get seasick. I was tired. I found I could climb into the aft cabin to take a nap. The rolling of the boat was not as pronounced there. I was sound asleep when Jim called, "Judy, come out here. I need you." Out I went, no shoes and no sweatshirt. Later, we figured my foot must have hit the battery switch and turned it to the off position. The fog had rolled in. *Misty* was two miles behind on a different course than we were, and they were unable to find us on their radar. Tom Frasca was not happy. Nearby, *2nd Wind* was supposedly on *Misty's* course, except that they were not together. Tom Isele was changing course to rendezvous with *Misty*. We needed to stay with *2nd Wind* and their radar. Jim wanted to go below to check the chart, to make sure there were no obstructions between us and the course *Misty* was on. I took the wheel and followed *2nd Wind*. How quickly things could change from orderliness to confusion.

We finally got together again on the inside route that *Misty* was taking. Shortly after, the fog lifted. Jim had stayed below too long and was getting seasick. Nevertheless, he went below again to check the fuel level. It was too close to the one-fourth mark for us to be comfortable. *Yankee Lady* had an unpleasant habit of picking up air in a rolling sea when she was low on fuel. He lifted the six-gallon jerry can of fuel out of the storage area and set it next to the fuel tank filler. It had been his idea to use a kerosene pump to transfer the fuel, and he had packed it at the beginning of this voyage. This consisted of a rigid twenty-inch plastic tube, a syringe-type bulb, and a flexible plastic tube, longer than the rigid one. He placed the rigid tube in the jerry can and the flexible tube in the fuel filler hole. He squeezed the bulb to start the flow of fuel. Presto, the fuel siphoned from the jerry can into the fuel tank, another successful fuel transfer at sea.

The rest of the trip to Liscombe was uneventful. The six of us learned we needed to communicate better. We agreed that if our paths started to diverge, we should ask about one another's courses and not take anything for granted. After our planning meetings, we should make sure we had specific steps to take and that we all knew what the others were going to do.

We heard a boat named *Aurora* calling *2nd Wind*. Evidently, Tom didn't have his speaker turned up because he didn't answer. After a few calls, *Yankee Lady* answered. *Aurora* actually wanted to talk to any of us. They had read my last article in *Points East* magazine and recognized the names of the boats. The captain gave us some tips for entering the Liscombe River. He noted that it was narrow but well buoyed. He told us that Liscombe Lodge had four moorings.

As we were following the charted passage into the river, we called Liscombe Lodge several times to ask about available moorings. There was no answer. We continued up the tree-lined river to the mooring field in front of the Lodge. We circled by the dock where a young man appeared. He told us we could use the moorings or the dock. So *2nd Wind* chose the dock; *Misty* and *Yankee Lady* picked up moorings. The river at our mooring was very narrow and rocky on both sides, but the current always flowed out so we would always face in the same direction. *No problem.* The moorings cost twenty-five dollars a night, the dock, thirty dollars. With either of these, we could use all the facilities of the lodge—showers, laundry, tennis court, swimming pool, Jacuzzi, recreation room, fitness room, bikes, canoes, and hiking trails. The lodge spread out behind the trees on the bank of the river and was owned and run by the provincial government.

After I shut the engine off, I looked at the fathometer. It was blank. I thought, *Hmm, that's funny.* I tried the cabin lights—nothing. What's going on? I tried to restart the engine—nothing. Jim and I sat there, puzzled for a minute. Then Jim said, "Go look at the battery switch." I did. It was off. I must have kicked it when Jim woke me from my nap in the fog. When I bought *Yankee Lady*, the salesman who was demonstrating the boat said, "*Never* turn the battery switch to off while the engine is running. You will burn out the alternator." Well, we figured some good designer must have made this system idiot-proof because our alternator was fine and everything worked after we switched on the battery.

Last night, we ate supper on our boats in the wilderness. Tonight, we sat at a round table with a linen tablecloth and linen napkins. We enjoyed dinner listening to romantic piano music, including "Star Dust," "Smoke Gets in Your Eyes," "Misty," and the like, played by a lady seated at the piano near our table.

We were too tired and not ready to leave the next day, Saturday. The weather wasn't favorable on Sunday. So we took advantage of what the lodge had to offer. We joined Tom and Rosie for breakfast at the restaurant. After eating lunch and another supper in the restaurant, I was actually tired of eating out. All six of us met in the recreation room to do some charting on the ping pong table. We plotted our courses from here to Halifax. After, Barbara and I played a game of ping-pong. Tom, Tom, and Jim played a little pool. Jim insisted that he won even though actually Tom, the better player, lost because he accidentally sank the 8 ball. Jim and I played tennis. He insisted that he won at that also although I would argue the better player was me. At various times, everyone went swimming and relaxed in the Jacuzzi. The other four used parts of the hiking trails and picked raspberries and blueberries. Rosie brought me a plastic bag full of blueberries. Jim and I took a short dinghy ride to the base of the waterfalls at the end of the river and then dinghied back up the main river to the first island. We were impressed that the showers at the pool, marina, and recreation room all had full dispensers of soap and shampoo. Rosie discovered that the marina shower had a bathtub! She indulged in some luxurious soaking. We did our laundry and froze gallon jugs of water in the marina freezer. On Saturday, Tom, Tom, Rosie, and Barbara hired the van to drive them to church and the grocery store in Sherbrook, about twenty minutes away.

Sunday was Tom Isele's birthday, the big seventy. At the grocery store on Saturday, Rosie couldn't find a suitable birthday cake, so she bought two frozen single layer cakes and stacked them together. Tom wasn't exactly surprised because at the store, the clerk had said to Rosie, "The birthday candles are over there," while Tom was standing next to them. *What's birthday cake with-*

out ice cream? None of us had a freezer, so ice cream storage was not possible. Undaunted, Rosie walked up to the restaurant, told them the situation, and returned with six paper coffee cups full of ice cream.

While she was on the ice cream run, Tom made the coffee. He started with water and coffee in the pot. When it started to perk, he said, "Rosie always likes it full." At this point, he didn't think it was full enough, so he took the gallon jug of water and poured a large amount of water into the spout. The coffee pot coughed and sputtered and then started perking again. We watched Tom blow out the candles, sang "Happy Birthday" (we rival the Salvation Army for off key), and enjoyed the joint efforts of Tom and Rosie. Rosie couldn't find paper hats, so she bought each of us a small tartan hat magnet as party favors.

After getting fuel and water, we left Liscombe on Monday. We would decide whether to leave the protection of the river when we could see the condition of the ocean. In case we needed them, we had identified two protected harbors behind islands in the river opening.

It's a go. We followed our charted route. The ocean was rough. We rolled around a bit in the three-foot waves, but it was a short trip, about four and one-half miles of open water before we reached the shelter of more islands. At times, there were shoals, rocks, and small islands close by either side of us.

Hawbolt Cove is a small, relatively shallow indentation in the shore. Because of the protection of its two peninsulas and the off-lying islands, it is rated as a harbor of refuge. We passed the first wharf, where colorful fishing boats were tied up, and approached the second, which belonged to the fish plant. Jim called to someone on the dock, "Can three boats tie up here?" The answer was yes, but it gets shallow toward shore. Since it was low tide, we figured that if we fit now, we would be okay for the duration. *Yankee Lady* tied onto the face of the wharf, as always near a ladder. *Misty* and *2nd Wind* found space and ladders on either side of the wharf. We rolled a bit during the day, but the fenders did their jobs.

We walked across the street to the small general store that stocked an amazing variety of things, from food to fishing supplies. If you blinked, you would miss this town called Marie Joseph. There are a scattering of houses along the main road, which is two-lane Route 7. Grassy sloping meadows led to a blueberry patch (we asked) and then to a small pine forest. It was too late in the day to pick blueberries. Jim and I bought ice cream cones.

We talked to one enterprising eleven-year-old boy who was fishing from the wharf. He caught mackerel and put them in the bait freezer at the fisherman's dock. The fishermen paid him for his fish. He came back later with a friend and a six-year-old boy who was probably one of the boys' little brother. The older boys caught a large number of mackerel, which they threw on the dock near *Yankee Lady*. Jim saw the younger boy pull something heavy in. He said, "Oh you caught a big one."

The older boy said, "Naw, it's just a boot!"

But the little boy stood as tall as he could and said, "But there's a crab in it" (about two inches across). The boot and the crab were catch and release. The boys walked back down the dock and caught more fish. Meanwhile, we noticed a congregation of seagulls near us. Then the boys noticed the seagulls eating their catch at our end of the dock. They ran over, hollering at the seagulls who then flew over their heads to the just caught fish at the other end of the dock. The boys decided they better use their bucket to stow the fish.

After supper, we met on *Misty* to discuss whether there would be enough visibility to leave the next day. The weather forecast was not favorable.

I woke in the middle of the night because I felt cold drips of water on my foot. *Yuk.* Jim used a knife to wedge a paper towel into the leaking spot we discovered overhead. It worked. We will investigate later. At least the wind had calmed, the waves had stopped, the boat was not rocking, and the squeaking fenders were quiet.

Jim cooked a delicious breakfast—coffee and blueberry pancakes. We did some chart and GPS work and occasionally looked out at the fog. The moisture inside the boat was second only to the moisture outside.

Should we leave or shouldn't we? The fog lifted a little to reveal the islands just past the harbor and then shut down again. It was up to *Misty* and *2nd Wind* to decide whether they could lead through the fog. But Tom and Barbara were not yet comfortable with their radar, and *2nd Wind* still had no autopilot. It was my feeling that unless we had everything going for us, we should stay put. Things could deteriorate rapidly in bad weather. We decided not to go.

We were getting to know some of the local people. Jim was in the store talking about our radar problems. A young fisherman, Richard Pace, who was the son of the lady who ran the store, told him about a couple of his friends, one who fixes radar and one who sold them in Halifax. When it looked as if we were going to stay, he called his radar-fixing friend, Claude, and asked him to come over. He arrived within a half hour. Together, Jim and he reviewed what Jim had done and rechecked the wires. The verdict—the radar was dead. No charge. He and Jim shook hands, and Richard gave Jim the name and phone number of his friend in Halifax. Jim called him to line things up when we get to Halifax.

We met another fisherman, Randy, who was Richard's uncle. Randy and his father, Elvin Turner, own the fish plant. It has been a family business since it was started by Randy's great-grandfather. Randy gave us a tour through the buildings. They were all impressively clean. One room contained a furnace, a blower, and a dryer. Layers and layers of trays lined one side of the wall. He told us that only a few years ago, five thousand pounds of fish, mostly cod, were dried here every day. What a contrast to the old, wooden drying racks earlier fishermen had to set out on the beach. I guess success had its price though. Now, there were not enough fish to keep this operation going. The buildings are for sale.

He showed us the lunch room, which reminded me of a teacher's room in school, only this one was for fishermen. There was a long white table with white benches placed in the middle of the room. There were bathrooms (which we could use) at the end of it. Another building contained ice. We looked inside at the mountain of finely crushed ice made from saltwater. Randy told us we could take some if we needed it. He told us that the shovel was in the building across the street at the head of the wharf. Before we left, we filled our ice chest. As in Dingwall, we almost thought it would last forever, much longer than freshwater ice.

The wind was forecast to change direction and come from the south or southwest. Jim and I decided to turn *Yankee Lady* around so she would be heading into the wind and waves. He organized the lines while I climbed into the dinghy. This time, I got to play tugboat captain. Jim attached the dinghy painter to the stern cleat. I backed out and to the left remembering that when backing, you point the motor in the direction you want to go, something I learned way back in my Boston Whaler Harpoon. *Yankee Lady* swung around, Jim retied the lines, and that was that. We also decided to put an anchor out midship off the port side. Jim wrote *Yankee Lady* Anchor on one of our orange buoys, attached it to the anchor line as a float, and took the anchor, float, and line out about seventy feet where he dropped the anchor. We used the winch to tighten the anchor line and keep ourselves off the dock. That eliminated the squeaking fenders.

While Jim was preparing to cook chicken on the grill, Elvin walked over to tell him that the forty-five-foot blue fishing boat at the end of the fishermen's dock would be coming over to this wharf to get ice around 9:00 p.m. *Misty* would have to move.

Tom and Barbara decided to move around to the other side of the dock and slip in behind *2nd Wind*. This proved to be a good choice. They were out of the way and sheltered from the wind and waves somewhat by the tall dock.

We met aboard *Yankee Lady* for dessert and our usual cards. Just about on the dot of 9:00 p.m., two fishing boats powered over to get ice. The first one was in and out with no problem. The forty-five-footer, however, was hovering near our buoyed anchor line. The captain shined his searchlight on it. I went out and shouted to him that it was an anchor line. While we were watching, Jim said to the group, "If he gets tangled in our anchor line, we'll be following him out to sea," but the captain avoided it and headed into the dock. *Crash!* The side of the fishing boat hit *Yankee Lady's* bow pulpit, which was perhaps sticking out a little too far. We all piled out of *Yankee Lady*; Jim checked for damage. The pulpit was a little loose, but everything was intact. The running lights on the bow railing were okay and still working. We figured later that the bow pulpit stanchions had been on the loose side anyway, which probably cushioned the blow. The fishermen on the wharf ran over to check for damage. Everyone, including the captain, was truly concerned.

The fishing boat was named Ocean Preacher. It took up most of the dock. Tom and Barbara were *very* glad they had moved *Misty* to the other side. We climbed onto the dock to watch the proceedings. It was getting dark, and the dock was illumined with bright vapor lights. Ocean Preacher's bright, white working lights illuminated her deck as if it were day; she also displayed the red over white lights on the mast above the cabin (red over white, fishing at night). Ice had been brought from the ice house to the dock in large plastic bins. Randy picked a bin up in the forklift, raised it to the level of an aluminum chute, and dumped the ice into the chute. He manipulated that forklift as if it were an extension of his hand. One of the crew members shoveled and pushed the ice down into the hold. Other fishermen were standing on the dock, which was now wet with melted ice.

We talked to the captain, Larry Whynot, while this was going on. He said the boat was an Indian boat and that he could fish as a native, but he preferred to fish under his commercial license. He said that he obeyed the Eastern Shore Fishermans Protection Association and provincial rules and did not support the outlaw Indian groups who were trying to seize power over the fishery. He said that sometimes these Indians were set up by the white man (telling where to sell their illegal fish, etcetera). Then he said, "Oh, I'm sorry. I shouldn't have said that."

Jim laughed and said, "As long as you don't call us pale faces, I guess it's all right."

This boat would be fishing for snow crabs. The crew was allowed to bring in seventy-five thousand pounds this season. There was a minimum size for male snow crabs. Female snow crabs were small and seldom caught in the traps because of the size of the netting. Sometimes, a government agent would go along to randomly check the traps. Sometimes, the captain had to take a black recorder box that would record the boat's location and date. Larry said that he also had his own smaller boat at home near Liverpool where he and his brother have fished for tuna as well as other legal fish.

We talked about our sailing adventures, radar, equipment, and charts. He apologized for hitting us. To explain why it happened, he said, "Come over here," and he showed us *Ocean Preacher's* wheelhouse. The wheel was three feet from the floor. The captain's seat was five feet from the floor. If Larry stood on the floor to steer, he couldn't see out the window. When he sat on the seat, he could see out the window, but he had to use his feet to reach the wheel. He explained that this should have worked, but then, he tapped one of his legs. It was made of wood; he could only steer with one foot! Having loaded the ice and boxes of frozen mackerel bait, Larry and his crew left to go fishing.

In the morning, the fog was so thick even the seagulls were grounded or flying on instruments. After breakfast, Jim removed the headliner panels over the V-berth in order to get at the bow pulpit stanchion bases. He also removed the wooden panel, which was just before the point of the bow. My job was to use a Phillips screwdriver on the outside of each stanchion to keep each bolt from turning while Jim tightened them from below. Three hours later, the stanchions were tight and not leaking, and my hands were stiff from holding the screwdriver for so long. We decided to move *Yankee Lady* back a few feet so her bow would not stick out over the end of the dock. We didn't want to get smacked again by a fishing boat. Jim manipulated the lines, and it was done.

Meanwhile, the two Toms were working on *Misty's* outboard engine. They took it apart, cleaned it, and put it back together again. *No improvement.* They requested Jim's help, so after lunch and a brief trip to the general store with me, he and Tom F., with Tom Isele watching, took apart the outboard. Jim found a speck of dirt in the high-speed jet of the carburetor. Tom cleaned it, and presto, good as new.

Barbara also asked Jim if he could look at their radar. They were having trouble adjusting the gain to get a clear picture on their LCD unit. Tom Isele had improved the picture, somewhat, but Barbara and Tom wondered if it could still be better. Jim may have improved it a little more. However, he told Tom, in his opinion, he didn't think the LCD unit could pick up the smaller targets that the CRT units could. Both *2nd Wind* and *Yankee Lady* had CRT units.

Rosie and Tom went for a walk and picked blueberries. We met on *2nd Wind* for dessert and cards. The men won. Rosie gave each of them a plastic bag of blueberries for a prize. If the women had won, we would have received the same prize.

The fishermen used cell phones to call in their arrival times two or three hours before they were due. We heard that *Ocean Preacher* and Claude's boat were due in at 9:15 p.m. and 9:20

p.m. to unload their crab catches. Elvin Turner scheduled the trucks, notified his workers, and called the officials from ACD so that everyone would be at the wharf on time. ACD was hired by the government to make sure no fisherman exceeded his quota.

Tom, Rosie, Jim, and I waited on the dock until the first boat arrived, and then we sat on top of *Yankee Lady's* cabin to watch this unfolding "fishermen's ballet." What an example of coordination and teamwork. Two tractor trailers were parked at the end of the dock near the road. They would take the crabs to a processing plant in New Brunswick. The workers arrived at 9:00 p.m. They set the stage on the wharf. They wheeled a scale to the end of the wharf, right next to *Yankee Lady*. They used a forklift to place a large bin of shaved ice near the scale, and they put a wooden pallet between the ice and the scale. Two forklifts waited by the pallet and the bin of ice; two tubs were placed upside down in front of the scale to be used as a working table. Over three hundred gray plastic tubs were placed nearby to hold the crabs. Some held sixty pounds, some held fifty pounds, depending on which company would be processing the meat. A man stood by the yellow crane ready to activate it. A lady wearing olive-green rubber bib overalls and gray boots stood by the hooks at the end of the crane's pulley. Two men waited by the scale. The ACD man stood behind the men at the scale, clipboard in hand. Bright vapor lights illuminated the whole scene.

Then, a white light appeared out of the dark as the first boat rounded the point. Speculation ended as to which boat it was when Claude's smaller, faster, thirty-eight-foot boat took shape out of the gloom. Claude, our radar helper, nosed the boat up to the wharf, and the crew secured the dock lines. The stern extended past the wharf in front of *Yankee Lady's* bow. We were glad we had moved back.

Claude and his crew of four were jubilant. They estimated they had taken 8,500 pounds of snow crab. The aft end of the boat was sectioned into boxes about six square feet. Each box was loaded with crabs covered with ice. It seemed to us that the whole deck was one big mass of slowly writhing crabs. We thought they would never run out of boxes to unload. A stack of empty gray tubs was passed over to the boat. Claude stood at the side of the boat next to the wharf. The four crewmen, wearing rubber gloves, threw chunks of ice overboard and scooped salmon-colored crabs into the tubs. The crabs were alive but docile, being almost frozen. It seemed like long crab legs stuck out everywhere. When a tub was full, they slid or lifted it over to Claude.

The lady on the wharf grabbed the hooks at the end of the crane's pulley, walked them over to the boat, and handed them to Claude. Claude hooked them onto a full gray tub. The crane operator lifted the tub while the lady guided it over to the upside down tubs. The crane operator let the full tub down. Two men grabbed it and placed it on the upside down tubs or on the scale. There was another empty tub nearby, which was used for overflow crabs.

Then the ballet went into high gear. The two men grabbed a tub, hoisted it onto the scale, checked the weight, and either added or removed crabs. The ACD man stood behind and looked over the shoulders of the men at the scale watching the weight recorded on the scale and making notes on his clipboard. In unison, the two men lifted the weighed tub and slid it onto the wooden pallet. The man at the ice bin shoveled ice over the top of the tub. The two men weighed another tub and lifted and slid it onto the pallet; the man shoveled ice. The boat crew scooped crabs, the lady walked back and forth with the hooks, Claude attached them, and the crane operator raised and lowered the gray tubs of crabs. The weighers adjusted their pace to keep up with the incoming crab tubs, faster at peak and slower toward the end. The forklift picked up twelve tubs at a time from the pallet and drove to the waiting truck backed onto the wharf. Other men loaded the tubs onto the truck making sure the load was balanced.

It was a perfect, rhythmic dance. No instructions were given; all knew their parts. No one collided; all moved gracefully around the wharf to the melodies of sliding tubs, the backing, beeping forklift, the slush of the ice hitting the crabs, the jangle of the chain being unhooked from the tubs, and the joking and talking of the workers.

It was cool and damp; we wore sweatshirts and jackets. Most of the crew and workers wore no coats; they were warmed by their physical exertion. At times, we sat on the cabin top; at times, we stood on the bow talking to the boat crew. Someone must have mentioned my journal to them. Jim climbed onto the wharf to take a picture of them scooping crabs. One young man said, "If it goes in a book, my name is Jeff." Three of the men on the wharf jumped when Jim used the flash; lightning had been seen nearby.

Finally, after a little over an hour, the boat was empty. When the final count was tallied, the crabs weighed in at 9,120 pounds—that was a lot of crabmeat! You could tell Claude was happy; he grinned and gave us a thumbs up sign.

Elvin buys the crabs for $2.60 a pound, pays his workers, and sells the crabs to the processing plant. Claude pays his crew a salary; some captains pay their crews on shares. There were boat expenses and association dues to deduct, but nevertheless, this was a good day. The boat left the wharf to motor back to the fisherman's dock while we called back and forth, "Good luck. Have a safe trip. We enjoyed watching."

Ocean Preacher had been waiting at the other dock. Larry motored her over to the wharf. As he approached, we called out, "We moved the boat back."

He called back, "I noticed." We gave him a good-natured cheer when he tied up without hitting *Yankee Lady*. His arrival was more subdued. He had lost twelve pots, some of them probably poached. He estimated his catch at 6,500 pounds. Incidentally, Claude had lost one pot with about 1,000 pounds of crabs in it. What happened to the crabs? The trap netting was biodegradable. Eventually, the crabs could crawl back onto the ocean floor, which in this case was 720 feet below the surface.

Larry stepped out of the wheelhouse and said, "I'm glad this day is over." The unloading process was similar except that *Ocean Preacher* had a hold; nothing was stored above deck. Larry opened the hatch to the hold and extended a ladder into it. The crew took some tubs, went below, and started loading crabs. They hooked two tubs at a time, and the crane lifted the crabs out. Larry guided the tubs to the lady on the dock. Since there were fewer crew members, it took longer to unload this catch. Finally, someone in the hold called, "Last tub coming up." This catch weighed in at 7,500 pounds. The wharf cleared quickly. The workers put the equipment away and left. All was quiet again. It was late. Larry decided to leave the boat at this wharf. In a low voice, he asked us if we wanted some crabs; he had saved some for us. He will keep them on ice until tomorrow.

Blueberry pancakes for breakfast again, compliments of Rosie. This was not exactly a hardship. Jim took apart *Misty's* radar while Tom F. watched. Jim was looking for any visible defects, such as broken wires, that could be fixed. *Nothing.* Midmorning, Larry walked over to ask what we wanted to do with the crabs. Jim talked about cooking them on the grill; Larry said he would be leaving overnight, and we could cook them in *Ocean Preacher's* galley. This would be a lot easier and less messy for us. Jim asked him how to cook them. Larry made a face and said, "You're not going to like this part." At this point, I said, "I'm not watching."

Here are the gory details. With two hands, grasp the legs, one set on each side of the body. Bend them down. Place the front of the upper shell, where the eyes are, on the edge of a protruding object, such as the edge of a table, and pull down, ripping the entire upper shell off the crab. A lot of black gelatin-like substance runs out. The upper shell falls into a waste container. Break the lower body in half. Remove the gills and other nonedible parts. Shake and bang the legs and joints against a solid surface to remove the rest of the black stuff. After preparing, steam in a small amount of water as soon as possible. Larry gave us a tour of the boat, showing us the still iced down crabs and the galley. He said that if he's not around later, we could just use the boat.

Even though it was damp and misting off and on, I decided to go blueberry picking on the hill. Rosie came with me. We hiked across the muddy path, up the meadow to the blueberry patch where there was a plentiful supply. There was also a plentiful supply of mosquitoes. The grassy meadow was decorated with glistening, intricately woven, spider webs, each silver strand clearly defined by the clinging mist, nature's artwork. I saw one small gold-colored spider making its way through the blueberry plants. Jim left the radar project and joined Rosie and me. When we were finished, I had a large bowl full of blueberries.

From this hill, we could see the harbor and the many shapes of the islands in Marie Joseph Bay, where we would go as we left the harbor. We had heard that some fishermen had attempted to grow mussels in this bay. Thousands of dollars of seed mussels had been placed inside their netting. When they grew big enough to crawl to the outside, the ducks had thought, *Dinner*, and eaten all of them. Elvin said not to mention ducks around here.

We returned to the boats. It was now time to clean and cook the crabs. Tom Frasca and Jim went down in *Ocean Preacher's* hold and followed Larry's directions. When the leg portions were sufficiently cleaned and separated, Jim and Tom F. put them in a bucket. Tom Isele pulled it up, put the crab legs in pots, and iced them until cooking time. When the cleaning was finished, Jim steamed the crabs in two batches. Meanwhile, I was playing with blueberries. I made a batch of cooked blueberry jam, a dozen blueberry muffins, and a no-bake blueberry pie.

We gathered on *Yankee Lady* for a feast of snow crab legs, blueberry muffins, steamed cabbage, carrots, and salad. It took us a long time to eat it all.

I heard *Ocean Preacher* leave in the middle of the night and went back to sleep until seven. The weather had cleared; we could actually see the islands in Marie Joseph Harbor. The forecast was for southwest winds, fifteen to twenty knots decreasing to ten to fifteen knots, and seas one to two meters, decreasing to one meter or less. This was a good scenario because we would be heading into improving conditions.

At 8:00 a.m., Rosie and I made some last-minute purchases at the store.

I said to the store owner, "This has been a great stop for us. We wanted you to have twenty dollars from each boat 'for the good of the dock.'"

She replied, "Thank you so much." She added, " Elvin really appreciated it but it wasn't necessary.

I added, "We knew that but we wanted to do it anyway."

Rosie and I returned to the boats and we prepared to leave. Jim cast our lines off the dock, and pulled in our anchor. The others untied also. As we motored out of the harbor, I waved at Elvin who was watching from the dock. He waved back. Since *2nd Wind's* fathometer was not working and we hadn't stowed all our gear, *Misty* led out of the harbor, following the GPS waypoints we had all plotted. During the last leg out, Jim put up the mainsail. The others did the same. Jim called *Ocean Preacher* on channel 6. Larry's reply was loud and clear. He said the seas were not as bad as they had been when he left; there were not as many white caps. His reply was loud and clear because he was almost back in the harbor. His crew, Albert, was seasick and unable to pull pots.

As we left the shelter of the islands, the seas built, probably to two meters (a little more than six feet), and the southwest wind was in front of us. It was a good thing we had a GPS waypoint for buoy VV1 because it was about one-half mile off station, appearing north of Long Island instead of south of it. We had charted our next course from that buoy. If we had been in the fog and depending on hearing the bell, we could have run into the island! We called the Coast Guard to report the discrepancy.

We could not hold our course of 266 degrees toward buoy XH1 because periodically, large waves would almost stop *Misty* and *2nd Wind*. As usual, *Yankee Lady* was not running at full rpm, but we felt we needed to stay with the others. Unless we tacked off the wind, our sails would not be full enough to give additional power. So we all did. Jim reefed *Yankee Lady's* sail to give us a more comfortable ride. We were still averaging only between three and four knots. At this rate, we would not arrive at our intended destination, Jeddore, until after dark. After a quick radio conference, we decided on our alternate port, Sheet Harbor Passage. Now we had to figure out exactly where we were and how to get in.

On *Yankee Lady*, Jim became seasick because he had been doing some work below. To add to his discomfort, his back also went out, which immobilized him temporarily—not the best thing to happen on a rolling boat. This left me to run the boat. Using the GPS, Jim read me the latitude and longitude of our current position. I plotted this point on the chart. It looked like we had a clear shot to buoy XK1; the others thought so also. From there, we could head to buoy XP7, which was part of our original contingency plan, should we need Sheet Harbor Passage. Tom F. and I both drew lines on the chart between the two buoys. We saw one small problem, this course would take us very close to a rock and a shallow area at Pumpkin Island Ledges. We decided that if we stayed to the left of the GPS road, it would take us to the left of the target; we would be in the clear.

Because of Jim's discomfort, I increased our speed and started a series of small zigzag tacks toward buoy XK1. I moved ahead of *Misty*, thinking to make all possible speed to get Jim into flat water as quickly as possible. At the same time, *2nd Wind* called to say he was having trouble keeping up. Even though he felt awful, Jim reminded me that we needed to stay together in case something happened to one of the boats, so I slowed down.

I don't know what happened to the improving weather conditions. The wind and waves increased. *Yankee Lady's* bow would descend into the trough of a wave, pick up some water, and toss it over the dodger. We were soaked. Fortunately for us, the autopilot kept right on working, and we could retreat behind the dodger—not so with *Misty* and *2nd Wind*. *Misty's* freeboard was too low, and the waves would fly over the dodger and hit them. *2nd Wind's* auto pilot was broken, so Tom had to stay behind the wheel.

We rounded XK1 and started heading toward shore and buoy XP7. At Jim's suggestion, I made a rough estimate of the distance of the rock at Pumpkin Island Ledge from buoy XP7. The rock was about two and a half miles before the buoy. This told me that when the GPS indicated we were three miles in front of the buoy, I should be especially vigilant and make sure I was well to the left of center on the GPS course. All three boats stayed to the left, and we passed by with no problem.

From our angle of approach, green XP7 was in front of an island. The color blended into the green of the island and was therefore difficult to see. It was obvious that we needed to turn before the island, but where? There was shoal water between the buoy and the island, so we couldn't overshoot the buoy. Thank goodness for the GPS. We spotted the buoy when we were about half a mile away. Just in front of it, we turned north toward our last waypoint, XP15. Our passage opened up between two islands. Our morale increased as we lined ourselves up with the range markers on shore. This extra boost made us feel better as we passed by Bad Luck Shoal and Deadman Island. We turned to port at XP15, motored by Factory Point into the protected bay of Sheet Harbor Passage, and anchored behind Sober Island. The waves never really let up until we made this last turn. How peaceful to sit in the cockpit enjoying the view—pointy pine trees, rocks and seaweed, boulders, a few houses, an old wharf.

A gentleman, who owned the moored sailboat near us, rowed over to *Misty* in his dinghy. He welcomed them and asked if any of us needed supplies. He also invited us to a church supper and said he could supply us with transportation. He said he hadn't done much sailing this year because of the bad weather. *Amen to that.* Misty thanked him and reported to us. We didn't take him up on any of his kind offers. We were too tired, and Tom, Tom, Barbara, and Rosie wanted to finish their leftover crab for supper.

After supper, we met on *Yankee Lady* to enjoy the remnants of the last blueberry-picking expedition: no-bake blueberry pie, graham cracker crust, and Cool Whip. The weather for tomorrow does not sound like a good day for traveling.

This eastern shore was not letting us through without a struggle. We woke to rain, which became rain and wind by noon. Jim and I spent the morning listening to the radio and talking. I typed some, and he worked on the charts. I decided to try another cooking endeavor—English muffins. The recipe was in the computer, and they did not require an oven for baking. I mixed the dough in the morning and let them rise. After lunch, I cut them out with an upside down glass, let them rise for twenty minutes, and then cooked them in my twelve-inch Revere Ware frying pan coated with corn meal, seven minutes on each side. They actually looked and tasted like English muffins.

After lunch we talked to 2nd Wind and Misty on the radio. Tom and Rosie were reading, warmly wrapped in blankets. Tom and Barbara were finding leaks and feeling damp. Tom found that *Misty's* battery needed water and the diesel fuel had "white stuff" in it—depressing thoughts for a cold, rainy day. Jim and I were keeping warm with our alcohol heater.

Jim picked the rest of our allotted crabmeat out of the shells; he was up to his elbows in crab. We heated the resulting crabmeat in butter and ate it, together with a tossed salad and three-cheese instant mashed potatoes. Another kindly gentleman, Mr. Levy, motored across the harbor in his small yellow boat. He also stopped at *Misty* to ask if anyone needed supplies. He told them his son was a boat builder. I'm sure he could not imagine we were eating a gourmet crab supper in this isolated place.

At 7:00 p.m., we conferred on the radio to establish tomorrow's courses. I then offered English muffins to anyone who wanted to come and get them. *Misty*, with a revitalized outboard motor, said they'd be over. They knocked on the hull and said, "Delivery boat." I gave them two packages: one for them, one for *2nd Wind*.

I said, "This is just like Block Island," where Aldo motors around the harbor in his Boston Whaler, selling baked goods from his bakery. They motored over to *2nd Wind* and said, "Bread delivery, Aldo's of the north."

We left at seven in the morning; it was cool and damp. The seas were almost calm with just a small ocean swell that I didn't think ever went away. We motor-sailed through small patches of light fog, but as the day progressed, the sun came out, and visibility improved under a blue sky.

Boat traffic increased as we approached Halifax. The presence of sailboats, powerboats, a freighter, and a Coast Guard ship made it seem more like familiar Long Island Sound. Halifax harbor is large and deep. The city is set on the port side. We passed cargo docks, Navy docks, and downtown Halifax. One long building displayed paintings of signal flags. I went below to consult our signal flag chart and figured out they said, "Welcome." We continued under the Narrows Bridge into Bedford Basin, turned to starboard, and approached the breakwater in front of the Dartmouth Yacht Club.

The dockmaster directed us to the breakwater. He told the other two boats to tie up on the face dock at the beginning of the first row of slips. He told us to turn right at the first channel and take the fourth slip on the right. The wind was blowing across this channel. *Misty* and *2nd Wind* tied up with no problem. Jim motored into the narrow space between the breakwater and our assigned channel. As he started to turn in, he saw a twenty-two-foot powerboat trying to back into another slip. Suddenly, we needed to wait while the powerboat jockeyed back and forth several times before successfully tying up alongside his slip. The wind was trying to blow us backward. *Misty* and *2nd Wind* were taking up space on the outside of the dock, which gave us less room to maneuver. But by continuously adjusting the throttle and alternating between forward and reverse, Jim held *Yankee Lady* in place. Finally, we eased into the slip, I jumped off to tie the lines, and Jim turned the engine off. *Thank you, Jim, for your expertise, and thank you,* Yankee Lady, *for being so maneuverable.*

We were welcomed to the Dartmouth Yacht Club by the dockhand who told us that the first night was free for members of other yacht clubs. Each night thereafter would be twenty dollars. *Fair enough*, we thought.

It was 6:00 p.m., and we were hungry. Some friendly members of the yacht club told us about Brewbaker's Restaurant, which was within walking distance of the marina. The six of us enjoyed a good meal and good conversation.

In the morning, someone gave Tom Frasca a ride to the Yanmar dealer who was on the other side of Halifax. He was able to get the parts he needed. Back at the slip, John, the dockhand, told Barbara she needed to move *Misty* over a few slips. Tom Isele went over to help her.

Somewhere along the way, Barbara had told me that docking *Misty* was one of her greatest anxieties. Today was no exception. The wind was blowing down the fairway; the slip was upwind. As Barbara backed away from the dock, *Misty's* bow turned the wrong way, downwind. This meant that Barbara had to back up the fairway past the assigned slip and then motor forward to enter it. She wrote in her journal, "Not a pretty picture. *Misty* doesn't back well or in a straight line. Tom Isele was embarrassed. He tied me up and left. Don't blame him! The dockhand, John, said, 'I see you have one of those boats that don't back up,' and said something about the rudder and the prop being too far aft. I felt vindicated because no one believes me." Oh well, I guess we all know, docking is not an exact science.

Jim spent the morning looking the radar over once more, wiggling a few connections, and, in general, not making any improvements. Then he called Gordon Hart, the name given to him by Claude back in Marie Joseph. Gordon picked up the radar and took it to his shop. Meanwhile, Tom Isele got his autopilot back, all repaired.

I needed a few groceries. Someone at the yacht club told me there was a coop store one block away. Barbara, Tom, Rosie, and I walked over. When I entered the store, I asked the manager if we could get a ride back to the boat. I explained that we would be able to buy more if we didn't have to carry it. She was doubtful, but she found a clerk who would take us in his car.

This was really a wholesale store; many items, including meats, were packaged in large quantities. Nevertheless, I filled a grocery cart half full. The others found necessary supplies also. Because they were finished before we were, Tom and Rosie left their packages in the front of the store for us to pick up. I was behind Barbara at the checkout counter. She paid her bill. The clerk rang up my purchases, $105. I got out my Visa card. Oh no, they didn't accept Visa. I did not have the necessary cash, and I did not have my checkbook. Thinking to use my Visa debit card to get cash, I asked for the nearest bank. It was next door, around the back of the building. The coop was due to close at 4:00 p.m. It was 3:45 p.m. I found the bank, which also closed at 4:00 p.m. They didn't take Visa cards either. The nearest Visa bank was blocks away. *What to do?* Then I remembered that I had never canceled my Mastercard when Jim and I were married. I was sort of sentimental about it because I had a ridiculous credit line—$40,000. I dug it out of my wallet and handed it to the cashier asking for a mere $125. I was back at the coop about one minute to 4:00 p.m. I paid the bill and joined Barbara and the young man who gave us a ride back to the yacht club.

Gordon Hart returned. The radar needed a new magnetron, which would cost at least $700. Even if we fixed it, we would still have a radar that was outdated and discontinued. It had served us well. But now, we decided to get a new one. Jim suggested that Gordon keep the old one for parts. Gordon recommended Atlantic Electronics in the nearby industrial complex. He told Jim to use his name and to bargain with them. The favorable exchange rate should also help us.

Jim needed to get to Atlantic Electronics and back to the boat with the new radar. He asked the friendly folks at the yacht club how he could get a ride. Someone suggested a powerboater working on his boat at the dock. Jim asked him. Yes, he could borrow the car until 5:00 p.m.

Jim bought the radar, took it back to the boat, and unpacked it. It was 4:00 p.m. The others decided to go to a restaurant called China Town across Bedford Basin from the yacht club. I would have liked to have gone, but Jim really wanted to get the radar in. Reluctantly, I agreed. That did make sense, and I would be glad when it was done. We waved as Tom, Tom, Barbara, and Rosie motored past us aboard *2nd Wind*. It was about a half-hour trip to the restaurant. Jim finished in time for us to walk to the restaurant near the coop grocery store where we enjoyed a leisurely meal. It was kind of nice to be just the two of us for a change.

The next morning, we left Dartmouth in calm weather and bright sunshine. We motored back under the Murray MacKay Bridge at the Narrows, an area that played a significant part in the history of Halifax. We had heard about floating docks near the Sheraton Hotel where we could tie up for the day, or perhaps overnight.

As we approached the floating docks by the Sheraton, *Misty* turned aside to investigate. The docks were attached to pilings placed next to a large concrete pier. Space was available for boats only on one side. The other side was too close to the concrete pier. *Yankee Lady* and *2nd Wind* continued to the Maritime museum.

There was no space there, so we radioed *Misty* and turned around. By the time we got back, *Misty* had already docked, and Tom was on shore trying to find a dock attendant.

Misty was tied up at the outside end, bow facing the channel. Another sailboat was tied up a boat length behind *Misty*. I estimated that there was enough room to fit *Yankee Lady* in between the two of them. There was another space, close to the city end, where *2nd Wind* could fit. The wind was blowing off the dock, which would make the approach more difficult. There was not a lot of space to maneuver.

Tom was at *2nd Wind's* helm; I was steering *Yankee Lady*. Jim started to put out fenders and get the dock lines ready. I was in a hurry to get in, so was *2nd Wind*. I should have learned from past experience that this was not good. As I started my approach, *2nd Wind* passed in front of me. I should have slowed down and waited, but I didn't. Barbara ran down the dock to take *2nd Wind's* lines. As I approached the dock, Jim climbed over the lifeline at the bow and stood on the edge of *Yankee Lady* with the bow line in his hand. I had the stern line ready to throw to him after he jumped on the dock with the bow line. I powered in bow first. Jim was poised to jump. I needed to make sure the stern would clear the sailboat behind us. The wind was blowing us off. I turned too soon, and the bow swung away from the dock. There was too much water for Jim to jump across. He lost his balance and saved himself from falling into the water by falling backward over the lifeline. Barbara let go of *2nd Wind's* lines and sped up the dock to us. I threw her the stern line; Jim regrouped and threw her the bow line. Somehow, *2nd Wind* managed to get tied up also.

I thought, *I should have learned this lesson by now, never hurry your approach to a dock. Yankee Lady* has a fiberglass scar on her side from the time I rushed things, years ago, at the Edgartown, Massachusetts, water barge. Jim could have fallen between *Yankee*

Lady and the dock. A scarred or injured Jim would have been unthinkable. Fortunately, his back survived, and he wasn't injured.

We found that this dock was free for the day, but to stay overnight would cost $1 a foot. The terminal for the Dartmouth-Halifax ferry was a short distance from this dock, and the wake from the ferries caused us to periodically bounce uncomfortably. The weather forecast for the night and the next day was for rain and winds from the south, twenty-five to thirty knots. The south wind could make this harbor rougher than we would care for. We decided to stay for the afternoon and motor to the Armdale Yacht Club at the end of the Northwest Arm later in the day.

Tom and Rosie left to find a restaurant. The rest of us ate lunch on our boats and then set out to explore the waterfront. Halifax has the world's longest downtown boardwalk, not quite two and one-half miles. Shops, restaurants, and tour boat ticket offices line this symbol of Halifax's revitalized shoreline. Historic old buildings, usually brick, line the narrow streets leading away from the water. Toward its seaward end, the boardwalk opens into a plaza, which is in front of the entrance to the Maritime Museum of the Atlantic. Vintage ships and boats were tied to the adjoining wharves.

Halifax boasts the world's second largest natural harbor. Ships and the sea have shaped her history. The displays in the Maritime Museum document this history. We visited two specific exhibits documenting maritime tragedies. Halifax was the closest harbor to the Titanic when it sank. Crews were sent out to search for bodies. Many bodies were lost at sea but one hundred fifty were retrieved. They are buried in three Halifax cemeteries.

During World War I two ships collided approaching the Narrows at Bedford Basin. One was loaded with munitions. The subsequent explosion created the largest man-made explosion prior to the Atomic Bomb. The entire north end of Halifax was destroyed. Over 1700 people died; more than 4000 were injured and 6000 people were left without shelter. Among the relief efforts the people of Boston immediately sent a train loaded with supplies and medical personnel. To this day, the people of Nova Scotia send a Christmas tree to Boston as a thank you gift.

While Tom and Barbara walked to the Citadel, we visited with Tom and Rosie aboard *2nd Wind*. We left at 5:00 p.m. to motor five miles around the tip of Halifax proper and up the Northwest Arm to Armdale Yacht Club. Once we entered the Arm, we were sheltered from the wind, and we glided through smooth water. As we approached the Yacht Club, I tried several times to reach someone on the radio. *No answer.* Finally, when we were almost there, the launch driver responded on his hand held radio. There were no slips available, but we could use the moorings on the outer edge of the mooring field.

It was my turn to pick up the mooring line. Jim turned *Yankee Lady* into the wind and approached the mooring ball. I snared the line with the boat hook and then grabbed it with my hands. *Yuk!* Wouldn't you know, my turn and the mooring line was slimy black-green with sharp little shells embedded in it. I secured it and went below to wash my hands.

We ate supper in the cockpit and watched a sailboat race take place around us. Since we were on the outer edge of things, boats sailed close by both the bow and stern of *Yankee Lady*. I sat forward and took notice. A short distance away was a sixteen-foot wooden sloop with a comet insignia clearly visible on the mainsail. As the couple sailed by, I called over, "I used to sail one of those when I was a kid. What year is it?"

They hollered back, "1947, my father used to own it." It had obviously been lovingly cared for. I thought back for a minute, remembering all those times on Long Island Sound when my girlfriend and I would take a picnic lunch and a portable radio and sail near Larchmont, New York. We would listen to the New York Yankees ball games, swim a little, and sail a lot.

We woke to a gray, cool, damp day. The wind blew, and fog drifted in and out. Someone at the yacht club found slips for our three boats. We moved gratefully, thankful to be able to walk around and use the clubhouse. We ate lunch at the restaurant, appreciating both the food and the warm, dry atmosphere. As we have found throughout this trip, the people were friendly and interested in our adventures. We asked permission to use some of the tables downstairs to lay out our charts to plan the next few days. *No problem.*

Later, Tom and Rosie went to a shopping center; Tom, Barbara, Jim, and I walked around the end of the Arm to the Binnacle Chandlery, the biggest in Nova Scotia. Jim had brought our big, colorful golf umbrella. It started to rain. Barbara and Tom left.

Someone had told us about the convenience store next door where they sell huge ice cream cones. We decided we couldn't let this ice cream opportunity go by. We bought two cones. There was nowhere to sit in the store, so we started walking back to the yacht club and eating under the outspread umbrella. We found that ice cream melts really fast in the rain. We exhausted our supply of paper napkins, but somehow, we both managed to finish in a relatively neat fashion.

We met again in the evening to finish charting. The weather report for tomorrow is iffy. We will wait and see.

AROUND CAPE SABLE: FOG, FISHING PORTS, AN OVERNIGHT ADVENTURE, HALIFAX TO NORTHEAST HARBOR, MAINE

Morning was gray and damp in Halifax. The tops of the city buildings disappeared and reappeared in the mist. We delayed our departure from 9:30 a.m. to 10:30 a.m. to see if the weather would improve. We sat in the clubhouse because it seemed warmer and dryer than the boats.

We left in slightly improved visibility. We rounded Chebucto Head and found our way through the prickly Sambro Ledges Passage. There was enough visibility (a little better than a mile) to see the buoys marking this passage and to see some of the rocks and ledges outside the marked passage. This part of the voyage would take us along the southwest coast of Nova Scotia, around Cape Sable to Yarmouth, and across the Bay of Fundy to Northeast Harbor, Maine.

The fog thickened as we entered the final leg for Taylor Island. Our course took us close to points of land and between islands, which would suddenly emerge darkly out of the fog. Our radar and the GPS gave us precision and comfort in navigating that we never knew in the old days.

Yankee Lady passed just in front of a red and white Coast Guard buoy tender, which was anchored in a stretch of open water. At first, it looked like an island in the fog, one that wasn't supposed to be there.

Finally, the proper buoys and Fleming Island appeared. Jim and I turned to starboard into a narrow slot of water behind Taylor Island, motored in slowly, and anchored, practically next to the trees. *Misty* and *2nd Wind* followed. There wasn't room for much anchor line scope. *Misty's* and *2nd Wind's* anchors held, but we dragged. We tried to anchor three more times in various places. We began to wonder if the anchor would ever dig in, but we had no choice; we had to keep trying. The last time put us in front of *Misty*, not too close. We had enough swinging room and enough scope.

The sun came out revealing several more islands and points of land at either end of our sliver of water. We heard the surf pounding the rocks on the ocean side of Taylor Island. Inside, though, the water was still and calm. We thought we were in a really secluded spot until several boats passed through. One was a small runabout with a tooting horn and a stuffed animal moose for a bowsprit. Another was a working fishing boat. I figured they may have come from one of the small towns on the nearby mainland. I wondered if they were curious to see who was anchored here or if this was actually a shortcut between islands. Since these boats were passing through our anchorage from east to west, I asked the fishing boat captain if our five-foot draft sailboats could leave through the western end of Taylor Island. "Yes," he said, "just steer clear of the point."

After dessert on *Misty*, Jim and I sat in the cockpit and watched the path of the Milky Way appear in the moonless sky. The stars sparkled against the dark; several shooting stars streaked toward the horizon.

We woke to calm wind, calm water, and sun shining on the cockpit drying up the morning dew. Breakfast was a delight as we drank in the view. Our narrow slot of water was flanked by Taylor (oceanside) and Moore (bayside) Islands. A few spruce trees stood out among the rocks, boulders, shrubs, and grass that covered these islands.

Although the fishing boat captain had said the western passage was okay, Jim and I prefer to check things out for ourselves. We took the dinghy to the west end of the island to observe this passage. We noted a ledge beginning to uncover on the ebbing tide, just off the first point of land. There was a large group camped on the ledge at the tip of Taylor Island. A fishing boat was anchored just offshore. We watched it leave, motoring between Taylor Island and the rocky islet in the middle of the opening. This looked like a good path for us. We reported our findings to the others.

Misty and *2nd Wind* left ahead of us, bound for the Town of Mahone Bay. We planned to detour to Deep Cove, slightly north of the town, to anchor overnight and join them on Sunday.

We decided to explore Taylor Island before we left. We took the dinghy to the eastern end, looking for a landing spot. From the water, we saw a pirate flag flying above a campsite, deserted for the moment. There were three army-type green tents, an outhouse, two picnic tables, and a rusty, old fuel tank, converted to some kind of stove. A bench and two transplanted front seats from a vehicle were placed on the rocks for rest and relaxation. There were two small moorings waiting for the next boat visit. It was not exactly wilderness, but it had character.

We turned around and found a small indentation on the shore. Jim powered the bow of the dinghy against the slippery, seaweed-covered rocks. I found a small toehold and fell (on purpose) forward to a large bare boulder. I climbed up and pulled the dinghy painter tight. Long-legged Jim stepped off onto the boulder. We climbed through brush and over rock ledges to the top of the hill.

We looked at the views surrounding the island. Shoreward, two peninsulas jutted into the water. There were two small fishing villages hugging the granite coast. The bay was dotted with islands and ledges, none of which we saw when we passed through in the fog. The lighthouse at Peggy's Cove stood tall to the northwest, about two miles away. Oceanside, small blue and white fishing boats were inside a fishing weir, outlined with orange buoys. The crews were hauling in their catches. We watched *Misty* and *2nd Wind* leave the harbor.

I had brought two plastic bags for berries but found only five blueberries and one raspberry. I had to eat them to keep my hands free for climbing rock ledges. We climbed back down by a different route, but it wasn't much easier. We found the dinghy, took giant steps across the seaweed to climb (fall) in, and motored back to *Yankee Lady*, now the only boat in the anchorage.

We left through the western opening we had noted from the dinghy. Two fishing boats were coming in from the ocean as we rounded the first point. One was towing three dories; they both turned toward shore and anchored off the ledges where the campers were. We proceeded out with no problems; we never saw less than twenty feet of water. Much later, when I looked back at the chart of Taylor Island, the slot of water looked tiny. I asked myself, "How did we do that?"

We sailed and motor-sailed. We passed by Peggy's Cove lighthouse where we could see tourists walking on the large, sloping rock ledge. We crossed St. Margaret's Bay and entered island-studded Mahone Bay where there are said to be 365 islands.

The others went directly to the town of Mahone Bay. We decided to inspect Deep Cove, which was supposed to be beautiful. It was a disappointment, but the trip through the islands of Mahone Bay was not. A series of vistas opened all around us. Islands blended together and separated, houses stood in small clearings, and channels appeared between forested islands. Other boats, slipping through this magical land, crossed our path or darted ahead bound for another island or anchorage. We saw numerous anchorages behind islands, some with sandy beaches, most covered with my favorite pointy pine trees. The small settlements were protected from the ocean surge by the many islands.

What a contrast these islands were from the rocky islands we left behind this morning. This could be the Casco Bay of Nova Scotia.

As we approached Mahone Bay Harbor, we saw *Misty* and *2nd Wind* on moorings. No one was on board, so we proceeded to the head of the harbor to ask about moorings at the marina. No one answered. We headed back out, met a launch, and found that we could pick up a mooring near the others. There was a dinghy dock next to the public wharf.

We took our laundry and dinghied ashore. The Laundromat was in the next building over from the wharf. We put our clothes in the washing machine and walked down the one main street of town, ignoring the ice cream store next to the Laundromat in favor of eating out later. We met Tom and Barbara and then Tom and Rosie as we walked about. I went to the grocery store at the other end of town while Jim went to the hardware store across the street. I thought he was coming to the grocery store and was judging my purchases according to the carrying power of two people. But I met Tom Isele in the store who said Jim was going back to the Laundromat. I put back the cantaloupe and was considering dumping some other things when Tom, who had two gallons of water to carry, said he would use a grocery cart to carry the packages back to the dock and then return the cart. We met Jim sitting on a step halfway back. It seemed I had most of the quarters for the laundry. Quarters were hard to get because the change machine was out of order. All the laundry doers had been asking nearby store owners for quarters, and they were running out. We put my quarters in the dryer and took the groceries out to the boat. We returned for the laundry later and ate at a small cafe overlooking the water.

The next day, Sunday, was a beautiful blueberry muffin morning. The sun was shining, the water was calm, and we were at rest on a town mooring. Jim and I cooked the muffins in the Revere ware pan "oven"; I ate two apiece and shared the second batch, by dinghy, with the others on *Misty* and *2nd Wind*. Tom, Rosie, Tom and Barbara went to church while we relaxed and/or worked on the charts. It was nice to not have to hurry.

They returned with a church story. There was no Catholic church in town, but there was an Anglican one. Tom Isele belonged to the Episcopal church in Old Saybrook, so the four of them decided to attend the Anglican service. Tom, saying that he knew the order of service, marched everyone to the front of the church.

The four of them were wearing their Sunday-go-to-meeting clothes (same ones for different ports). Barbara and Rosie wore dresses, and each had on a wide-brimmed hat. Hats were not required in church; they were the only ones wearing them. The men wore long khaki pants. Tom Frasca had on a checked shirt. Tom Isele, at the head of the procession, wore his Fourth of July American flag shirt. Not only did they feel conspicuous because they were in the front, but their clothes announced that they were not locals. It got worse.

Tom Isele did not know the order of the service and neither did the other three. The ladies, trying to be subtle, peaked over their shoulders to see what the people behind them were doing. The men, however, pivoted around and took a good look. All four of them did this at the same time. Sometimes they were sitting when everyone else was standing, but more obviously, sometimes they were standing when everyone else was sitting. Undaunted, Tom Isele sang loudly in his best barbershop voice. Rosie and Barbara were thinking, *Wait until we get Tom Isele outside.* After the service, the curious ones greeted them and asked where they were from, but Barbara, Rosie, and Tom Frasca vowed that never again would any of them follow Tom Isele into church.

We left our moorings at 1:00 p.m. We tried sailing downwind, but the wind wasn't strong enough and the sun was hot, not that we were complaining about sunshine. When we changed direction at our GPS Spot G, we were heading too close to the wind to sail. But the motor-sailing was fine with beautiful scenery, no big waves, and blue sky.

We rounded the breakwater at Lunenburg, and the brightly colored town buildings, perched on a hill, appeared before us. We followed the buoys until we were opposite the Fisheries Maritime Museum, then turned to port, and picked up mooring buoys. The guidebooks had not been clear at all about these moorings, but there was nothing to it. We were opposite the famous *Bluenose II* schooner.

Jim and I sat in the cockpit and admired the view—famous Lunenburg. There was a gentle breeze with blue sky overhead. We were secure and at peace. It was times like this that made us forget damp, gray fog, soggy clothes, mildew in the boat, and cold feet!

Lunenburg is a picture postcard town. The waterfront is lined with functional, wood frame buildings—brick red, bright red, blue, and white. Wooden wharves, supported by evenly spaced pilings, extend out from most of the buildings. Each slot between the wharves is occupied by boats, some fishing, some pleasure, and some antique. The *Bluenose II* was berthed at the Fisheries Museum of the Atlantic. The streets ascending the hill are lined with residential houses, and a church was situated near the top.

You've heard of Camelot? Well, around here, it is slightly different. A large, black, deep sea fishing trawler was called *Cachalot I.* We hoped they did.

Tom and Rosie went ashore for dinner. Jim roasted potatoes and onions on the grill and then cooked steak for me and hot sausage for him. Roasting potatoes and onions, individually wrapped in aluminum foil is one of Jim's signature culinary accomplishments. It doesn't come without risk. I remember the time the grill wasn't securely tightened on the aft rail. It tilted slightly downward while potatoes and onions slid off and plopped into the water. But Jim, in his black Speedo, was equal to the challenge. Instantly, he dove into the water and recovered all of them.

The next morning, we ate breakfast ashore, joined by Tom and Rosie. Barbara and Tom arrived just after we finished. We stood on the dock next to the *Bluenose II* while her crew prepared her to leave for Halifax. The *Bluenose II* is the pride of Nova Scotia. She is a replica of the original *Bluenose*, a fishing schooner that fished the Grand Banks and competed in schooner races. She never lost a race. What a stately magnificent sight she was, all two hundred ten feet of her, as the captain backed her away from the dock. She gave three long blasts from her horn to signal her departure. As her sleek, dark hull left the harbor, all the other boats at their wharves saluted her with long blasts from their horns. It gave us goose bumps.

Jim and I walked to the marina at the other end of the harbor to see if there would be a place to dock for fuel. We decided that there was not enough room for three boats to tie up. We would use the dinghy and the jerry can. We paid our bill for the mooring ($11.50) at the Yacht Shop, bought a few souvenirs and walked back to the Fisheries Museum of the Atlantic.

We toured the Theresa E. Connor, a Grand Banks dory fishing schooner built in 1938. Except for the engine, I wondered if this was the kind of boat my great grandfather Stillman Nickerson captained off the coast of Nova Scotia.

Misty and *2nd Wind* motored over to the marina to get fuel. *Misty* was tied to the floating dock, and *2nd Wind* was tied to the next wharf because there was no more room at the floating dock. When Jim arrived in the dinghy, they were both sitting and waiting for fuel. It seemed that one of the owners was attending a funeral. He had shut off the electricity needed for the fuel pump because the painters were working around the electric wires. He would be back in an hour. Undaunted, Jim went to the Yacht Shop office and found a ride to the nearest gas station for himself and Tom Isele. They took their jerry jugs, filled them with fuel, and called it good. *Misty* waited for the owner to return.

I was busy while all this was happening. I plotted the GPS waypoints for the day (sometimes it's hard to keep up with the charting), took off the sail cover, and generally prepared *Yankee Lady* for leaving.

We left at 1:30 p.m. motor-sailing downwind in smooth water. Suddenly, off Rose Point, *Yankee Lady's* engine began to sputter and surge. Jim diagnosed the problem—dirty fuel. He went below to change the primary fuel filter (we always try to have spares). I shut off the engine so he could work on the fuel system. Then I adjusted the sails for downwind sailing, jib on one side and main on the other—wing and wing.

Jim changed the primary filter, and I restarted the engine. There was no improvement; it must be the secondary filter. I shut off the engine again, and Jim changed that filter. Then he had trouble bleeding the engine to get the air out and the fuel in. The little lever attached to the fuel pump was not sufficient to pump the fuel. Finally, Jim took the oil-changing syringe and put it in the opening. That worked; he got rid of the air, and the engine purred again.

Meanwhile, I was sailing. The wind changed slightly, I put jib and main on the port side, and we picked up speed, not that I wanted to. We were approaching the next buoy on our course where we would change direction. That new course would put us closer to the wind, and the boat would heel over more. I figured this would not be a good thing while Jim was balancing himself and the filters below. I consulted the chart and found that there was clear water straight ahead. I furled the jib to slow down and continued past the buoy. Shortly after, the engine was fixed. Jim rejoined me in the cockpit, and we retraced our path to the last buoy. Then we followed our planned course into the La Have River. The wind, now from in front of us, was blowing at twenty knots with gusts to thirty. I was very glad we did not have to tack into that strange territory under sail with no motor backup although I'm sure we could have done it if we had to.

We found the large red building with the sign, "LaHave Bakery and Outfitters. Welcome". This was our destination. We approached the dock to the smell of freshly baked bread. *Misty* and *2nd Wind* tied up to the floating dock across from two other boats. We picked up the mooring nearby. Two small wharfs jutted out far enough into the river to protect us from the wind and the white caps. The bakery occupied the front of the building. There was a small dining room furnished with this and that tables and chairs. Jim and I ate soup and a sandwich for supper. Barbara and Tom had sandwiches. Tom and Rosie snacked. Barbara, as dessert hostess, got creative. She told us each to pick out a dessert square, featured in the bakery showcase. She would pay for them, and we would meet on *Misty*.

The next morning, I made French toast from the Portuguese sweetbread we bought yesterday at the bakery. Jim is from a Portuguese family; he has many fond memories of his mother's sweetbread, especially the ones prepared during holidays. We swung on our mooring and ate outside in the sunshine enjoying the ambience of the scene. The La Have River is wide here, still buoyed and navigable for fishing trawlers as well as us. Neat houses grace the road next to the river. A few had small docks with two or three fishing boats tied to them. Small rolling hills, plowed or wooded, rose behind the road and houses. *Misty* and *2nd Wind* sat quietly against the floating dock.

We were underway at 10:00 a.m., again in light wind and bright sun. The mouth of the La Have River was dotted with islands, not as friendly as Mahone Bay, because of the many lurking rocks and ledges, but it was a smooth trip. The ocean was as flat as we've ever seen it on this trip. We motor-sailed, just off the wind. Jim waited to put the jib out until I finished assembling a salad for lunch. It was much easier to function below when *Yankee Lady* was upright.

As we neared Liverpool/Brooklyn, I called *Ocean Preacher* on channel 6 on the VHF radio. Larry's father answered. The *Preacher* was still up north, but Larry was here in Brooklyn, working on his boat, *Ohma*. I told his father how much we enjoyed meeting Larry and that we would try finding him on his boat. Larry's father signed off, saying, "Finest kind."

We motored toward Liverpool Harbor just to see it because it was strictly commercial. As we passed by the entrance to Brooklyn, someone at the marina called, "Sailboats entering Liverpool Harbor" on channel 16. Tom, aboard *2nd Wind* answered. The man told him there was no docking in Liverpool (we knew that) but that there were plenty of slips at the marina. That was a first—the marina calling us about slips. We continued around the bend in the Mersey River to Liverpool. One large, old ferry was tied to a wharf. There were also four fishing trawlers, one of which partly belonged to Larry's father. The harbor ended at a small bridge. We turned around, motored back around the curve and across the river to Brooklyn. The three of us tied up at the long face dock, *Yankee Lady* on one side, *Misty* and *2nd Wind* on the other.

Some members from the marina/yacht club helped us tie up. They were extremely friendly. They told us that showers and water were available. There was no charge for dockage or services, but donations were accepted. Buddy, the large black dog, supervised the activities on the dock and gladly played throw the stick, catch the stick with me later while Jim called Larry from the clubhouse.

Larry's wife said he was working on *Ohma*. Jim and I walked over to the fisherman's dock and found him deep down in the boat. Jim had to climb down the ladder and get on the boat to get Larry's attention because he was cleaning the bilge with a noisy high-pressure water wash pump. We invited him and his family out to dinner.

Larry borrowed his mother's car so we wouldn't have to ride in the back of his pickup. His wife drove the three children and took Jim (who elected to ride with the kids) to the Chinese restaurant in Liverpool. Besides a good dinner and a visit with Larry and his wife, we got our grandchildren fix for the trip. To us, this family represented the real Nova Scotians, native or not—down-to-earth, hard working, honest, and sincere.

Larry returned with us to the boats. We visited with him on *Yankee Lady*, and then all went to *2nd Wind* for dessert and coffee. It was interesting to listen to Larry talk about his boating life—we shared the same water but different worlds.

We left Brooklyn at 9:00 a.m. in calm water and calm winds. It was cool and partly cloudy. As we motor-sailed, Jim and I let the autopilot do the work. We sat under the dodger on our navy blue "chair" cushions, out of the breeze, warm and comfortable, looking here, looking there, and checking our course on the GPS.

We passed a small rocky islet. On it, a lighthouse pointed toward the sky. We thought we saw a small house next to the lighthouse, but when we looked through the binoculars, we saw that it was a small cruising/fishing boat sitting high and dry. Tom Frasca called over the radio, "I guess he found the lighthouse all right." For that boat, the name of the island was certainly appropriate—*Little Hope*.

We found our way to Lockeport Harbor and motored by the breakwater entrance. The marina was in front of us. There was no room at the dock. Jim and I tried to pick up one of two mooring balls. We found they were not moorings but some sort of line rigged by the fishermen. Jim and I motored across the harbor to the fishermen's wharf, a public dock. We asked a man working at the end of the wharf about dockage. *No answer.* We circled around to the other side and saw no one. We decided to raft to a fishing boat, climb up on the wharf and find someone to ask. Just before we did that, a young man parked his truck on the wharf and climbed down to his boat, which was tied to a floating lobster car raft. The raft was tied to the wharf. We asked him about available spaces. He said he would move his boat to the other side so the three of us could be together on the raft—another example of Canadian hospitality. We tied up on the face of the raft and then decided to move around to the side so the other two could tie together against the face. Jim stood on the raft so he could manipulate bow and stern lines to slide us around, bow into the wharf. I ran around *Yankee Lady's* deck, changing lines from one side to the other and moving the dinghy, it seemed, all at the same time. It all worked; we tied up and then helped *2nd Wind* come in. *Misty* rafted onto *2nd Wind*. We sat comfortably in our little corner of the harbor, cockpits facing each other, ready for the conversations to come. We dinghied across the harbor to the dinghy dock.

The six of us ate supper at the White Gull Restaurant. The proprietor also owned the marina. The fish was fresh; the scallops, also fresh, came from the fish plant up the block. It was relaxing not to cook after a day on the water.

We woke to fog and light winds. The marina owner said we would not be able to get fuel until midday. This was too late for us to pick up a favorable tide, so we relaxed and didn't worry about the fog. The sun came out in the afternoon.

Lockeport Harbor is man-made. Breakwaters define the outer edges and shelter the harbor from any direction of wind. It is an active fishing harbor. The large fish plant processed scallops, crabs, and lobsters. We noticed another, smaller fishing wharf at the northern end. The town is compact; it was easy to walk to any of the stores.

In the afternoon, Jim and I took the dinghy out of the harbor entrance and motored in shallow water among some of the nearby islands. My perspective was definitely different when cruising over shallow spots worry-free.

We sat on the boat and watched a group of young teenage boys jump or dive into the water. They jumped from a nearby fishing boat or from the wharf and climbed up on our lobster car raft and then up the ladder back to the dock. They invited us into the water. For me, it was no way, but Jim considered it. He decided the water was too cold. We gave them some chocolate/caramel cakes wrapped in cellophane.

Jim cooked pork chops on the grill. We sat outside in the sunshine to eat a dinner of pork chops, stuffing, carrots, and applesauce. It looked like the weather was a no-go for tomorrow.

Morning was foggy again. Barbara returned from her foggy morning run with a report of a miniature harbor scene. When she ran out in the fog, she noticed a bunch of model-sized boats all sitting in the mud. But when she returned, the tide had come in, the sun was out, and they were all floating. She saw a regular flotilla of miniature boats. The Coast Guard vessel was painted red with a white stripe. There were gray navy vessels, colorful fishing trawlers, two- and three-masted schooners, and sturdy dories. A red sea buoy and a green one marked pretend channels. The whole scene sat there, waiting for the people who take the walking tour of Lockeport to imagine their own salty stories.

The six of us spent quite a bit of time talking about the next part of our voyage. Our next major challenge would be rounding Cape Sable, sometimes called the Cape Horn of Nova Scotia. There were two possible passages: inside and outside. The outside was smoother and safer. The inside was shorter, more adventurous, and scenic, but tidal streams were powerful, and the bottom was shallow and irregular. Sometimes there was an upwelling of deep, cold water that could create thick fog when the sun was shining everywhere else. I reminded everyone that we would be entering the Bay of Fundy, which is famous for tricky currents and fog. We agreed that we *must* go with the current. When even a light wind opposes the current, a lively chop could develop. One cruising book noted that in these conditions, you would have green water all over your deck. Once you were committed to the inside passage, there was no turning back. You would not be able to buck the current and you would be sitting in some of the roughest water on the East Coast.

A look at the names on the chart readily revealed the nature of this area: Horse Race, The Rip, Tail of the Rip, Rock on the Rip, etcetera. We figured that at the worst, it was bigger and farther to go through than our familiar Long Island Sound Race (where Jim lost a dinghy to a standing wave that overtook him) plus you would have to go around a corner at the same time.

The boys came back to swim again. This time, Jim decided to go in and check the propellers on all three boats. *Misty's* had a lot of grass, which he removed. Then he went to the other side of the raft where the boys were diving into the water. They challenged him to see who could swim under water the farthest. He dove in and surfaced near the fishing boat across the way. Guess who won? Gramps.

We left at eight the next morning to take advantage of the favorable current. It was a gray day; rain was predicted, but the seas were relatively calm, and there was good visibility. Predictions were for northwest winds ten to fifteen knots becoming light by evening. In reality, we left in north*east* winds, which put the wind slightly behind us. This was a little warmer than if it were blowing in our faces. Nevertheless, a few more degrees of warmth would have been welcome.

We arrived off a bony mess of rocks and ledges, called The Salvages, around 11:30 a.m. We had watched the waves breaking over some of the outlying rocks for some time before we arrived there. We gave these ledges plenty of room and began our turn into Port La Tour, about two miles away.

The wind increased. It always seems to increase when you start to head into it, but this time, it really did pick up. Looking to windward, the seas were black, with waves topped by whitecaps; they looked formidable and cold. We were glad to be heading toward a harbor. Jim and I and the others turned our boats into the wind at the red and white (MoA) fairway buoy to take down our mainsails. We made excellent time, arriving off Port La Tour by 12:30 p.m.

There were two public wharves: one on the north side of the harbor, Upper Port La Tour, and one on the south side, Port La Tour. We motored *Yankee Lady* into the southern one first. There were some floating docks, but fishing boats took up all the space. We called the others to say there was no room. We all crossed over to the north side. By now, it was blowing hard. 2nd Wind peeked in, saw some fishing boats rafted 3 deep, left and announced it was too crowded. Feeling we didn't have much choice, Jim and I slowly motored through the opening. Immediately to our starboard was an empty spot on the dock. We decided to tie up and try to find someone to ask about space. There was not much time to think about it, not enough time to get out fenders and lines. The wind was blowing us toward the dock. Jim headed for it, and, smush, *Yankee Lady's* rub rail was hugging a square timber.

We were at the dock; the wind was pushing us against it, and we weren't going anywhere. Then we tied up properly. Meanwhile, *Misty* came in with fenders out and lines ready. They rafted to the fishing boat in front of us. Jim went to find someone to talk to. *2nd Wind* came in and saw a space against the dock in the corner, in front of the fishing boat. The wind wedged him against the wharf also. Then he adjusted his fenders and lines. We may not be able to get out until the wind lets up, but at least we were secure and safe for the moment. Jim couldn't find anyone around. We will investigate later.

We had arrived at high tide. We needed to calculate the depth of the water at low tide. We didn't want to sit in the mud. Jim consulted Reed's almanac to find the range of tide for Port La Tour. We figured there would be a drop of 7.6 feet, which would give us 5.4 feet at low tide. There would be just enough water! I wouldn't have wanted to be a lobster trying to crawl under our keel.

Jim and I ate lunch—hot soup, cocoa, crackers, and peanut butter—comfort food. After, as we stood on the dock, talking to the others, a pickup truck drove out. The fisherman had come to shut the hatches on his boat (the one *Misty* was rafted to). He said there was no problem with where we all are. No one else should be coming in, and he was not going anywhere.

It started to rain and continued to blow. This mess was not predicted, but we had found space for the three boats again, and we were safe and dry.

Jim and I lit the alcohol heater, which warmed the cabin. We took long naps, relaxed some more, made chili for supper, and joined the others on *2nd Wind* for dessert and cards. Barbara reported that when she returned from a walk at suppertime, Tom was so cold that he sat hugging the warm pressure cooker.

It was low tide. To get to *2nd Wind* required climbing from *Yankee Lady* twelve rungs up to the dock and then down twelve rungs to *2nd Wind* by vertical ladders. The ladders were built in between the dock pilings; they had metal rungs and a metal hand hold on top. No problem, we were all used to these ladders by now. It looks iffy for rounding Cape Sable tomorrow. We will listen to the weather tomorrow morning at 7:00.

At 6:50 in the morning, I climbed out of bed, put the coffee on, and looked out the companionway hatch to see fog. I crawled back into the warm bunk and turned on the handheld radio in time for the seven o'clock weather. As I snuggled under the covers, I heard predictions of fog, clearing later in the day, with light winds becoming ten to fifteen knots by afternoon, and seas one meter or less. Tomorrow's forecast was for strong winds. I would have loved to stay in that warm bunk a little longer, but it was not possible. We held an early morning radio conference and voted to go. Even though it was longer, we all agreed to take the outside route around Cape Sable. None of us wanted to encounter the tricky currents and narrow passages of the inside route when we couldn't see around us.

Jim and I had time for breakfast before we left at 8:00 a.m. Thank goodness for hot coffee. We left the harbor slowly in about two hundred yards of visibility. The water was so clear we could see the bottom ten feet below, but we really didn't have time to study it. We were concentrating on the radar and peering into the fog. The radar showed the buoys we had noted on the way in: the red buoy at Whale Rock and then the clanging red and white "safe water" buoy. We saw each of these visually as they loomed out of the fog just before we passed them. After the red and white buoy, there were no more obstructions on our course.

Other than the three of us, the radar indicated one boat behind us. It was outbound heading toward the buoy where we made our right turn. The rest of the time it was just *Misty*, *Yankee Lady*, and *2nd Wind*, alone in our shroud of fog. We stayed close to each other for companionship and security. Jim set the radar range at one mile, taking it up every now and then to look farther and check for traffic. For miles, there were no targets ahead of us and just the two small blips behind us—*2nd Wind* and *Misty*.

We all had entered a GPS waypoint for an imaginary spot in the ocean three miles off Cape Sable, an imaginary spot, which we called spot 8. As we neared it, the fog became thicker. *Misty* and *2nd Wind* briefly dropped out of sight. Even though Jim and I could see them on radar, we slowed down. It was more comforting to see them visually. We all turned up the ranges on our radars, trying to at least see Cape Sable electronically. *Nothing*. Then we remembered the cruising guide had said the land was so low it wouldn't show up on radar. It was disappointing not to see this symbol of our adventure: the southernmost point of Nova Scotia where ocean currents meet the swift currents of the Bay of Fundy.

We encountered a few strange seas, lumpy waves, and eddies of current but nothing to really shake us up or set us off course. After we rounded the cape, the seas became calm. It didn't matter which direction we faced in the cockpit, the view was the same— basic gray. Riding with the swift current, we hit a top over-the-ground speed of nine knots, a lot for our sailboats. Because of the marvels of the electronic age, this was not a difficult trip. The radar, the GPS, and the autopilot took us where we wanted to go.

I should also describe "boat hook" steering. One of my favorite positions was to sit on the chair cushion placed aft of the wheel, leaning against the backstay, and facing forward. From there, I could watch the water slip by the boat and view the scenery off to starboard (or port, depending which side of the boat I was on). The controls for the autopilot were near the companionway. To push the buttons and steer from aft, I had to climb around the wheel and move forward. I wanted to relax; this was a lot of work. Jim had attached a small piece of PVC tubing to the aft starboard stanchion. This was home port for the boat hook. I looked at the boat hook and said, "*Hmm*" to myself. I took it out, extended it, and pushed the point of it into the correct button on the autopilot. Presto, boat hook steering. That was how I rounded Cape Sable.

It cleared about an hour before we reached West Pubnico. We saw the dark shapes of land appear through the mist and then become clear as the sunshine arrived. *Misty* led the way, following the charted buoys and avoiding a rock by the cardinal buoy near the entrance to the harbor. She entered the small harbor crowded with fishing boats—draggers, trawlers, and lobster boats. We followed and saw a spot at the large public wharf immediately on our starboard. We quickly tied up while *Misty* landed at the wharf in front of us just past the blue fishing boat. *2nd Wind* followed and tied onto a raft of two fishing boats in front of *Misty*. The harbor shoaled just in front of *2nd Wind*. It was a little strange to see barnacle-covered rocks and gravel only a short distance away while we sat in deep enough water.

We climbed onto the dock where cars were parked and people were walking about. Everyone was friendly and talkative. This was an Acadian community. All the local residents were bilingual. Still not used to being welcomed at fishing docks, Jim and I asked several people for permission to stay. They all looked slightly puzzled that we should ask and said, "Sure, no problem." Jim and I asked one gentleman about obtaining drinking water on the dock. He said there wasn't any, but he would be glad to drive us to his house to fill our five-gallon container.

We learned a lot about M. LeBlanc, our driver. He was the captain of a 135-foot scallop dragger, based in Yarmouth. He had worked on the water for over forty years and planned to retire next year. He owned half of the Red Cap restaurant where his wife and daughter work. His two sons sailed with him on the dragger as they were growing up. While they were young, he gave the two of them one fisherman's worth share of earnings. One of his sons is mate with him now on the dragger. I asked him if he could give the six of us a ride to the restaurant around 5:00 p.m. He said he would have, but he was going to a picnic at that time.

We returned to the dock and put the water container on the boat. We continued to learn more about Canadian hospitality. Someone suggested to Tom and Barbara that they should move because *Misty* was tied up underneath the crane where returning boats unloaded their fish. *Misty* joined *2nd Wind* on the fishing boat raft. *Misty* and *2nd Wind* needed fuel, which was also not available at the dock. Another local gentleman said he would give them a ride to the gas station. Jim and I went along.

They got fuel, and then we also got a tour of the area. He drove us to the next town, Argyle, to see a large sailboat mooring area. He said he was a lobster fisherman and would have to wait for winter lobster season before he could go fishing. Jim asked him to stop at the restaurant to see if he (Jim) could arrange for a ride for the six of us to go to dinner. Jim talked to Mrs. LeBlanc. She said to be ready between six and seven. When she got a break, she would come get us.

When we returned to the dock, the tide had gone down eight feet. We looked at our radar. We were so low that any wave would rock *Yankee Lady* and smash the radar against the dock. We had to move. We joined *Misty* and *2nd Wind* on the raft. Now the raft consisted of two fishing boats and three sailboats. To get to the dock, we would have to climb over all those boats. We elected, instead, to take the dinghy the short distance across the harbor to a floating dock for small boats. It was a lot easier to climb in and out of the dinghy than it would have been to climb across five boats.

At six, all of us were waiting on the dock. It seemed wherever we went, we were a conspicuous group. Several people stopped to talk to us as they were driving off the dock. All offered to give us a ride to the restaurant, which we declined. Around 6:15 p.m., a young man in a van drove up. He was our ride; he was also one of M. LeBlanc's sons. His mother had recruited him to get us. He was very polite, but he was in a hurry to get back home to finish watching an auto race on TV. At the restaurant, M. LeBlanc's daughter waited on us. After dinner, Jim went into the kitchen to talk to the mother again. She came out and met all of us. M. LeBlanc, back from the picnic, was recruited to give us a ride home. It was a pleasure to get to know this Acadian family as much as we did.

At seven in the morning, we listened to the weather (this was getting to be an early morning habit). Predictions were for possible showers and fog patches with light wind becoming ten to fifteen knots. The current would be favorable around 10:00 a.m. We decided to leave for Yarmouth at 8:00 a.m.

Everyone was busy eating breakfast, entering waypoints into the GPS, and preparing the boats for leaving. Jim and Tom F. started *Yankee Lady's* and *Misty's* engines. Oh no, cranky *2nd Wind* wouldn't start. Sighing with frustration, Jim climbed over *Misty* to *2nd Wind*. He replaced the spark plugs and dried out the carburetor. The engine started. We left at 9:00 a.m.

Hoping for clear weather, we had plotted a course through Schooner Passage, a shortcut through several of the Tusket Islands. Jim and I were leading when we arrived at the decision point, whether to turn toward the shortcut or head into the Bay of Fundy. We decided that the weather looked too unsettled to take this unknown, narrow passage in potentially poor visibility.

This meant everyone had to reprogram their GPS settings. The last-minute change was a bit unsettling to Tom F. who liked to plan farther ahead, but he was a good sport about it.

We motored to the south of Bald Island under a gray sky, in light wind and calm seas. After we passed it, we turned north toward Yarmouth. The gray day made the scenery seem more dramatic, sort of like a stark black and white movie. These islands were oval-shaped drumlins, leftovers from the glacial age. They were all oriented north-south, the direction of the retreating glaciers. High cliffs at the southern ends revealed the glacial gravel that formed the islands. The flattops sloped toward the north. Many were barren with just a fringe of grass and no trees. A lone, deserted house sat atop Bald Island, gaping at us through hollow windows and doors.

It started to rain. We could see the showers approaching and leaving on the radar. At least we could tell when the rain would let up, and we could come out from under the dodger.

It cleared again as we approached Yarmouth. We talked to Fundy Traffic, channel 14, who advised us there was no traffic at this time. It was an easy, buoyed entrance, especially because we could see. We passed the old and new government docks and the ferry dock where the huge CAT was tied up. We found Killam's wharf and tied up at the floating docks next to each other.

The tidal range here is eleven feet. Each dock had a sign posted that gave the approximate depth at low tide. We chose docks with six feet. The ramp leading off the dock had two parts. On the left was a straight ramp with slats nailed across every foot so that you wouldn't slide; on the right was a set of steps designed to be walked on at low tide. At high tide, they look like this: ^^^^^^^. At low tide, they looked like stairsteps. Yarmouth represented another milestone completed. We ate dinner at the local family restaurant, Wilson's, and then went to bed early.

Gales were forecast for the night, but the wind didn't get that high. It calmed down toward morning and then picked up during the day. It was a cold wind out of the northwest, twenty to twenty-five knots. This meant that our sterns faced into it. Jim and I kept the hatch closed most of the day to keep the wind from blowing in. The electric heater kept us warm and toasty.

The marina at Killam's wharf was new this year. There were washing machines and dryers in both the men's and ladies' washrooms. There were also showers. Jim did the laundry in the men's room, which meant I couldn't help. I enjoyed a long, hot shower in the ladies' room. There was a small park and gazebo next to the dock, in front of the marina office.

We did errands and chores, actually grateful for this lay day to get caught up. I typed, cleaned some, and reorganized the V-berth. Jim walked all over Yarmouth trying to find a washer for our still leaking fuel pump and a piece of copper tubing for *2nd Wind's* carburetor. No luck, so he made a new washer (from a penny) for our fuel pump and replaced *2nd Wind's* copper tubing with a piece of plastic tubing. Everything worked again.

After a group conference, we decided to make an overnight trip to Northeast Harbor, Maine, as soon as there was favorable weather. We figured it would take approximately twenty hours to make this one-hundred mile crossing. We planned to leave at three in the afternoon and arrive in Northeast Harbor around nine the next morning. This would eliminate about four days of travel north and then west. Jim and I went to Saan's a clothing store to find warm gloves for me for the trip. Other than that, we were pretty well set for clothes. Tom Isele bought long underwear. We anticipated the night trip would be *cold*.

We watched the Scotia Prince leave bound for Portland, Maine. This was particularly meaningful to me since when I lived and sailed in Maine, I would sit in the cockpit of *Yankee Lady* watching her majestic departure from Portland Harbor, dreaming of sailing to far-off places. Now I was doing it.

I invited everyone to *Yankee Lady* for dessert. Tom, Rosie, Jim, and I ate supper at an excellent Chinese restaurant. Rosie, the bakery finder, appeared with a twelve-piece, freshly made carrot cake. Well, that settled the menu for dessert; I didn't have to prepare anything.

Between the sleeping bag and the warm heater, it was a cozy night. In the morning, the revised weather forecast sounded favorable for leaving in the afternoon. This speeded up our preparation time. We filled our water tanks. The marina lady called the fuel delivery man to ask him to bring diesel and gasoline to the dock. After talking to me and Tom Isele, he decided not to bring the big truck. He walked down to the boats and said he would drive someone to a gas station in his car. Tom Isele took all our jerry cans and went with him.

Jim and I walked to the ferry terminal to get the latest information on the CAT's schedule. The CAT was 300 feet long, held 900 passengers, and 240 cars. It had four 9,500 horsepower diesel engines and could travel at a cruising speed of 55 mph. We did not want to be in its way! It was painted black with a white stripe that curved sort of like a speeding cat, and to us, it looked formidable. When it entered the harbor, we could hear and feel its throbbing engines vibrating through the water. Good news, it would leave this afternoon at 3:30 and would leave Bar Harbor tomorrow morning at 7:30. This meant we wouldn't meet it in the middle of the night! We planned to leave at 3:00 p.m. We talked to Fundy Traffic to find out about any other activity and to let them know of our plans.

We finished getting ready for our overnight journey. Just as we were getting ready to untie our lines, Rosie crossed the dock to each boat and gave Tom, Barbara, Jim, and me each a piece of leftover carrot cake to fortify us during our night voyage. Then, we all dropped our lines and backed out of our slips promptly at 3:00 p.m.

We passed the old and new government docks, fishing boats tied alongside, and the big black CAT tied up at the ferry dock. We put up our mainsails and followed the buoyed channel out of the harbor. The buildings of Yarmouth, in muted earth shade colors, lay behind us, clustered on the hill.

To be prudent, Jim filed a float plan with Yarmouth Coast Guard. Because of the distance away from Yarmouth, they gave him a phone number to call when we reached Maine, emphasizing that a search would be started if we failed to report. Jim assured them that he would contact them.

When we were about a mile out, we watched the CAT leave and pick up speed leaving a white rooster tail behind. *Good-bye, CAT, hope we don't see you again.* Suddenly, our engine started to lose rpm and then gain it again. It would not keep a constant speed. We were starting to bounce in the waves and beginning to have misgivings about continuing. Jim sighed and said, "I guess I'll have to go look at it." He suspected air in the fuel line because he had replaced the leaking washer on the bleed screw of the secondary fuel filter. He opened the screw and bled some air out. The engine straightened out. It could be a long night.

The wind settled to west southwest, ten to fifteen knots. The waves were mostly three footers all night long although some were bigger. It was a beautiful evening with a beautiful sunset. I fixed dinner from the Chinese restaurant leftovers. We asked *2nd Wind*, who was ahead of us, to keep an eye on us for twenty minutes or so. We left the autopilot in charge and went below to eat dinner. This was the first time we ever needed the built in ridges (fiddles) at the edge of the table to keep dishes from falling off.

Dark came. The half-moon provided some light to see by and sent a silvery path to our boat. Spray from *Yankee Lady's* bow hitting the waves splashed outward, white and foamy, partially lit by our red and green running lights and white steaming light. The dim lights of the compass, fathometer, knotmeter, GPS, and radar shone in the cockpit. We motor-sailed on through the night.

We saw a target on the radar eight miles away. We watched as the blip approached our path and closed in the distance. We could see a red cruise ship in the distance lit up like a city. Jim called, "Cruise ship with a red hull heading southwest, this is the sailing vessel, *Yankee Lady.*" Fundy Traffic interrupted to ask our location. Jim gave it to the operator, reading our latitude and longitude position from the GPS. They told us we were not in the Fundy Traffic area anymore, but the name of the boat was *Big Red Boat II.* They had been tracking it earlier. Jim contacted the captain directly, and they determined that we would pass port to port within a mile of each other. How reassuring it is to be able to use radar in this manner. Thank you, Fundy Traffic, for your help.

Later, while Jim was sleeping, I saw another cruise ship, first as a distant light and then becoming closer. I was pleased to be able to figure out the radar. It indicated that the ship would pass behind us and to the right, no problem. The ship was totally outlined with white lights, looking like a large crystal Christmas tree ornament for some nautically minded giant.

Every now and then, the faint lights of fishing boats would appear in the distance. We knew that men and women were working their nets and trawls under bright deck lights, but all we saw were small dots of light.

The moon set about midnight. The water became dark and black. The waves seemed more ominous, rolling toward us one after another, many topped with white caps. The stars and the Milky Way arched over us, horizon to horizon, pinpointed lights against the black sky, looking like they were set in an upside down bowl. The blurred shape of the Pleiades rose behind the radar and climbed skyward. Orion marched overhead. The red, green, and white running lights of the other two boats appeared brighter. Jim and I could easily keep track of both boats as they bounced along behind us. The radar, set at eight miles, showed nothing except the two very small dots that were *2nd Wind* and *Misty.* We could almost think it wasn't working, nothing changed on the screen. As we traveled through the night, I thought, *We experience only half of the beauty of nature when we sail only in the daytime.*

About thirty-five miles from Maine, we started to see the mere shadow of a rotating white light sweeping the horizon. We figured, correctly, that it must be the tall Petit Manan light beacon shining twenty miles northeast of Mt. Desert Island. It was amazing to pick it up so far away. Then, Barbara and I saw pinpricks of red lights very distant to starboard. The chart indicated no big town or city in that direction; they weren't moving, and there were too many of them, close together, to be boats. If I had wanted to, I could have let myself get spooked. My imagination could have run away with thoughts of aliens. But I did keep wondering, *What were they?* Aha! They must be the huge radio towers built to detect submarines stationed over forty-five miles to starboard in Cutler. Some of them were ninety feet high. *Mystery solved.*

Yankee Lady continued her rocking chair progress through the water. After awhile, we were sort of used to it. It was cold. We each had on many layers of clothing. Jim lit the alcohol heater and left it glowing in the main cabin all night long. We took turns going below to warm up and to try to sleep. *How nice*, I thought, *to have someone to trade with, to trust, and to share this adventure with.* When it was our watch, Jim or I sat on two cushions at the top of the companionway. We shut the top of the hatch, put the towel around us in the opening, and left our feet and legs hanging down the ladder into the cabin—warm feet and warm legs. The rest of our bodies were behind the dodger, out of the wind.

Trying to sleep was a challenge. There was enough wind to heel the boat over. The aft cabin was on the high side, so that is where we tried to sleep. I kept trying different techniques. First, I put my back against the inside wall so I wouldn't roll anywhere. My head and pillow were near the table that covered the engine. That was not comfortable. Then I tried lying on my stomach. There was too much bouncing. Then I put my head and pillow at the far end (toward the stern) and covered myself with the fuzzy mohair blanket. That way, I managed to sleep a little, maybe three hours total—one hour at a time. Jim didn't have much success at sleeping either; he managed about one hour.

It was my watch. We were about twenty-five miles from the Maine shore when Tom Isele called over the radio, "I've lost my engine!" Oh no, not again! Not here! Jim had just fallen asleep. He was slightly groggy when he responded to Tom. What were our options? *Yankee Lady* slowed down to stay with *2nd Wind*. Slower *Misty* maintained course and speed. We knew that in these waves and the darkness, it would not be safe for Jim to transfer to *2nd Wind* to help. It would also be very difficult to try to tow her. Jim suggested that Tom put out the jib so *2nd Wind* could keep moving while Tom looked at the engine. After untangling the jib sheets in the dark, Tom succeeded in unfurling the jib. *2nd Wind* couldn't hold our current heading under sail, so we started tacking back and forth. *Misty* became our locator boat so we could keep track of our original course.

Rosie took the wheel. Tom went below to see if there was anything obviously wrong with the engine. He found water again and removed as much as possible, all the while bouncing up and down and rolling back and forth. When he returned to the cockpit, he found that he could start the engine with the choke out. When he pushed the choke in, the engine stopped. He called Jim who replied, "Run it anyway you can for the rest of the night." The two boats rejoined *Misty*, and we continued on our planned course. Talk about anxiety, Tom had no trouble staying awake for the rest of the night.

I went below for an hour's sleep. When I awoke, it was dawn. I saw a freighter passing by about two miles off our stern to port. I asked Jim how close it had come. He said it had come very close to *Misty*. Judging distance and direction could be very confusing in these circumstances. Tom Frasca had talked to the captain who, I'm sure, knew what he was doing. However, he didn't choose to communicate that to *Misty* right away. He asked Tom to change channel frequencies twice, which perhaps was just to keep Tom on edge. Finally, after Tom said that he was the boat on the freighter's port side, the captain said, "Yes, I have you in sight. I will pass astern of you." He had already changed course to do that. Tom, relieved, politely said, "Thank you. Have a nice day." I don't think Jim would have been quite so polite.

The rising sun tinted the sky a rosy pink. When I looked forward, a familiar scene greeted me. The rounded hill at the end of the Schoodic peninsula was to starboard. The mountains of Mt. Desert Island were straight ahead. Egg Rock appeared just inside the wide entrance of Frenchman's Bay. We all watched the sun's rays touch the top of Cadillac Mountain and gradually creep down to shore. I'm sure there were people who had driven to the top this morning to be the first to see the sunrise on the eastern coast of the United States. We were privileged to see it from the water.

When it was light enough to see their deck clearly, Barbara looked at the cover of the lazarette in the stern. There, plastered against the deck, was a dead jellyfish. It was undoubtedly alive and gooey when the wave that carried it splashed onto *Misty*. To say the least, Tom and Barbara were grateful that the wave had not been aimed at them.

We were back in lobster pot buoy country. We considered it good timing that we arrived during daylight when we could see them before we ran over them. I don't think the lobster fishermen realize how fortunate they are to be able to fish year around. In Canada, the majority of the lobster season is during the winter only. Nice for us, I suppose, we didn't have to contend with dodging buoys. We couldn't help but notice the difference in attitude toward us between the fishermen here and those in Canada. In Canada, they went out of their way to be helpful, including moving a fishing boat off the floating dock to make room for us. We were welcomed at every dock we went to.

Sadly, though, it was not the same in Maine. I have the greatest respect for most of the lobstermen. They are hardworking and proud. They are known for their dry wit and independent spirit. But some have carried this too far. On this trip, they monopolized most of the radio channels, and when we talked too long in their opinion, they played music and jammed the radio channel. Their comments were sometimes filthy, and instead of being funny, they were sometimes cruel. I could make the excuse that they are threatened by the increased pleasure boat traffic and the tourists, but who else is going to support them by buying their lobsters?

We most definitely did not want to forget to close our float plan with Yarmouth Coast Guard. Rather than waiting to get to a telephone, Jim decided to try calling them on channel 16. To his surprise, he reached them. Jim closed the plan and thanked them again for their courtesy and friendliness.

After we motored by Bunker's Ledge (where the seals hang out in the sun—too early this morning) and Bear Island, I called the harbormaster's office. Yes, we could have three slips, one was easy enough for *2nd Wind* should the engine stop. We tied up first; Jim took the dinghy to play tugboat to *2nd Wind*, but he didn't need it. Tom glided into the dock like a pro.

The overnight trip was over. We had increased our knowledge of what it's like to be at sea at night. We had enjoyed the beauty of it, protected ourselves from the cold of it, navigated through it, and dealt with the problems that arose in it.

As soon as we tied up, Tom, Tom, and I went ashore to call customs. The harbormaster's office gave me the number. I called them on the nearby pay phone, and each of us answered a few simple questions. We were cleared in with no problems.

I had cooked breakfast four miles before we reached the R2 buoy off Bunker's Ledge. The others ate after we docked. Jim and I took long naps and slowly cleaned the boat. We put away our winter clothes, shook the rugs, and did breakfast dishes. We switched the money in our wallets from Canadian to American, saving the Canadian for some future trip.

Not wanting to impose on Jim, Tom I. spent time on the telephone trying to find a mechanic to help him with his engine. No one in Northeast Harbor had time to do it. He found someone to tow him to Southwest Harbor where a mechanic said he could work on it if it were tied to his dock and he could run down and look at it between jobs. Tom said he would call us at 5:00 p.m. on channel 78.

The mechanic in Southwest Harbor found water in *2nd Wind's* fuel tank and drained it out. Tom left, thinking the engine was fixed. *Wrong.* He called at 5:00 p.m. as he was motoring back to Northeast Harbor. We helped him tie up; his engine stopped again when he throttled down. He'll deal with this another day.

Northeast Harbor is a major hub of boating/yachting activities. The marinas and repair shops in Northeast and Southwest Harbors are the last major facilities on the Maine coast. The guidebooks caution that beyond the Schoodic Peninsula, boaters are pretty much on their own. Jim and I have cruised this territory on other trips. It is beautiful and rugged, but without self-sufficient Jim, I would not have enjoyed it half as much.

The six of us went to dinner at the Colonel's restaurant in town. Jim and I stopped for ice cream cones at the Dockside restaurant on the way back to the dock. It was a cool evening, and we froze while we ate them, but it made us appreciate the warm comfort of the electric heater when we got back to the boat.

We enjoyed the luxury of electricity at the dock. In the morning, I plugged in the coffee pot and went back to bed until I smelled the aroma of fresh coffee. The new toaster we bought at the discount store in Yarmouth made excellent toast. After breakfast, I sat in the sunny cockpit thinking about the many times I have sailed here.

Our slips were near the commercial docks. Last night, we watched the captain of the *Capn'B*, a lobster boat converted to a tugboat (he pushes a small barge attached to his bow), single handedly land a dump truck, back it onto shore, and park it.

He did this by driving the barge onto the ramp on shore until it wouldn't go any farther. Leaving the boat motor in forward gear, he walked to the front of the barge and flipped the stopper for the winch to let the barge ramp down. While the ramp was going down, he walked back to the cabin, climbed the three steps to the wheelhouse, and drove the barge a little further onto the land. Again, he left the motor in gear, climbed in the dump truck, backed it off the barge and parked it.

The *Capn'B* commutes back and forth to the Cranberry Islands, a group of islands that guard the entrance to Mt. Desert Island. This morning, we were standing on our dock when it left with a loaded fuel truck on deck. The captain took the opportunity to refuel the boat from the fuel truck after he left the dock. Tom Frasca commented that the captain carried a really big fuel tank, given that an entire fuel truck was on board. I called the captain on the radio and asked him if he was planning to go far. After a few seconds, he laughed and said he guessed he had enough fuel to go to Florida.

Tom Isele spent a good part of the morning and early afternoon working on *2nd Wind's* carburetor. Jim found a see-through, in-line filter at a Down East automotive repair shop. It was Jim's kind of place—no computers, lots of junk, and an owner and secretary who knew where everything was. He installed the filter in *2nd Wind's* fuel line, and then he and Tom cleaned the carburetor, which was full of dirt. *2nd Wind* was like new again—maybe.

We moved *Yankee Lady* to a mooring. It was soul-satisfying to be swinging into the wind again with our own little private space of water around us. Pleasure boats of every kind filled the harbor. Smaller sailboats occupied moorings closer to the head of the harbor. Larger and more luxurious yachts were moored in deeper water. On other trips, I have also seen multimillion-dollar cruising palaces tied to the long face dock of the marina, some with a car and/or a helicopter on the top deck. Beyond boat chartering, there is very little commercial activity here. Northeast Harbor is definitely not a fishing harbor.

Jim adjusted the stuffing box on *Yankee Lady* and installed an outboard motor fuel pumping bulb between the fuel tank and the first filter. This would improve the air bleeding process; he won't have to fuss with the tiny lever that didn't work well back at the La Have River. It would also pressure test the fuel system when filters were changed.

Tom and Rosie insisted on taking us out to dinner. We ate at the Kimball Inn, which is probably the most posh that Northeast Harbor gets. We met on *Misty* for dessert after our huge meals. We had fun recalling our overnight adventures.

In the morning, I enjoyed a hot shower at the Yachtsman's Center, the little building just up the hill from the harbor. Four quarters will buy four minutes of hot water. I had four extra quarters ready just in case. There was also a sitting room for cruisers, stocked with paperbacks, magazines, and coffee. Cruising dogs could enjoy the dish of water outside on the porch.

Jim took the diesel jerry can aboard *2nd Wind*. Tom, Tom, and Jim motored to Clifton's dock where they bought fuel and/or ice. Then Tom, Tom, Rosie, and Barbara stayed in Northeast Harbor to go to church.

Jim and I decided to motor around the corner to Somes Sound and spend the night either in Valley Cove or at Somesville. We were looking for a place to spend time away from civilization. Somes Sound is a deep indentation into Mt. Desert Island, the only fjord-like waterway on the Atlantic coast of the United States. Valley Cove, in particular, reminded us of the Saguenay River in Quebec although it was not as long or as much of a wilderness—no beluga whales here.

We decided to motor into Valley Cove before trying Somesville at the head of the sound. Valley Cove is near the entrance to the sound. It was practically hidden from view until we rounded the point and headed to port toward the green buoy. There was a small powerboat tied to the Hinckley mooring. As we motored by, they said they would be leaving in a couple of hours. That settled it; we would stay in beautiful Valley Cove. We tied up to the white, nun-shaped Coast Guard buoy to wait. That buoy seemed very solid, especially should we hit it in the changing winds and tides. We left a long line out. Toward suppertime, the powerboat left. The Hinckley mooring had no pick-up line on it, so Jim made a large loop in one of our lines, lassoed the mooring, and fastened the line onto *Yankee Lady's* bow cleat. We were secure for the night. We were still rather full from eating out so much. We had cold cereal and wild blueberries for supper.

Valley Cove is spectacular. Deep water extends almost to shore. The mountains, green firs and hardwoods mixed in with boulders and cliffs, rise directly from the water. It looked as if the water ended abruptly at the cliffs. The water was almost a deep green, repeating the color of the trees above. We felt like a small speck underneath the majesty of these mountains. Boats came and went during the afternoon and evening, some just to see the view, some to tie up at one of the other three moorings for a while. During the afternoon, a green Friendship sloop, white sails full (two jibs and a mainsail), sailed across the sound heeling over gracefully in the wind. When it came close to shore, it looked like a toy against the cliffs. Singlehandedly, the sailor jibed around and sailed out. By late evening, we were alone.

We sat in the cockpit until after dark. The sun set over the mountain to the southwest. The few puffy clouds turned a cotton candy pink. The moon appeared over the mountain to the southeast, outlining the points of the mountaintop trees against the sky. The Big Dipper pointed to the North Star. The wind stopped. The water was calm and clear, revealing the reflections of dark mountains and bright stars. The lights from a few houses sparkled across the sound. *Yankee Lady* obliged us by turning 360 degrees during the evening and night so that we saw this panorama from our cockpit seats. We were at peace.

HOME, MAINE COAST, HEALTH SCARE, CIRCUMNAVIGATION COMPLETED

We were reluctant to leave Valley Cove, but it was time to meet the others. We were ready to begin the last leg of our voyage home to Connecticut. We joined *Misty* and *2nd Wind* near Greening and Sutton Islands. We motored through Western Way on a glassy sea. We turned to starboard at the large green buoy number 1 and crossed Bass Harbor Bar, noting the little lighthouse with the red light nestled into the cliff. We crossed Blue Hill Bay and followed the well-buoyed winding channel through York Narrows. As we passed through island-studded Merchants Row, the buildings and fishing boats in the town of Stonington peeked through openings between islands.

These Maine islands are a feast for the eyes. They are uniformly covered with conical-shaped green fir trees and ringed with white/gray granite ledges .They are not very high, except for Isle au Haut, which curved gently skyward off to our port. Interesting potential anchorages begged us to stop; the islands invited exploring, but that was for another time.

This passage rivaled any place we've been for beauty. The only difficulty for cruisers was the colorful forest of lobster pot buoys. This was not autopilot country. However, lobsters were good to eat, so I guessed we would have to put up with it.

Fox Island Thorofare is a well-buoyed scenic passage between the islands of Vinalhaven and North Haven in Penobscot Bay. As we entered this sheltered route, the water remained calm and the sun shone on water and land. It was peaceful, relaxing, and beautiful. Then we heard the fateful words from Tom on 2nd Wind, "I've lost my engine." *Oh no, not again.* There was enough wind to keep sailing slowly at two to three knots. Jim took the dinghy over to *2nd Wind*. Even at two to three knots, it was no easy task to climb in and out of the dinghy against the force of the water. I told Rosie who was steering *2nd Wind* to follow me. Jim diagnosed water in the gas again. He got it cleaned up, and we were off again. Tom will use the other gas tank from now on.

After passing two more buoys, we turned to port into the basin at the entrance to Perry Creek. The island at its mouth appeared attached to land until we motored past it and saw several boats inside. This creek is so sheltered that it is considered a hurricane hole. Several boaters from the Rockland area have put moorings in here to use in case of a big storm. When I lived in Maine and was sailing by myself, I stopped here several times. It was common practice for visiting cruisers to use the moorings belonging to local boaters with the understanding that they would move if the owner showed up. Jim and I thought we knew of one mooring far inside the creek belonging to a couple from Rockland whom we had met in Florida and who said we could use it. We decided to look for it. *Misty* and *2nd Wind* picked up moorings before the creek narrowed. It was low tide, and I was ready to give up, but Portuguese navigator Jim wasn't. We motored past the last boat, a small, classic-looking wooden daysailer. The creek was narrow with rocky ledges on either shore, but we were still in eight feet of water. We saw two more moorings. I wondered how any deep draft boat could get in this far, but Jim kept going. The last mooring was about twenty feet from the shoaling part of the creek. I picked it up with the boat hook. Ahead, the almost dry creek meandered around low banks of gravel, covered with mussels. We could never have anchored in this spot; the creek was too narrow and too close to the shallows to put out enough anchor rode, but the heavier mooring system used less scope. We sat secure, not in total seclusion, because we could see other boats, but it would do.

There were hiking paths on either side of the creek, maintained by the Land Trust. We followed one of these the last time we were here, hiking through sweet-smelling pine trees, ledges, grasses, and soft moss.

Toward high tide, the gravel shoals disappeared, and the creek looked very passable. This would be the time to take the dinghy to the head of the cove, "gunkholing" along the granite shores and, perhaps, landing for a brief walk. But if we didn't keep track of the tide, it would be a longer walk (and swim) to get back to the boat. We were so far up the creek that we could not see the opening into Fox Island Thorofare. We could hear the wind in the trees and the birds calling each other. Then a cruising trawler picked up the mooring next to us. They probably saw us and figured it was deep enough to come in. Thankfully, they did not run their generator.

After supper, the others dinghied over for dessert, blueberry pie made from the last of the wild blueberries I bought in Northeast Harbor. We reviewed the day and planned for tomorrow. We will probably go to Port Clyde or Boothbay Harbor.

During the night, Jim and I woke up around 3:00 a.m. It was absolutely still. We stepped out of the companionway. It was damp and cold, but the stars were brilliant spots in an absolutely dark sky—no city or town lights anywhere. The silence was almost touchable.

We left Perry Creek at eight in the morning, almost feeling as if we should muffle our engines so as to not disturb the silence. We continued along Fox Island Thorofare and passed the town of North Haven, a small island community. It is linked to the mainland by the ferry from Rockland and by a small dirt strip airport. The Thorofare sometimes ices over in the winter. Then the islanders are dependent on small airplanes to bring in supplies.

The Rockland ferry was leaving just ahead of us. We followed its path to the first red and white buoy. I guessed the lobster fishermen were smart enough not to put their pots where the ferry would wipe them out. We enjoyed a mile or two of pot buoy–free cruising. After that, we played dodg'em again. We angled across West Penobscot Bay, passed Two Bush Light, and headed for Mosquito Island and the buoyed passage toward Port Clyde. We reached it by noon. The weather for the next day did not sound good. When thinking about how far to go, we sometimes asked ourselves, "Where would we rather get stuck?" Port Clyde could get a little bouncy in a south wind. We decided to continue to Boothbay Harbor.

We passed through Davis Strait, not as skinny as the chart implied, turned slightly toward starboard and motor-sailed past Old Hump Ledge. We passed close by Eastern Egg Rock, which is possibly the southernmost habitat for puffins. I used to circle the island and maybe see one or two puffins, nothing like the many we saw on the Bird Islands off Cape Breton.

We crossed Muscongus Bay. *Misty* was dropping farther behind; they suspected grass on their propeller. *2nd Wind's* engine was still causing problems. It seemed to run best at cruising speed, so we felt we should match their speed in case they needed help. *Misty* dropped farther behind.

We passed Pemaquid Point with its tall lighthouse and dramatic sloping ledges, and then approached Thrumcap Island, noting the profile of Fisherman's Island which appeared in the hazy distance. The chimneys and roof of the large house perched on top of it punctuated the skyline.

After we passed the lighthouse near Ram Island, *Yankee Lady* and *2nd Wind* turned to starboard and motor-sailed into Boothbay Harbor. We found three moorings belonging to the Tug Boat Inn Marina and asked the dockmaster if he could save the third one for *Misty*. He said there would be no problem; it was not crowded. *Misty* arrived a short time later.

The others ate in town. We had filled up on peanuts and crackers and cheese; we chose cold cereal for supper. Later, we went to town, made phone calls, and walked around. Some things had changed, others hadn't. There was a "new" restaurant (three years old) across from the Ebb Tide restaurant. We bought coffees to go and then saw Tom and Rosie at a table. We joined them and talked while we drank the coffee. We were planning to stay in Boothbay the next day.

How nice to have a leisurely morning. Jim and I didn't eat breakfast until nine; then we sat outside and watched the activity of the harbor. I always loved to do this when I was on a mooring in this busy harbor. Now, while not as busy as midsummer, there was enough to watch. A long blast of a horn signaled that one of the tour boats, loaded with passengers, was leaving for its scenic cruise. A few small boats darted about. The moored boats swung back and forth gracefully on their mooring lines. The passenger schooner, *East Wind*, motor-sailed gracefully out of the harbor. The church across the harbor chimed the hours away.

Tom Isele was still trying to solve his engine problems. Jim went over to consult. He checked the leak on the exhaust manifold. It was not getting worse; he showed Tom how to try to tighten it when it cooled down. It will need attention when he gets home. They talked about how to clean the contaminated gas tank also.

It was humid and hazy in the early morning, but the front passed through, the wind shifted to northwest, and we were in the clear by the time we left for Portland.

Yankee Lady led through scenic Townsend Gut (her former home territory). The same bridge tender opened the Boothbay, Southport Island, swing bridge for us, asked our names and home port, and told us to have a safe voyage. The osprey nest constructed on top of the green day marker just before Ebenecook Harbor was empty and rather forlorn-looking. I thought that maybe the birds had already left for southern waters. We motor-sailed across the harbor to Dogfish Head and entered the Sheepscot River. To starboard, we could see my friends' Peggy and Karen's island, one of the Five Islands.

We enjoyed a sprightly sail across Casco Bay although we left our engines on for maximum speed. I called DiMillo's marina after we rounded Ram Island light. They responded that they did not have space for the three of us. Well, we'll look for moorings across the harbor at Centerboard Yacht Club. Just before motoring toward the mooring field, I called DiMillo's again. Things had changed, one boat had unexpectedly left, and they had space— two slips and a spot at the long face dock.

We thought it was expensive, but this would be only a one-night stop; it gave us quick and easy access to Portland and to DiMillo's restaurant. The restaurant is in a former car ferry boat and has become a Portland institution. While some would call it only a tourist place, I have never been disappointed by the food there. After we registered the boat, I made a phone call while Jim said he would get a reservation for the six of us for dinner. When I was done, I couldn't find Jim, so I went to the front desk at the restaurant to see if he had been there. I was told, "No, we don't take reservations."

I found Jim back at the boat. He said he had a reservation. *Hmm.* The mystery was solved when we went to eat. Instead of stopping at the front desk, he marched us right to the dining room and gave his name to the hostess. She escorted us to a round table for six, already set with a white tablecloth and freshwater poured into the water glasses. How did he do that? He had ignored the front desk before and had asked the hostess for a reservation. She said, "Is your name Schwartz?"

He replied, "No, but it can be if that will get me a reservation."

She laughed and said, "I can give you one anyway." That's Jim! All agreed that their meals were delicious.

It was dark when we returned to the boats. Jim went below, but I sat in the cockpit, facing the water and absorbing the sights and sounds of Portland Harbor. The full moon rose over South Portland. The ever-moving water broke the reflection of the moon into rippled patterns. The dark shape of a boat slid by; the white over red light pattern signaled that it was a pilot boat (white over red, pilot ahead) heading out of the harbor to meet an incoming freighter. The bright yellow, black, and white Peaks Island commuter ferry announced its leaving with a toot, toot, toot. A long, deep blast of a horn signaled that the Scotia Prince was leaving her dock, bound for Yarmouth, Nova Scotia. She glided by looking like a small city, white lights shining from almost every window and from spotlights on her decks. I could hear the creaking of our dock lines as the waves from the passing boats caused *Yankee Lady* to roll gently at the dock. Overhead, the rumble of jets flying low and slow, runway lights shining like beacons, indicated their approach to nearby Portland airport. The beep, beep of backing trucks, the hum of cars, and the occasional fire siren all said, "City, city." To me, Portland was a comfortable city, small enough to have a sense of community and big enough to have a variety of services.

We left Portland Harbor at nine in the morning. *Misty* left first because the resident boat assigned to her slip was returning from maintenance at a nearby boatyard and wanted to use it. *2nd Wind* left with her. We untied our lines and started to head out, but a large freighter, escorted by a cheery red tugboat, was passing. We decided the better part of valor was to wait and follow it.

The sun was out, the seas were calm, and the wind was variable. The other two boats took a divergent track from ours, but we all converged at CP buoy off Cape Porpoise. This part of the coast is relatively low. There was not much scenery until we passed close by Nubble Light just before arriving at York Harbor. We found the entrance buoys and powered through the curving passage and five-knot ebbing current into the harbor. We called the harbormaster who directed us to guest moorings.

Jim and I were going to eat on the boat when Barbara invited us and Tom and Rosie to join her and her sister, Jean, at the Dockside Restaurant right next to York Harbor Marine Service. It was a peaceful evening. A beautiful orange, harvest moon rose over the trees to the east, a sure sign that this was September. We should be getting home. However, we went to bed expecting rain and gales tomorrow. We were not planning to go anywhere.

The rain came, and the wind came, although I didn't think it was a gale. We stayed aboard until midafternoon. It cleared some; at various times, all of us dinghied to the Agamenticus Yacht Club dock across the harbor. Jim and I started walking to the beach when the rain came again. We walked to the Stage Neck Inn for shelter and encountered civilized luxury with oriental rugs and comfortable chairs. It was a warm and dry place to be. The barroom had windows overlooking the beach. We asked the hostess if we could get coffee and sit awhile. She said, "Yes," then, after thinking a minute, added, "You can get free coffee and cookies in the lobby. It's okay if you bring them in here." It cleared. We walked the smooth, gray sand of this small beach, where I used to bring my children when they were small. We took the cliff walk partway. The waves were not as high as we had expected from all the wind.

We met on *2nd Wind* in the evening. We decided to stay over tomorrow. The others will go to church; we will meet my daughter, Cathy, and her husband, Jon.

We relaxed in the morning and then, toward noon, motored over to the fuel dock to get diesel and water. The dock boy said we could stay at the dock until someone else wanted it. Cathy, Jon, and Maureen, their potter friend, arrived within the half hour. They brought lunch and dinner.

After lunch at the mooring, we left the harbor on a slack tide. Jon took the wheel; there was no problem with current. The wind was blowing about twenty knots with gusts to twenty-five knots. Jim put up the mainsail and then let the jib out three-fourths of the way. Downwind, outbound, the wind was no problem—smooth, upright sailing, flat seas.

Maureen had never been sailing before; she loved it. We turned upwind and started to heel over—a lot. Maureen, up on the foredeck, still loved it. So did Jon. In fact, Jon never stopped smiling when he was sailing on *Yankee Lady*. He used to say his teeth would get sunburned. Cathy and I weren't so sure about heeling over that much, so Jim released the jib. It luffed and whipped around noisily while Jim and I were discussing how much to bring it in. The jib answered for itself by promptly ripping. Jim furled it, and that was that. It was as old as *Yankee Lady* (fourteen years). It didn't really owe us anything. We continued to sail with just the main—a pleasant sail over to Nubble Light and back. Jon deftly avoided the lobster pot buoys as we headed toward the harbor. Shortly before the entrance, Jon's hat blew overboard, so we did a man (hat) overboard drill. Maureen got the credit for almost falling in while grabbing the hat with a too short boat hook.

Jim broiled the chicken, which Jon had marinated, on the propane grill; I cooked rice and made a salad. Cathy had picked up a decadent chocolate mousse cake at the grocery store. It was so rich we couldn't finish it. Too bad, Jim and I will have to eat the leftovers another day. It was dark; time for the three to leave. Jim took them in the dinghy to the public dock. It gave me a good feeling to be able to share part of this adventure with some of my family. We are very close and comfortable with one another, more so I think because I was a single parent when they were growing up.

In the morning, *Misty* and *Yankee Lady's* engines were running, ready to leave. Then we heard those words again from *2nd Wind*, "My engine won't start." We shut off our engines. Tom, Tom, and Jim spent most of the morning doing the usual things to *2nd Wind's* engine. *No luck.* Barbara and I tried to cheer up Rosie while we waited on *Yankee Lady*.

Tom hired a mechanic to look at *2nd Wind*. The mechanic did the same things that Tom, Tom, and Jim had done: dry the spark plugs and clean the carburetor. In addition, for good measure, he changed the points. *2nd Wind* started again.

A little later than planned, we left York Harbor, happy to be on our way again. We motor-sailed across the open ocean to the Annisquam River, passing close by the Isles of Shoals.

We had originally planned to stay at the Annisquam Yacht Club, but the weather was too good to stop so early. During the summer, the Annisquam waterway is one of the busiest stretches of water in New England, but on this September weekday, it was relatively quiet. We enjoyed smooth seas and a warm breeze as we motored along.

The Blynman Canal begins after the tall highway bridge. It cuts through a narrow part of Cape Ann and opens into a passage to Gloucester. There are two bridges over it; both channels are only wide enough for one boat to pass through at a time. The railroad bridge is located on a sharp turn in the channel. It is impossible to see if another boat is coming the other way until you make the right turn into the narrow slot. It is impossible to go slow, either the current is behind you giving you a two- to four-knot push or you needed full power to counteract the opposing current. When we were less than a quarter of a mile away, we could see that the bridge was down. The bridge tender told us over the radio that he would open in ten minutes. We waited by the marina where there was room to turn around. We also heard him call a boat on the other side telling him to wait for three sailboats. *Phew, that was easy.*

The second bridge opened as we approached. We motored through, entered Gloucester Harbor, and turned slightly to port. Here, the road to Gloucester follows the edge of the harbor. Just behind the harbor bulkhead was the famous bronze statue of the Gloucester fisherman standing behind the wheel of a fishing schooner eyes gazing out to sea. We paid our silent respect to this memorial built to honor those who had lost their lives at sea.

Jim called the harbormaster who directed us to some floating docks next to a closed restaurant. After we paid the dock fee to the owner, Frank, we dinghied across the harbor to a town dock, walked three blocks and found the restaurant that Frank had recommended.

Gloucester is a well-protected harbor. It was used by English fishermen even before the pilgrims landed at Plymouth across the bay. Probably here, as in maritime Canada, one would have found camps ashore and long drying tables set up to cure the cod brought in by the fishermen. Later, Gloucester became one of the leading Massachusetts ports. While it has been overshadowed by Boston, it is still a significant fishing community as well as a safe harbor for pleasure boats.

We planned to leave early. Barbara, our local weather recorder, knocked on our hull around 6:00 a.m. We had planned to cross Massachusetts Bay to the Cape Cod Canal, about fifty miles from Gloucester, but she said the weather didn't sound favorable. Predictions for the end of the day were for twenty-five- to thirty-knot winds. Tomorrow didn't sound much better. It seemed we were dealing with an approaching tropical depression followed by a Bermuda high. We didn't want to be traveling toward such conditions.

Jim and I suggested Manchester-by-the-Sea as a good place to be stuck for a few days. The harbor was sheltered from most winds, and we knew that the Manchester Yacht Club was most welcoming, offering reciprocal privileges to members of other clubs, including free moorings and use of their clubhouse. The town of Manchester-by-the-Sea was also appealing. There were groceries, restaurants, and gift shops within a short walking distance from the dinghy dock.

We left to an ominous-looking sunrise. The sky became hazy; geometric zigzag clouds lowered and covered the sun. However, the sky cleared somewhat as we motored closer to Manchester-by-the-Sea. The entrance was fairly straightforward, as long as we paid attention to the proper sequence of buoys. There were rocks and shoals on either side of the dredged channel.

The harbor looked crowded. We called Manchester Yacht Club—no answer. Then, Jim and I saw the launch in the outer harbor. We continued in but slowed down by the clubhouse. The launch motored in, and we waved it down. The driver, Jack, looked skeptical when we asked for three moorings, but bless him; he found them for us. We found out later that he was the general manager of the yacht club.

We were not disappointed in the town of Manchester-by-the-Sea. At various times, all six of us went ashore, shopped and ate out. Since the weather was still too windy, Jim decided to install a new toilet in the head. We dinghied to the two boatyards, which shared the same driveway. Crockers had one in stock at a really good price. They wouldn't take a credit card, so Jim opened his wallet and said, "This is all I've got for cash." It was less than the stated price, but they agreed to take it. We ate lunch again in town, and then Jim started the installation.

Suddenly, he felt like the boat was rocking violently (it wasn't), and he became dizzy and nauseous. He managed to climb into the cockpit and lean over the side. He said, "Oh no, not vertigo again." He waited a few minutes to see if he would get better but then said, "Get help." He also said, "Ask Tom Frasca if he could finish installing the toilet." I grabbed my pocketbook and Jim's wallet and dinghied to the yacht club. Jack was right there. He had someone call an ambulance while he took me back to *Yankee Lady* in the launch. With Jack's help, Jim was able to roll over into the launch. I asked Jack to tell *Misty* and *2nd Wind* what was happening. The ambulance was there when we arrived at the dock. We were taken to Beverly Hospital Emergency room. Jack and the ambulance attendants were cool, calm, and professional—a big help at a time like this.

JUDITH SILVA

Even though he felt terrible, it made Jim smile when I wouldn't let the policeman help me into the ambulance. I had been climbing around a boat for three months; I didn't need help getting up a couple of steep steps.

Jim was treated, basically for vertigo. He started to feel a little better. I needed to rent a car to get around on land, so I called Enterprise Car Rental. They were unable to pick me up at the hospital ("We'll pick you up?"), so I called a cab. When it arrived, there was an Indian (from India) woman and her two small sons seated in the backseat. I squeezed in with them while the cab picked up another passenger. The woman had a difficult time speaking English to give the cabbie her directions. I told him where Enterprise was. It was a good thing I had kept the address and phone number because his dispatcher kept saying there was no Enterprise company in Beverly. I insisted there was. Between the no-English lady and me, he was getting frazzled. I said, "You drive like a New York cab driver."

He said, "I was." Well, that took me back to my growing up years in Larchmont when I took trips to New York City with my grandmother. Eventually, he delivered the Indian lady to her house and me to Enterprise. Helpful people gave me directions back to the hospital and from the hospital to Manchester-by-the-Sea. I memorized those two routes.

I checked back with Jim. He needed clean clothes, so I drove to Manchester Yacht Club. Fortunately, it was still light, which made it a lot easier to find my way. As soon as I saw the Manchester-by-the-Sea harbor, I could orient myself by water and then aim myself toward the yacht club. I followed the winding roads until I reached the parking lot. I stepped into the dinghy and stopped at *Misty* and *2nd Wind* to keep them informed. The two Toms had basically finished the toilet except for one small leak. I thanked them for their help and their good thoughts and prayers. I, of course, had been doing a lot of praying myself. I got the clothes and drove back to the hospital.

By evening, Jim felt well enough to go back to the boat. Although he couldn't walk really straight, the doctor released him. Jim drove the dinghy back to the boat, and we climbed aboard. He inspected the toilet, found the leak, and fixed it! What can I say?

When we woke in the morning, Jim said part of the left side of his face felt numb. He felt he should go back to the hospital and have it checked; maybe this wasn't vertigo after all. He was readmitted and given a series of tests, which took half the day. The conclusion was that Jim had had a mild stroke, which primarily affected his balance. The neurologist emphasized that it was done and over with. Jim should deal with it and get on with his life. Jim should also take steps to prevent a reoccurrence. We decided we better go home for a few days. Jim could relax and see his own doctor.

I called my son-in-law, Jon, in Manchester, New Hampshire. He called Cathy at her new job, and they arranged to leave midafternoon. We took the car back to Enterprise and a cab to the yacht club. Jim waited on the dock while I packed on *Yankee Lady*, cleaned the ice chest, and did the breakfast dishes. I did not like doing this alone. After all those years of being single, *Yankee Lady* suddenly seemed lonesome. An important part of my life was sitting on the dock. Tom and Tom helped carry stuff in their dinghies.

Cathy and Jon arrived just after dark. They were wonderful. We stopped for dinner at Chili's in Burlington, Massachusetts. Jim wanted a Blooming Onion. Actually, so did the rest of us, but it struck me as an odd thing for someone to order who was just out of the hospital. Jim's navigation was a little shaky; he tended to walk to port, but otherwise, he was all right. We arrived home around 10:00 p.m. Cathy and Jon left to drive back to New Hampshire. It was a good thing they were night people. With gratitude, I thought, *Relatives do count, and come through, when they are needed.*

After a few days at home, we were back! Jim was feeling better although he still got tired and was a little out of balance. He had started taking blood pressure medication and had another doctor's appointment after we finished the trip. We had talked to Tom and Rosie. Crocker's Boat Yard had replaced *2nd Wind's* head gasket, and she should be healthy again. They would be ready to leave tomorrow. The weather forecast was good for the next few days although Hurricane Isaac was lurking to the south. *Misty* left last Friday.

It was raining and cold. I wrote a letter of thanks to the Manchester Yacht Club praising Jack for his help and included a donation for their Christmas party. We took the dinghy back to the boat. *Yankee Lady* looked wonderful and welcoming. We lit the alcohol heater and shortly; the temperature rose to sixty-five degrees from fifty. We discovered that if we opened the table and put the heater under it, the table dispersed the heat toward the seats. We were very comfortable, cozy, and grateful for Jim's progress.

We left the next day for the Cape Cod Canal. *2nd Wind* was ready to go by 9:30 a.m. We decided that Jim shouldn't do any deck work until his balance improved. I dropped the mooring line, and Jim steered *Yankee Lady* out of Manchester Harbor. Jack was in the launch and waved at us as we left. *Bon Voyage.* It was a beautiful day but slightly cool. When we left the shelter of the islands near Manchester, we rode easily up and down the five-foot swells.

The Boston skyline appeared in the distance. We crossed the shipping lanes, noting a large freighter outbound and a tug and barge inbound. Then Boston faded away, and the south shore grew larger, distant blue turning to green and brown. The wind picked up, and the swells turned to white caps as we approached the canal. I called the Sandwich Cape Cod Canal Marina on the radio. Yes, they had slips available for us.

We made it just before dark. The sun was setting as we entered the canal. The current was against us running about three knots. A tug pulling a large barge was just rounding the corner by the marina entrance on the south side of the canal. The current was pushing him. The tug needed to make a slight left turn. The barge wanted to go to the right. It looked like it was sliding slightly sideways. The tug moved way to the left to control the barge, which made it look like it was heading toward us although we were hugging the north side of the channel. This was a little disconcerting, but the tug and barge straightened out; we slowly crossed the canal and motored to the marina. It became calm as soon as we entered the small harbor; we were out of the current.

We tied up at the fuel dock to get fuel and water and then the dock attendant directed us to a slip. We plugged in and turned on the electric heater. The cabin soon warmed up. After a long and chilly ride, we cherished the quiet, calm, and warmth. *2nd Wind* pulled in next to us. It was dark; we walked across the street to an excellent restaurant. How relaxing to sit with friends, enjoy a good meal, and look forward to a warm, calm, dry night.

We enjoyed the benefits of electricity again in the morning—heater, coffee pot, and toaster. We waited to leave until 10:30 a.m. in order to pick up a favorable current. The Cape Cod Canal is a major waterway for all kinds of vessels, quite a contrast from the solitude of Canadian waters. Swift runabouts darted through it, ponderous freighters, awkward tugs and barges, fishing boats followed by clouds of seagulls, efficient pilot boats, luxurious motor yachts, and sleek sailboats all took this short cut to avoid the greater distance and the shoals off Cape Cod and Nantucket. It was a thrill to be part of this activity.

Thousands of people drive over the Sagamore and Bourne Bridges to travel to Cape Cod. It was a special experience for Jim and me to pass under them in our own boat. We waved at several people walking along the path by the side of the canal. The water was flat, the breeze was gusty, and the sky was blue. A large barge, tug pushing behind it, passed us going in the opposite direction. We picked up speed at the end of the canal; the GPS read up to 9.4 knots over the ground.

The water remained flat as we left the canal and entered Buzzards Bay. I decided to make English muffins. No sooner did I get started then Buzzards Bay turned choppy, living up to its reputation for rough water. No matter, I had my sea legs.

We considered a number of stopping places for the night including Point Judith Harbor of Refuge. However, we calculated that we would arrive there after dark, which we didn't want to do. We decided to stop at Westport, Massachusetts, which was just after New Bedford. We had never been there; it was supposed to be a challenge to navigate. However, we had entered so many new harbors on this trip that it did not seem daunting to add this one to the list. We entered the waypoints into our GPS and proceeded. We passed the sunken cement barges and sailboat at the end of the point and turned toward the red and white safe water buoy. We continually consulted the chart to make sure we were where we thought we were.

The shallow river was well buoyed. It was low tide; *Yankee Lady* and *2nd Wind* each brushed the bottom once. We called the restaurant mentioned in our 1995 (outdated) *Waterway Guide*. The harbormaster responded and told us F. L. Tripp handled the restaurant slips as well as their own. He called them on his cell phone because they didn't answer the radio. Tripp then talked to us and directed us to the dock. They only had two free spaces. One was at the face of the fuel dock; the other was between four pilings behind the fuel dock. *2nd Wind* was to tie up to the outside dock; we would slide in between the four pilings.

In order to reach the ladder to the dock, it was necessary to back in. Jim, still not feeling quite himself, said, "I'll let you back it in." As I set up the approach, the wind was blowing across the dock and the current was flowing out. They both hit *Yankee Lady* broadside as we tried to turn. I first tried to turn the bow out and back in from the channel side of the harbor. *Yankee Lady* wouldn't turn. Jim and I both thought of motoring forward, making a U-turn in front of our space and then trying to back in. I did this, but in order to get *Yankee Lady* to turn, I had to gun the throttle forward and spin the wheel to the left and then gun it backward, spinning the wheel to the right—several times. Jim was practically biting his fingernails, waiting for the boat to turn. He thought I was too slow and stood up to try to help. I gave him *the look*. He said, meekly, "I guess I better sit down." Finally, the stern was in between the pilings. I backed *Yankee Lady* in and gave the stern lines to the dock attendant. Then we handed him the starboard bow line. He climbed onto the trawler next to us, walked to the bow, and tied the line onto the piling. Jim used the dinghy to tie the port line onto the other piling. I said to Jim later, "That docking was three-fourths skill and one-fourth luck."

Tom and Rosie walked to a nearby restaurant. It was cold; we decided to eat aboard. They stopped by *Yankee Lady* after dinner.

In the morning, *Yankee Lady* was ready to leave when Tom walked over, saying, "There'll be a slight delay. I can't get the engine started."

I thought, *Maybe it's time to get out the chewing gum and Band-Aids*. Yet again, Tom dried the spark plugs, drained the carburetor, and cleaned the fuel filter. *2nd Wind* started.

Leaving the slip was a little easier than backing in. We still had to plan our strategy, though. Jim stepped down into the dinghy, a big step, from *Yankee Lady's* port side and pulled himself over to the front piling. This was on the lee side of the boat, so the dock line was slack. He untied it and brought it back to the boat. I untied the slack aft line on the dock. We were now left with the two windward lines holding the boat in place. Holding one end of the last dock line to keep it taut, I untied the knot, placed the line around the piling, and handed the free end to Jim on the boat. He wrapped it loosely around the stern cleat. I climbed back on the boat and put the long boat hook on the bow. While Jim eased the stern line, I pulled on the bow line until I reached the front piling. I had trouble trying to release the line on this piling. Jim released the stern line, left the wheel, and came forward. He used the boat hook to catch the looped line on the front piling. It came free. I hurried to the wheel to motor forward. Jim fended off the port piling; I gunned the engine, and we were out of there.

We left the Westport River and headed west. It was a crisp, cool day. The profile of Cuttyhunk Island gradually faded below the horizon.

We passed the red buoy off Sakonnet Point. We noticed the pinkish rocks jutting toward us, and the lighthouse, which we thought was shaped like a spark plug. I was below fixing lunch when I heard Jim say, "Oh my." I stuck my head out the hatch. It seemed like there were a hundred racing sailboats, colorful spin-nakers flying, heading across our path. We were motoring; they had the right of way. We had to admit we felt like that powerboat you may have seen on a poster or on T-shirts trying to make its way through a fleet of sailboats. The captain was saying, "Oh ——! We flew across Narragansett Bay, averaging seven knots. The racers turned around before we reached them. The current changed shortly before we reached Watch Hill.

We motor-sailed through familiar Watch Hill Passage, mak-ing sure not to cut buoy R2; there were rocks hiding over there. I called Spicer's Marina in Noank on channel 68. Even though the current was against us, we figured we could get there before dark. There was no response from them, but a Towboat/US captain answered. He said Towboat/US kept their boats at Spicer's and offered to call Spicer's with his cell phone. He radioed us back that no slips were available. We thanked him for his help. Plan B was to call Dodson's Marine in nearby Stonington. They told us they were totally booked for a regatta. *Now what? Should we continue to Old Saybrook, arriving after dark?* As Jim and I were discussing this, Spicer's called us on the radio. Yes, they could find room for us. Tom Isele, listening on his radio, said, "Thank goodness."

Now we were in Fishers Island Sound, really familiar territory. Around the corner from Stonington was the winding passage leading to the anchorage behind Napatree Point. Jim and Carol in *Albatross* and I in *Yankee Lady* had anchored or rafted there many times with family and friends. We passed Latimer Light, which I always thought had a wimpy horn; it was high pitched and not very loud. Ram Island and the entrance to the Mystic River appeared to starboard. To port, we could see West Cove on Fishers Island, which is where the original *Yankee Lady*, an O'Day 23, and *Albatross*, a Coronado 25, first rafted twenty years ago.

We carefully approached Mouse Island, noting the mine field of rocks off Noank Point. We kept the green daymarkers to port, passed the tip of the man-made breakwater, and were guided to our slip by the waving arms of the dock attendant. Spicer's was huge, a forest of masts interspersed with powerboats. *Yankee Lady* was docked here for a year before I moved to Maine. *Albatross* stayed here on a mooring for three years.

Our mouths were watering, anticipating dinner at the Seahorse Restaurant. We plugged in, tidied up the boat, and joined Tom and Rosie for the short walk to the Seahorse. We were early enough to get seated right away.

What a celebration dinner! We all ordered prime rib. Jim asked for separate checks. Rosie, trying to be subtle, whispered to the waitress that she wanted the bill. *Thanks, Rosie.* We looked at one another. We've almost made it, just under three thousand miles of adventures, challenges, and victories. Here we were among friends, joined in the common bond of this great odyssey. Tom said, "Just one more start, one day to go." Jim thought, *We'll get 2nd Wind back if we have to tow them.*

One more day. *2nd Wind* was not behaving; she wouldn't start. Tom and Jim walked to Spicer's store and bought new spark plugs. Tom put them in the engine; *2nd Wind* started, purring away as if to apologize for all the trouble. At least we didn't have to worry about getting a late start. The current was favorable until early afternoon, and we only had a short distance to go. (After this voyage, Jim and I talked about *2nd Wind's* engine troubles. He concluded that many of the problems were related to the introduction of ethanol into gasoline supplies.)

In flat water, we motored past Seaflower reef and then by the mouth of the Thames River. The wind picked up as we approached Bartlett's reef. At first, the breeze ruffled the smooth water. Just after Bartlett's reef, where the swift current from the Race pours over the uneven bottom, the waves boiled up in every direction, frothy and bouncy. This was no surprise to us having cruised this passage many times. Then the light wind turned into a sprightly southwest breeze, accompanied by fair weather waves consistently approaching from the same direction. Soon we could see the lighthouses at the mouth of the Connecticut River. We cut buoy 8 and headed toward the breakwater.

As we passed the outer light, I said to Jim and radioed to *2nd Wind*, "We have just circumnavigated New England!" Just under three thousand miles of adventure, laughter, joy, tears, frustration, fears overcome, and challenges met had been completed. Jim and I worked together as true co-captains in every sense. We gained even more respect and love for each other as we shared the thrill of the adventure and as we overcame the obstacles put in our way.

We motored through the entrance to North Cove and up to the dock. Several of our friends and acquaintances were at the club. I handed the dock lines to Bob Cika and Paul Dubuq, and then Jim and I jumped down to tie them off. With tears of joy in my eyes, I gave Jim a big hug. Then we took *2nd Wind's* lines as Tom docked in front of us. I gave him a big hug too and then called Rosie. We hugged and hugged and cried a little. Tom said to Jim, "Thank you for all your help."

Rosie hugged Jim and said, "Thank you for taking us on this trip. Without you, we wouldn't have made it." But they did make it. They had every right to enjoy the victory of it.

We all made it—*Yankee Lady*, *2nd Wind*, and *Misty*. Here's to the three boats that carried us and to the three crews who shared the dream and completed the adventure.